The Three-Star Recipes of
ALAIN
SENDERENS

The Three-Star Recipes of

ALAIN SENDERENS

of l'Archestrate, Paris

by ALAIN SENDERENS
with EVENTHIA SENDERENS

Translated and adapted by PHILIP *and* MARY HYMAN

WILLIAM MORROW AND COMPANY, INC.
New York   1982

BOOK DESIGN BY SALLIE BALDWIN, ANTLER & BALDWIN, INC.

Color photography by Jean-Louis Bloch-Lainé with Jacqueline Saulnier

Translation copyright © 1982 by William Morrow & Company, Inc.

Originally published in French under the title *La Cuisine Réussie*,
copyright © 1981 by Éditions Jean-Claude Lattès

Library of Congress Cataloging in Publication Data

Senderens, Alain, 1939-
   The three-star recipes of Alain Senderens.

   Translation of: La cuisine réussie.
   Includes index.
   1. Cookery, French.   I. Senderens, Eventhia.
II. Title.
TX719.S4413   641.5944   82-6488
ISBN 0-688-00728-7   AACR2

Printed in the United States of America

First Edition

1 2 3 4 5 6 7 8 9 10

About the Author

ALAIN SENDERENS was born in the southwest of France in 1939. When he was twenty-one, he came to Paris after having served as an apprentice chef at the Ambassador Hotel in Lourdes. In Paris, he started out at the Tour d'Argent where he was *chef rôtisseur,* responsible for all the roasts served in the restaurant.

He moved on to the Lucas Carton, where he worked under the great chef Soustelle. Later, after serving as chief saucemaker and chief fish cook at the Berkeley, then second chef at the Orly Hilton when it opened, he opened his own restaurant on the Rue de l'Exposition in Paris, in 1968. He called it the Archestrate, after a famous gastronome of ancient Greece, who traveled the world over in search of the finest foods and wines.

For many years, Senderens had been fascinated by recipes in early cookbooks, so when he opened his own restaurant, he began to work with forgotten old recipes, adapting them and serving them to his clients. His particular interest is exploring combinations of flavors—be they new or old. "I'm sure," he says, "that there are thousands of mixtures and combinations of tastes that have never been tried." His success, both as an innovator and culinary archeologist, was crowned in 1978 when the Michelin guide awarded him its highest, three-star rating. This, in Paris as opposed to the rest of France, is a rare feat for a *chef-propriétaire*—the owner of a restaurant who is also its chef.

Author's Preface

This book is dedicated to those who love to cook and who cook at home.
All of my recipes presented here have been adapted to home use by my
wife, Eventhia, in our home kitchen. In this book, you will find a chef's
recipes made accessible to you. The instructions are as clear and precise
as possible, as are measurements and cooking times. But remember
that cooking is an inexact art, so be relaxed when you cook. Once you
understand the basic principles, don't be afraid to adapt, to use other
products (they are sometimes suggested), to invent new recipes—in
short, to use what you learn here to develop your own personal style of
cooking.

ALAIN SENDERENS

7

Acknowledgments

Our special thanks to Alain Senderens for his help in adapting the recipes when necessary for this American edition of his book.

P.H./M.H.

Contents

Introduction by Eventhia Senderens

One of the first things I learned when I started to adapt these recipes for my own kitchen was how important it is to be perfectly organized and to have every ingredient called for in a recipe within arm's reach.

Before starting any cooking, the work surfaces, stove top and oven need to be completely in order. *La mise en place*—the preparation, measuring, and "lining-up" of ingredients in advance—must be thought through by reading the recipe carefully to understand the steps that lie ahead. Such mundane things as dish towels and potholders should be at hand the moment they are needed. Avoid the exasperation of having to search for things, whether tools or ingredients.

The success of a meal cooked at home depends, much more than when you are ordering in a restaurant, on the way the menu is planned. If a dish you choose is time-consuming, see how much of it can be prepared in advance, and precede or follow it with simpler dishes. This means not only that you will not spend too much time in the kitchen when your guests arrive; it will also help you to control the excellence of each part of the menu.

I have carefully tested all these recipes. Many of them I have found demanding at home without the help of a kitchen staff, but all of them have worked well if I did not try to do too many things at once—essentially, to repeat, to plan my menus carefully. The measurements are written as specifically as they can be. Do give the recipes a try, as they are, before trying to improvise. The subtle balance of flavors is calculated in each one of them. But later, with experience, you can make your own adjustments and variations.

Next, there are some techniques of cooking that present themselves repeatedly for ingredients you will use often. It is good to remember them as general methods, even though they are described in each recipe.

First, of course, always use fresh products. The cooking techniques used in the cuisine of Alain Senderens aim at preserving the maximum flavor of each food (and the vitamins, too). Therefore, cooking times tend to be short. Vegetables should be tender but still slightly crunchy, and meats (except for pork and veal) should be served rare.

VEGETABLES:

You will notice that vegetables are rarely boiled if they are to be served as a garnish. Generally, they are cooked in very little butter, over low heat; the water they contain is usually sufficient to cook them. If not, a spoonful or two of water is added so that there will be enough steam to allow them to become tender without scorching.

MEAT:

Meat for roasting is often seasoned before it is cooked. But large pieces of meat will not be sufficiently seasoned this way, so salt and pepper will have to be added when they are sliced and served.

The best method to insure a nice crust on meat is to brown it rapidly in a mixture of butter and oil; a teaspoon of each is often enough because the meat itself contributes its own fat to the browning process. Once the meat has browned, pour off the fat in the pan. If it is heavily glazed with fat, pat the pan with paper toweling, being careful to leave the caramelized meat juices. These juices give a wonderful flavor to sauces, so don't wash the pan after browning meat unless the contents have burned and blackened—which can happen; do discard anything that has scorched in a pan.

FISH:

The same simple method is used for the initial cooking of most fish throughout this book. Chopped shallots and mushrooms are allowed to melt down and soften in a baking dish or roasting pan. Fish filets are laid on top of them, white wine, or a mixture of white wine and water, is added, and the pan is placed in a hot (425° F) oven to bake. Cooking times are short, generally between 7 and 10 minutes. (There is nothing worse than overcooked fish.) The fish are served with sauces, made either separately or with the cooking liquid, which is reduced and enriched with cream, simmered to thicken it, and seasoned in different ways to give each recipe its particular quality.

SAUCES:

Alain Senderens follows a hard and fast rule for sauces: They are never thickened with flour. Cream, boiled down to a velvety consistency, or egg yolk, whisked in at the last minute, make for lighter sauces that are not only easier to digest but much more delicate in flavor than sauces thickened with flour.

SALADS:

I have noticed that many people do not season salads enough. The first thing to remember about them is that lettuce leaves should be as dry as possible. After washing (very thoroughly), dry them in a spin dryer or pat each leaf carefully in a towel. Then remember that the dressing you make will taste stronger alone than it will when mixed with the salad. For variety, try mixing oils or vinegars. There are many different ones available today, each with its distinctive taste. But some are very assertive; combinations can modulate them in pleasantly surprising ways.

LAST BUT NOT LEAST, THINK ABOUT:

Your butcher and fish seller: They will be glad to prepare your meat or filet your fish for you. All it takes is clear instructions . . . and a smile.

Organizing your menu: Plan carefully so that you spend the least time possible in the kitchen once your guests arrive.

Your budget: You can splurge on one part of a meal and save on another. For example, if you want to serve a lobster salad as a first course, follow it with a main dish of chicken or pork.

Serving and presentation: Very often, I have suggested serving directly onto individual plates, rather than from a platter. This saves time and makes for the best presentation to each guest. However, it may be inconvenient if you have limited space on which to arrange the plates. If you present a dish on a platter, divide it first into serving portions. In either case, remember that plates and platters must both be warmed.

And now, in conclusion, we wish you all . . . *Bon appétit!*

Editors' Note

The recipes in this edition of THE THREE-STAR RECIPES OF ALAIN SENDERENS have been tested by the translators for American home kitchens. This produced information that does not appear in the original French, including substitutions for ingredients that might not be readily available to most cooks here. All such material not contained in the French text is given in **Notes** printed in *italic* type.

Alain and Eventhia Senderens themselves propose substitutions and variations in their SUGGESTIONS, which precede the translators' notes.

Les amuse-gueule
APPETIZERS

Palets de Bleu d'Auvergne
BLUE CHEESE WAFERS

Ingredients for 16 appetizers:
- ¼ pound French or Italian blue cheese
- ¼ pound softened butter
- 1 egg yolk
- 1 scant cup all-purpose flour

UTENSILS:
Blender or food processor
Mixing bowl
Spatula
Baking sheet
To serve: Serving platter

TO BLEND AND SHAPE:
Remove any hard outer rind from the cheese, then cut it into slices and place in the blender or food processor. Blend to break up the cheese, add the butter and egg yolk, and blend until smooth and creamy. Place the mixture in a bowl and stir in the flour to make a soft, sticky dough.

15

Spoon the cheese dough onto a large sheet of aluminum foil. Using the back of a spoon or a spatula, spread it into a rectangle about 6 inches wide and 8 inches long. Lift up one end of the foil; the dough should start to roll onto itself. (It may be necessary to detach the edge from the foil with a spatula; after that, push on the foil behind the dough to make it detach from the foil and roll up.) When the dough has been shaped into a thick cylinder, wrap it in the foil, rolling and pressing on it lightly, and seal the ends. Refrigerate for 2 to 3 hours to stiffen before baking.

TO BAKE AND SERVE:

Preheat the oven to 425° F. Lightly butter a baking sheet.

Unwrap the roll of dough and cut it into 16 slices a little more than ¼ inch thick. Place them on the baking sheet with plenty of space between them.

Bake for 15 minutes or until golden brown, place on a serving platter, and serve immediately.

Crêpes de riz farcies
MINIATURE SPRING ROLLS

Ingredients for 32 small spring rolls, serving 4:

¾ pound boneless chicken breast
½ tablespoon butter
2 tablespoons finely chopped onion
2 tablespoons finely chopped apple
2 teaspoons mild curry powder
1 teaspoon tomato paste
Salt, pepper

3 tablespoons dry white wine
7 large round spring-roll wrappings or skins (*see Note*)
Cooking oil

UTENSILS:
Food processor (optional)
Small frying pan, with cover
Large kitchen towel
Large frying pan
To serve: Serving platter, or 4 small plates

THE STUFFING:

Finely chop the chicken breast with a knife, or use a food processor.

Melt the butter in a small frying pan, add the onion and apple, and cook over moderate heat for about 30 seconds. Sprinkle in the curry powder, cook 30 seconds more, add the tomato paste, lower the heat, and cook 1 minute. Add the chopped chicken, salt, pepper, and white wine. Cover and simmer very slowly for 20 minutes, stirring frequently. Remove from the heat and reserve.

THE SPRING ROLLS:

Dampen a large kitchen towel and spread it on a table. Separate the spring-roll wrappings and cover half the towel with them, then fold the towel over to cover them. Pat the towel lightly and leave for about 3 minutes, or until the wrappings have softened and become flexible.

Cut each wrapping into 4 pie-shaped pieces. Place a heaping teaspoon of the stuffing on each piece, and fold it to enclose the stuffing: Fold the curved side over the stuffing, then fold the pointed end opposite over this. Fold the right side over the top and then the left side. Press the top and bottom gently to seal. Continue in this manner until all the stuffing has been used.

TO COOK AND SERVE:

Heat 3 tablespoons of oil in a large frying pan; when it is very hot, place half the spring rolls in the pan (do not crowd), and brown over moderate heat for about 2 minutes. Turn them over and brown 2 minutes on the other side. Remove from the pan, drain on paper toweling, and remove to a platter or plate. Add another tablespoon of oil to the pan and cook the remaining spring rolls in the same manner.

NOTE: *Spring-roll skins or wrappings are sold in Oriental groceries. They are very thin, white, crêpe-like sheets of dough made from rice flour. They are generally sold in packages containing from 10 to 25 skins, and they can be kept refrigerated for several days without drying out in their package or a plastic bag. Ed.*

17

Beignets de lotte
ANGLERFISH FRITTERS

Ingredients for 4 servings:

FOR THE BATTER:
¼ cake fresh baker's yeast or ¼ teaspoon active dry yeast
½ teaspoon salt
½ cup beer
¾ cup all-purpose flour

½ pound anglerfish (monkfish) fillets, cut into ½-inch cubes
Juice of half a lemon
3 tablespoons olive oil
1 tablespoon chopped parsley
Salt, pepper
Oil for deep frying

UTENSILS:
Small mixing bowl
Large saucepan or deep fryer
Deep-frying thermometer
Slotted spoon
To serve: A platter, or several small plates

THE BATTER:
Make the batter as described for **Fritter batter** *(see p. 266)*, using the measurements given here.

TO MARINATE:
Place the pieces of fish in a small bowl with the lemon juice, olive oil, parsley, salt, and pepper. Mix with your hands, then marinate in the refrigerator for at least an hour before frying.

TO FRY AND SERVE:
Heat the oil to 385° F in a large saucepan or deep fryer.

While the oil is heating, remove the fish from the marinade and pat it dry with a cloth or paper towels. Drop the pieces of fish into the fritter batter, stir to coat each piece well, and carefully place them, one by one, in the hot oil. Fry for about 2 minutes, then, using a spoon,

18

turn the fritters over and cook for 2 minutes more, or until each one is perfectly brown. Lift the fritters out of the oil with a slotted spoon, to drain on paper towels for a minute or two, sprinkle with salt, and serve on a platter or individual plates.

SUGGESTION:
Any firm-fleshed fish may be used in this recipe, or, for that matter, chicken livers, which are excellent cooked this way.

NOTE: *The fritters will puff up in the oil, so don't crowd them. Cook them in several batches if necessary. Ed.*

Beurre d'anguille
SMOKED EEL BUTTER ON TOAST

Ingredients for 6 to 8 servings:

4 ounces smoked eel *(see Note on purchasing)*
4 tablespoons softened butter
3 tablespoons *crème fraîche (see p. 331)* or heavy cream
½ loaf sandwich bread, sliced
Butter (for the toast)

UTENSILS:
Blender
Mixing bowl
Toaster
To serve: Small bowl and plate, or a serving platter

THE BUTTER:
Place the smoked eel in the blender and blend to a purée. Blend in the butter, add the cream, and blend until smooth.
    Place the smoked fish butter in a mixing bowl, beat a minute more with a wooden spoon, then place it in a small serving bowl, and refrigerate until ready to serve.

19

TO SERVE:

Toast each slice of bread. When it comes from the toaster, lightly butter it, cut off the crust, and cut it into bite-sized pieces of any shape you like: squares, circles, triangles, and so on.

Serve the toast on a plate with the bowl of eel butter, or spread each little piece of toast with the eel butter before serving on a platter.

SUGGESTION:

Smoked salmon or any other smoked fish may be prepared in the same way.

NOTE: *The weight of fish given in the list of ingredients is for the smoked eel flesh. Often smoked eel is sold with skin and bones still attached; in this case you will need to buy about 6 ounces, and remove the skin and bones in order to have the 4 ounces needed for this recipe. Ed.*

Tartelettes aux asperges
ASPARAGUS TARTLETS

Ingredients for 8 servings:

10½ ounces (300 g) **puff pastry dough** *(see p. 271)* or **short pastry** *(see **Tarte Tatin,** p. 317)*
2 quarts water
2 teaspoons coarse salt
1 pound asparagus

4 egg yolks
¾ cup heavy cream
Salt, pepper
Pinch cayenne pepper
Pinch nutmeg

UTENSILS:
8 tartlet molds, 3 inches in diameter
Rolling pin
Large saucepan
Mixing bowl
Wire whisk
Baking sheet
To serve: Large serving platter

THE DOUGH:

Lightly butter the tartlet molds.

On a lightly floured table roll out the puff pastry into a rectangle about 9 × 18 inches and cut it into 8 squares about 4½ × 4½ inches. Line each mold with a square of dough, cutting off any excess with a knife. Refrigerate while preparing the asparagus.

THE ASPARAGUS:

Place the water and coarse salt in the large saucepan and bring to a boil.

Break off the sandy ends of the asparagus, peel, and cut in half. Drop the stems into the boiling water, bring back to a boil, and boil 4 minutes. Add the tips and boil 5 minutes longer. Drain the asparagus, cool under running water, and drain thoroughly on a cloth.

Cut each asparagus stem in half lengthwise, then crosswise into ½-inch cubes. Cut the tips in half lengthwise. Reserve.

TO BAKE AND SERVE:

Preheat the oven to 425° F.

In a bowl beat the egg yolks, cream, salt, pepper, cayenne, and nutmeg until perfectly mixed together.

Place equal amounts of asparagus cubes in each tartlet, lay the tips on top, then spoon the egg-cream mixture over each one until full. Place on a baking sheet and bake for 16 minutes, or until the surface of the tartlets is golden brown.

Remove from the oven, allow to cool about 5 minutes, and serve warm but not hot on a platter.

Sherry is excellent with this appetizer.

Les soupes
SOUPS

Crème de concombre aux herbes
COLD CUCUMBER SOUP WITH MINT AND CHIVES

Ingredients for 4 servings:

3 large cucumbers (1¾ pounds)
2 teaspoons butter
1 small onion, finely chopped
¾ cup water
⅔ cup heavy cream, whipped until stiff
10 fresh mint leaves, cut into thin slivers
1 heaping teaspoon finely chopped chives
Salt, pepper

UTENSILS:
Large saucepan
Blender
2 mixing bowls
Wire whisk
To serve: Chilled soup tureen, or 4 chilled soup bowls

THE CUCUMBER PURÉE:

Peel the cucumbers and cut in half lengthwise. Using a small spoon, scoop out all the seeds. Dice one quarter of the cucumber and reserve for garnishing the soup. Coarsely chop the remaining cucumber and reserve for the purée.

Heat the butter in a large saucepan, add the onion, and cook to soften without browning, over moderate heat (about 4 minutes). Add the chopped cucumber and continue cooking over low heat for 2 minutes. Add the water, season lightly with salt and pepper, and bring to a boil, then lower the heat and simmer for 10 minutes. Purée until smooth in the blender, then place in a bowl, and refrigerate, stirring occasionally, for about 30 minutes, or until the purée is completely cold.

TO FINISH AND SERVE:

Carefully stir the diced cucumber, mint, and chives into the whipped cream. Slowly pour the cold cucumber purée into the cream, gently stirring until a smooth mixture is formed. Add salt and pepper to taste and chill the soup for at least an hour before serving.

Serve either from a chilled soup tureen or in individual soup bowls.

SUGGESTION:

Yogurt may be used instead of whipped cream. If this is done, diced raw mushrooms may be added to the soup with the diced cucumber and herbs.

Vichyssoise de courgettes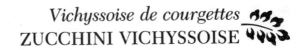
ZUCCHINI VICHYSSOISE

Ingredients for 4 servings:

  2 pounds zucchini
  1 large potato
  2 quarts water
  2 teaspoons coarse salt
  Salt, pepper
  ¾ cup heavy cream
  4 teaspoons mixed chopped parsley, chervil, and chives

UTENSILS:

Large saucepan
Blender or food processor
Large bowl
To serve: Soup tureen

TO MAKE AND SERVE:

Peel the zucchini, cut them in half lengthwise, and scoop out the seeds with a spoon or melon-ball cutter. Cut each zucchini half into pieces about 2 inches long.

Peel the potato and cut into ½-inch cubes.

Bring the water and salt to a boil in a large saucepan. Add the squash and potato and boil for 13 minutes once the water comes back to a boil.

Drain the vegetables and save the cooking liquid. Allow to cool for 5 minutes, then place the vegetables and 1 cup of the cooking liquid in a blender, season with salt and pepper, and blend to a smooth purée. Pour the purée into a bowl and allow to cool for 10 minutes.

Rinse out the blender and blend the cream in it for 10 seconds. Fold the beaten cream into the purée, as you would beaten egg whites. Taste for salt and pepper, pour the mixture into a soup tureen, and chill for at least 2 hours.

When ready to serve, sprinkle with the chopped herbs.

Soupe de moules brésilienne
MUSSEL SOUP BRAZILIAN STYLE

Ingredients for 4 servings:

1 whole coconut *(for substitution, see Note)*
1⅔ cups heavy cream

FOR THE MUSSELS:

3¼ pounds mussels *(see Suggestion)*
1½ tablespoons butter
5 shallots, finely chopped
1⅓ cups dry white wine

FOR FINISHING THE SOUP:

3 small tomatoes, peeled, seeded, and chopped

½ green bell pepper, seeded, chopped, boiled 1 minute, and cooled
under running water

½ red bell pepper, prepared like the green

1 teaspoon finely chopped fresh ginger

4 tablespoons drained canned corn

Salt, pepper

1 teaspoon chopped coriander leaf (cilantro)

UTENSILS:

Knife or ice pick

2 large bowls

Hammer

Vegetable grater or food processor

2 clean dish towels

2 large saucepans

To serve: 4 heated soup plates

THE COCONUT:

Prepare the coconut the night before making the soup.

With a knife or ice pick, puncture the 3 indentations in the top of the coconut and pour the "milk" that comes out of it into a bowl. Break the coconut in half with a hammer, then use a knife to pry the meat away from the shell of the nut. Grate the meat, or grind it in a food processor, and place it in the bowl with the "milk." Add the cream, cover, and refrigerate overnight.

The next day, line a bowl with a clean cloth and pour the coconut-cream mixture into it. Lift up the corners of the towel and twist together, squeezing and pressing on the towel to extract as much liquid as possible. Discard the contents of the towel and reserve the liquid for later use.

THE MUSSELS:

Clean and cook the mussels as described for **Mussels with tomato and basil** *(see p. 70)*, using the measurements given here. Once the mussels have opened, remove them from the pot and take each one out of its shell. Place in a bowl and reserve.

TO FINISH THE SOUP AND SERVE:

Strain the mussel cooking liquid through a clean cloth into a large saucepan. Boil to reduce it to 1⅓ cups. Add the coconut liquid, simmer for 2 minutes, add the tomato, green and red peppers, and ginger, and simmer 2 minutes more. Add the corn, simmer 4 minutes, then add the mussels, salt and pepper as needed, and simmer a final 3 minutes.

Ladle the soup into hot soup plates, sprinkle each serving with a little fresh coriander (cilantro), and serve.

SUGGESTION:
Clams may be used instead of mussels.

NOTE: *If a fresh coconut is unavailable, use 1⅔ cups of dessicated (grated) coconut. Add ¾ cup of water and use this mixture as described for the fresh coconut and its "milk."*

If you do have a fresh coconut, but it has no milk inside, add 6 tablespoons of water to the coconut-cream mixture. Ed.

Soupe arabe
ARAB SOUP

Ingredients for 4 to 6 servings:

   ½ cup dry chick-peas
   ½ cup dry white beans *(see Note)*
   Salt, pepper
   1¾ pounds breast of lamb (riblets), cut into 12 pieces
   3 tablespoons olive oil
   2 quarts cold water
   2 teaspoons salt
   Bouquet garni

   3 tablespoons olive oil
   1 large onion, diced
   2 small bell peppers (one red, one green), seeded and diced
   1 medium zucchini, diced

3 cloves garlic, diced
2 medium tomatoes, peeled, seeded, and chopped
Salt, pepper
⅛ teaspoon powdered saffron
½ teaspoon thyme leaves
5 mint leaves, chopped

UTENSILS:
Large bowl
2 large pots, one with cover
Ladle
To serve: Large soup tureen

THE BEANS AND LAMB:
Soak the chick-peas and beans overnight. Drain and reserve.

Generously salt and pepper the lamb. Heat 3 tablespoons of olive oil in a large pot and quickly brown the meat over high heat; remove the lamb from the pot and drain on a towel or cloth. Discard the fat in the pot, then add the chick-peas, beans, cold water, salt, *bouquet garni*, and pepper. Bring to a boil, lower the heat, and simmer for 1 hour. Add the lamb and simmer 45 minutes longer, spooning off any fat that surfaces.

THE VEGETABLES:
Heat the remaining 3 tablespoons of olive oil in another pot, add the onion, and soften over medium heat, then add all the remaining vegetables. Season lightly with salt and pepper, then add the saffron, thyme, and mint. Stir well, cover the pot, and simmer slowly for 30 minutes without adding any liquid (the vegetables cook in their own juices); if necessary, a little more olive oil may be added.

TO FINISH AND SERVE:
Pour the cooked vegetables into the pot with the lamb and beans and bring to a boil. Simmer for 5 minutes; add salt and pepper if needed. Remove the *bouquet garni* and skim off all the fat from the surface of the soup. Ladle the soup into a large soup tureen and serve immediately.

SUGGESTIONS:
Duck or chicken may be used instead of lamb, and a pound of green

peas instead of the chick-peas. Broad beans, lima beans, rosemary, or basil may all be added to this soup.

NOTE: *A pound of fresh white beans or lima beans may be used instead of dried beans. Simply bring the seasoned water to a boil and add the lamb and fresh beans; cook 45 minutes. If using fresh peas, cook them for the last 20 minutes only.*

This very meaty soup could easily be turned into a main dish by doubling the ingredients listed here. If served as a soup, you will find it easier to eat if you bone the pieces of lamb just before serving. Ed.

Les salades
SALADS

Salade de raie au persil simple
SKATE SALAD WITH ITALIAN PARSLEY

Ingredients for 4 servings:

FOR THE VINAIGRETTE:
6 tablespoons salad oil
2 tablespoons red-wine vinegar
Salt, pepper

FOR THE COURT BOUILLON:
3 quarts water
2 tablespoons salt
2 large carrots, diced
2 medium onions, diced
20 whole peppercorns
Bouquet garni
2 pounds skate *(for substitutions, see Suggestions)*

FOR THE GARNISH:
2 medium tomatoes, peeled, seeded, and diced
½ pound lamb's-lettuce *(for substitutions, see Suggestions)*
1 teaspoon finely chopped parsley

1 teaspoon finely chopped chives
1 teaspoon finely chopped chervil
1 tablespoon capers
2 shallots, finely chopped
Salt, pepper
6 to 7 sprigs Italian parsley, leaves only

UTENSILS:
Small bowl
Wire whisk
Sauteuse or large pot (5-quart capacity)
Skimmer or slotted spoon
Large saucepan
To serve: 4 salad plates

THE VINAIGRETTE:
Whisk the oil, vinegar, salt, and pepper together in a bowl and reserve.

THE SKATE:
In a large *sauteuse* or pot wide enough to hold the skate, make a court bouillon: Bring the water to a boil, add the salt, carrots, onions, peppercorns, and *bouquet garni,* bring back to a boil, and simmer, uncovered, for 30 minutes, skimming off any foam that appears.

Wash the skate thoroughly in cold water to remove any slime, then place it in the court bouillon. Cover the pot and poach the fish for 17 minutes.

THE GARNISH:
Five minutes before serving, place the diced tomatoes in a large saucepan, warm over low heat, and add the lamb's-lettuce, herbs, capers, and shallots. Toss gently to barely warm the salad; do not allow to wilt. Whisk the vinaigrette. Add 3 tablespoons of it and a little salt to the garnish, toss again, and place equal amounts on each plate.

TO SERVE:
Lift the skate out of the court bouillon. Using a fork, remove the skin, then lift the meat off of the bone. Divide the fish into 4 equal portions.

Whisk the remaining vinaigrette, dip the skate into it, and place a piece on top of each salad. Dip the Italian parsley leaves into the vinaigrette and place on top of the skate. Lightly salt and pepper each portion of fish and serve immediately.

SUGGESTIONS:
A mixture of lettuces of your choice may be used instead of lamb's-lettuce; and flounder, mackerel, or whiting may be used instead of skate. A little chopped lemon zest may also be sprinkled on the fish just before serving.

Salade de coquilles Saint-Jacques au céleri frit
SCALLOP SALAD WITH FRIED CELERY LEAVES

Ingredients for 4 servings:
   12 small sea scallops (3 pounds) purchased in shells; if unavailable, buy 10 ounces shelled scallops (*see Note*)

   FOR THE STOCK:
   1 teaspoon butter
   6 tablespoons dry white wine
   4 tablespoons water
   Salt, pepper
   1 teaspoon chopped fresh dillweed

   FOR DEEP FRYING:
   1 pound goose fat (preferably), or lard
   Leaves from 8 branches celery

   FOR THE SCALLOPS:
   2 teaspoons butter
   Salt, pepper
   ½ teaspoon chopped fresh dillweed

   UTENSILS:
   Saucepan
   Skimmer or slotted spoon
   Bowl

31

Saucepan, with cover
Deep fryer or pot
Deep-frying thermometer
To serve: 4 heated plates

THE STOCK:

If using scallops in their shells, open them yourself. Cut off the wrinkled strip surrounding each, wash it, chop it coarsely, and reserve on a plate. Wash and dry each scallop, then place it with its bright orange appendage on another plate, and reserve. (*See Note* if using shelled scallops.)

Melt the butter in a small pan and add the chopped scallop strips. Stir and simmer, uncovered, for 3 minutes. Add the white wine, water, salt, and pepper. Bring to a boil, add the dill, and simmer for 20 minutes, skimming off any foam that appears with a skimmer or slotted spoon. Strain the stock into a bowl and reserve.

THE SCALLOPS AND CELERY LEAVES:

Wash the celery leaves, discarding any that are very dark green (their taste is too strong). Pat the leaves dry in a clean towel.

Heat 2 teaspoons of butter in a saucepan; when very hot, add the scallops (they should all fit in one layer), season with salt, pepper, and the dill. Shake the pan or stir the scallops with a wooden spoon, add the strained stock, bring to a boil, then cover and simmer for 2 minutes (*see Note*).

Heat the fat in a deep fryer or pot to 375° F. Drop the celery leaves into the hot fat and cook for 2 to 3 minutes; cook them in 2 batches. Drain the fried celery leaves thoroughly.

TO SERVE:

Place some of the celery leaves on each plate and salt lightly. Remove the scallops from the pan with a slotted spoon and cut each one into thin slices. Salt and pepper lightly, place them on top of the celery, and serve immediately.

NOTE: *This recipe calls for sea scallops, but bay scallops may be used. Cook them for only 1 minute and leave them whole to serve.*

American scallops are most often sold out of the shell. The orange appendage, as well as the wrinkled strips used for making the stock, have been removed. When this is the case, buy ¼ pound extra scallops (or fish) for making the stock. Ed.

Salade de Saint-Jacques et mâche
SCALLOP AND LAMB'S-LETTUCE SALAD

Ingredients for 4 servings:

FOR THE VINAIGRETTE:
1 tablespoon lemon juice
2 tablespoons olive oil
1 tablespoon salad oil
Salt, pepper

FOR THE SALAD:
6 ounces lamb's-lettuce *(for substitutions, see Note)*
2 shallots, finely chopped

FOR THE SCALLOPS:
1 tablespoon chopped fresh dillweed, or 1 teaspoon powdered dill
Salt, pepper
8 large sea scallops weighing about ¾ pound *(for substitution, see Note)*
2 tablespoons butter
3 tablespoons dry white wine

UTENSILS:
Small mixing bowl
Wire whisk
Large mixing bowl
Large frying pan
Slotted spoon
To serve: 4 heated salad plates

THE VINAIGRETTE:

In a bowl whisk together the lemon juice, olive oil, and salad oil; season with salt and pepper and reserve.

THE SALAD:

Place the lamb's-lettuce in a large bowl with the shallots, add 3 tablespoons of the vinaigrette, and toss. Place in very slow oven to barely warm while cooking the scallops.

THE SCALLOPS:

Season the scallops with salt, pepper, and the dillweed. In a large frying pan heat the butter until very hot, add the scallops, and brown lightly for 1 to 2 minutes, then turn them over and brown for 1 to 2 minutes more. Lower the heat, add the wine, cook for 1 minute more, then remove the scallops with a slotted spoon. Cut each into 5 thin slices and add them to the bowl with the remaining vinaigrette.

TO SERVE:

Remove the lamb's-lettuce from the oven, place some on each plate, stir the scallops in the vinaigrette, and arrange the slices on the salad. Serve immediately.

SUGGESTION:

You can vary the salad by sprinkling finely chopped herbs (parsley, chives, etc.) or thin strips of truffle over the scallops just before serving.

NOTE: *Bay scallops may be used instead of sea scallops in this recipe. Purchase the weight given for sea scallops, season as described, but cook the bay scallops only half as long as sea scallops. Leave bay scallops whole.*

Fresh spinach or dandelion greens may be used instead of lamb's-lettuce. Ed.

Salade de truffes
SALAD WITH TRUFFLES

Ingredients for 4 servings:

> 4 large truffles (3½ ounces), fresh or canned
> 4 tablespoons salad oil
> 1 tablespoon sherry vinegar
> ½ teaspoon wine vinegar
> Salt, pepper

> FOR THE SALAD (*see Note*):
> ⅔ cup tightly packed lamb's-lettuce
> ⅔ cup tightly packed red *trévise* lettuce
> 1 cup tightly packed chickory leaves
> 1 cup tightly packed Batavian endive

> 3 tablespoons finely chopped chives
> 2 tablespoons finely chopped chervil
> 2 tablespoons finely chopped parsley
> Salt, pepper

> UTENSILS:
> 2 small mixing bowls
> Wire whisk
> Large mixing bowl
> *To serve:* 4 salad plates

THE TRUFFLES:
Brush fresh truffles clean, or drain canned ones, place them in a bowl with the salad oil and roll them around to coat them with the oil. Cover tightly with plastic wrap and leave overnight to marinate.

TO MAKE THE SALAD AND SERVE:
Drain the oil from the truffles into a small mixing bowl. Whisk in the two vinegars, salt, and pepper.

Cut the truffles into thin slices, place them on a plate, lightly salt and pepper, and spoon 1½ tablespoons of the vinaigrette over them. Place all the different lettuces and herbs in a mixing bowl, add the remaining vinaigrette, toss, and add salt and pepper as needed.

Place some of the salad on each serving plate, arrange the slices of truffle around the salad, and serve.

SUGGESTION:
A pound of potatoes can be peeled, boiled, sliced, seasoned with the herbs and vinaigrette while still warm, and served with the truffles instead of the greens—a really splendid combination!

NOTE: *A variety of fresh greens may be used instead of those listed; spinach, cos lettuce, watercress, and Belgian endive, for instance. Ed.*

 *Salade de lentilles*
LENTIL SALAD

Ingredients for 6 servings:

FOR THE LENTILS:
1 pound lentils
1 tablespoon coarse salt
2 onions, stuck with a clove
2 carrots, cut in half
16 peppercorns, tied in a cloth
Bouquet garni

FOR THE GARNISH:
4 medium carrots, diced
2 medium turnips, diced
3 medium leeks, white only, diced

FOR THE VINAIGRETTE:
2 tablespoons Dijon mustard
¾ cup salad oil
¼ cup wine vinegar
Salt, pepper

6 shallots, finely chopped
¼ pound boiled pork rind *(for substitutions, see Suggestions)*

1 boiled pig's foot, boned and diced *(for substitutions, see Suggestions)*
6 tablespoons finely chopped chervil or parsley

UTENSILS:
Large saucepan
Skimmer or slotted spoon
Large mixing bowl
Medium saucepan
4 small mixing bowls
Wire whisk
To serve: 6 salad plates

THE LENTILS:
Wash and drain the lentils. Place them in a large saucepan with 2 quarts of cold water, add the coarse salt, and bring to a boil. Skim off any foam that appears, then add the onions, carrots, peppercorns, and *bouquet garni*. Lower the heat and simmer for 30 to 45 minutes, or until the lentils are tender but not mushy. Strain the lentils and remove the onions, peppercorns, carrots, and *bouquet garni*. Place the lentils in a large mixing bowl, cover with aluminum foil, and keep warm while preparing the garnish.

THE GARNISH:
Cook the diced carrots in a saucepan of lightly salted boiling water for 3 minutes. Drain and reserve the water. Bring the water back to a boil and cook the turnips for 2 minutes. Drain the turnips and again reserve the water. Place the turnips in a bowl separate from the carrots. Cook the leeks for 5 minutes in the reserved water, drain, and reserve in a third bowl. Cover each vegetable with foil to keep warm.

TO SEASON AND SERVE:
Make a vinaigrette by whisking together in a bowl the mustard, oil, vinegar, and a little salt and pepper.
    Season the warm lentils with ¾ cup of the vinaigrette, stir in the chopped shallots, and place some of the lentils on each plate.
    Spoon a tablespoon of the remaining vinaigrette over each of the three vegetables used as garnishes and place a little pile of each one on each plate around the lentils.
    Place the remaining vinaigrette in a bowl with the boiled pig's foot

and rind, stir, and sprinkle this over the lentils. Finally sprinkle each salad with chopped chervil or parsley and serve barely warm.

SUGGESTIONS:
One-half pound of bacon, cut into thick "lardons" and fried just before serving, may be used instead of the pork rind and foot. Drain the fat from the pan the bacon cooked in, deglaze the pan with 2 tablespoons of vinegar, and pour over the salad with the bacon just before serving.

Salade d'écrevisses aux fonds d'artichauts et confit de canard
ARTICHOKE, CRAYFISH, AND PRESERVED DUCK SALAD

Ingredients for 4 servings:

FOR THE VINAIGRETTE:
9 tablespoons salad oil
3 tablespoons vinegar
Salt, pepper
2 teaspoons finely chopped parsley
2 teaspoons finely chopped chives
2 teaspoons finely chopped chervil

FOR THE SALAD:
20 live crayfish (*for substitution, see Note*)
4 tablespoons cooking oil
2 legs, or 1 leg and 1 breast of **Preserved duck** (*see p. 228*)
2 tablespoons duck fat (or goose fat)
½ pound lamb's-lettuce or spinach
4 cooked or canned artichoke bottoms, cut into thin slices
Salt, pepper

UTENSILS:
Mixing bowl
Wire whisk

Large frying pan, with cover
Skimmer or slotted spoon
Small frying pan
Large saucepan
Small saucepan
To serve: 4 heated salad plates

THE VINAIGRETTE:

In a bowl whisk together the oil, vinegar, salt, pepper, and herbs and reserve.

THE CRAYFISH:

Remove the central fin from the tail of each crayfish as described in **Lamb with crayfish** *(see p. 177)*. Heat 2 tablespoons of cooking oil in a large frying pan, add half the crayfish, cover the pan, and cook over moderate heat, shaking the pan frequently, for 4 minutes. The crayfish should turn completely red; if not, cook a few minutes longer. Remove the crayfish from the pan with a skimmer or slotted spoon, add the remaining oil and crayfish, and cook in the same way. When the crayfish are cool enough to handle, detach the tails from the heads and remove the tail meat from the shell. Reserve the tail meat on a plate.

THE DUCK:

Debone the pieces of duck and cut the meat into slices ¼ inch thick. Heat the duck or goose fat in a frying pan, add the slices of duck, brown on both sides, and drain on paper towels.

TO FINISH THE SALAD AND SERVE:

Place the lettuce or spinach in a large saucepan, season with salt and pepper, and toss over low heat until barely warm; do not allow to wilt. Remove from the heat and add all but one tablespoon of the vinaigrette and the artichoke bottoms, toss to mix, then place a quarter of the salad on each plate.

Place the crayfish tails in a small saucepan with the remaining vinaigrette, salt, and pepper, heat to lukewarm, and arrange them around the salad on each plate. Quickly reheat the duck in the small frying pan, place on top of the salad, sprinkle with pepper, and serve.

SUGGESTIONS:

Cooked asparagus or green beans may replace the artichokes. If green beans are used, sprinkle each plate with a julienne of raw carrot just before serving.

NOTE: *The garnished salad plates can be placed in a 350° F oven for a minute or two to reheat the salad just before serving if necessary; the salad should be served barely warm, not hot.*
   Boiled shrimp may be used instead of crayfish. Ed.

Salade de langouste à la mangue, au canard, et au basilic
LOBSTER, MANGO, DUCK, AND BASIL SALAD

Ingredients for 4 servings:

FOR THE VINAIGRETTE:
1½ teaspoons wine vinegar
1 tablespoon sherry vinegar
¼ cup salad oil
Salt, pepper

1 medium carrot, peeled and cut into strips with a vegetable peeler
   (for the garnish)
Pepper
Zest of ⅓ medium orange, cut into julienne strips (about 1
   tablespoon of strips)

FOR THE COURT BOUILLON:
3 quarts water
1 tablespoon coarse salt
3 medium carrots, sliced
2 medium onions, cut in half
Half a stalk celery
8 whole peppercorns
Bouquet garni (including the green of a small leek)
1 live lobster, weighing about 2¾ pounds *(see Note)*

FOR THE GARNISH:
¾ pound lamb's-lettuce, fresh spinach, or other lettuce
2 tablespoons finely chopped chives
1 tablespoon finely chopped parsley
1 tablespoon finely chopped chervil
10 medium basil leaves, cut into thin strips
1 tablespoon finely chopped shallot
½ **Preserved duck** *(see p. 228)*, or about ¾ pound boned and diced; leave skin attached *(see Note)*
Salt, pepper
1 ripe mango (¾ pound), peeled, seeded, and cut into thick ¼-inch julienne strips

UTENSILS:
Small bowl
Wire whisk
Medium saucepan
Large pot
Tongs
Large saucepan
Frying pan, preferably nonstick
To serve: 4 heated salad plates

PRELIMINARY PREPARATIONS:
Make a vinaigrette by whisking together in a small bowl the two vinegars, oil, salt, and pepper.

Sprinkle the carrot strips with pepper and drop them into a saucepan of lightly salted boiling water. Cook for 10 seconds and drain. Cool under running water, drain again, and reserve.

Place the julienne of orange in the rinsed saucepan, cover with cold water, bring to a boil, then drain immediately. Cool under running water, drain again, and reserve.

THE LOBSTER:
In a large pot bring the water and coarse salt to a boil. Add the carrots, onions, celery, peppercorns, and *bouquet garni*, lower the heat and simmer, uncovered, for 12 minutes. Bring the liquid back to a rolling boil, drop in the live lobster, return to a boil, and cook for 9 minutes. Lift out the lobster with tongs, place it in a colander, and make a little hole between its eyes with a knife. Place it head down in the colander

41

and allow to drain for 5 minutes. Remove all the meat from the tail and claws. Cut the tail meat in half lengthwise and remove the blackish intestine, then cut all the lobster meat into thin slices and reserve.

THE GARNISH:

In a large saucepan combine the lettuce, herbs, shallots, orange julienne, carrot strips, and ⅓ of the basil over very low heat and toss until the garnish is barely warm; do not allow to wilt. Remove from the heat, add 3 tablespoons of the vinaigrette, toss to mix, and place the salad on the warm plates.

TO FINISH AND SERVE:

Heat a frying pan with no fat in it. Lightly salt and pepper the diced preserved duck and fry quickly until brown and crisp, about 2 to 3 minutes. Drain on paper towels and sprinkle over the salad on each plate.

Place the rest of the vinaigrette and the lobster slices in a clean saucepan and warm over low heat. Arrange the lobster around the edges of the plates.

Place the strips of fresh mango in the center of each salad, sprinkle over the remaining basil, and serve immediately.

NOTE: *One-fourth pound of diced salt pork may be fried and used instead of duck.*

If necessary, the plates garnished with salad may be placed in a very low oven to keep warm while preparing the duck and lobster. Ed.

Salade de mâche au confit de canard
PRESERVED DUCK SALAD WITH LAMB'S-LETTUCE

Ingredients for 4 servings:

FOR THE VINAIGRETTE:
½ teaspoon salt
Pinch pepper
2 teaspoons wine vinegar
4 teaspoons sherry vinegar
5 tablespoons salad oil

FOR THE SALAD:

½ **Preserved duck** *(see p. 228)* (about ¾ pound)
¾ pound lamb's-lettuce or spinach
2 tablespoons finely chopped parsley
2 tablespoons finely chopped chervil
2 tablespoons finely chopped chives
5 shallots, finely chopped
1 medium apple, peeled, cored, and cut into julienne strips
1 medium turnip, cut into julienne strips
1 truffle, cut into julienne strips (optional)

UTENSILS:

Small bowl
Wire whisk
Large frying pan
Skimmer or slotted spoon
Large saucepan
To serve: 4 heated salad plates

THE VINAIGRETTE:

Place the salt in a small bowl, whisk in the vinegars, oil, and pepper, and reserve.

THE PRESERVED DUCK:

Place the pieces of duck and a little of their fat in a large frying pan and heat over low heat for about 9 minutes to warm through; do not allow to brown. Remove the duck from the pan with a skimmer or slotted spoon, debone the leg and thigh, and cut the meat into julienne strips. Cut the breast into 12 slices, cover with aluminum foil, and reserve.

TO MAKE THE SALAD AND SERVE:

Place the lamb's-lettuce, herbs, shallots, apple, turnip, and truffle and julienne strips of duck in a large saucepan and toss over very low heat to barely warm; do not allow to wilt. Remove from the heat, add 6 tablespoons of the vinaigrette, toss to mix, and place some of the salad on each of the warm salad plates. Quickly dip the 12 slices of breast meat in the remaining vinaigrette and arrange 3 of them on each plate. Serve immediately.

SUGGESTION:
Julienne strips of beet and celery may be used instead of turnip.

Salade de ris de veau aux cèpes frais
SWEETBREAD SALAD WITH WILD MUSHROOMS

Ingredients for 4 servings:

14 ounces sweetbreads
3 tablespoons salad oil
1 tablespoon olive oil
2 tablespoons red-wine vinegar
Salt, pepper

1 generous tablespoon finely chopped parsley, in all
1 generous tablespoon finely chopped chervil, in all
1 generous tablespoon finely chopped chives, in all
2 shallots, finely chopped (total)

10 ounces fresh boletus mushrooms *(cèpes)*, cut into thick strips *(for substitution, see Suggestion)*
1 tablespoon cooking oil (for sweetbreads)
¼ pound lamb's-lettuce or spinach
1 cup tightly packed chickory leaves
1 cup lightly pressed red *trévise* or batavia lettuce leaves

UTENSILS:
Large bowl
Small mixing bowl
Wire whisk
Small saucepan
Frying pan (preferably nonstick)
Large saucepan
To serve: 4 heated salad plates

PRELIMINARY PREPARATIONS:
Soak the sweetbreads in a large bowl of cold water for 24 hours before cooking. Drain and use a knife to remove any gristle or fat, cut the sweetbreads into ¼-inch slices, and reserve.

THE VINAIGRETTE:
Whisk the oils and vinegar together in a small bowl, season lightly with salt and pepper, stir in a third of the fresh herbs and shallots, and reserve.

TO MAKE THE SALAD AND SERVE:

Place the mushrooms in a small saucepan with a third of the vinaigrette, add half of the remaining herbs and shallots, and reserve.

Heat a tablespoon of cooking oil in a nonstick frying pan. Lightly salt and pepper the slices of sweetbread, brown them quickly, about 2 minutes to a side, and drain on paper towels. Keep warm while heating the lettuce and mushrooms.

Place the lettuces and the remaining herbs and shallots in a large saucepan over very low heat and toss until barely warm; do not allow to wilt. Add the remaining vinaigrette, toss to mix, and divide the salad among the plates.

Heat the mushrooms, stirring, until barely warm (not hot), then sprinkle them over the salad on each plate.

Place the slices of sweetbread around the edges of the plates and serve immediately.

SUGGESTION:

Fresh mushrooms must be used in this recipe; ordinary mushrooms may replace the boletus mushrooms used here.

Salade de foie de veau aux blancs de poireaux CALF'S LIVER SALAD WITH LEEKS

Ingredients for 4 servings:

FOR THE VINAIGRETTE:
1½ teaspoons Dijon mustard
Salt, pepper
2 tablespoons sherry vinegar
½ cup salad oil

FOR THE SALAD:
2 to 3 large leeks, white only (1 pound as purchased)
10 ounces calf's liver (one thick slice)
1½ tablespoons butter
Salt, pepper

4 slices Canadian bacon, cut into thin strips
1 tablespoon red-wine vinegar
3 cups tightly packed mixed lettuces (lamb's-lettuce, *batavia* and
  trévise lettuce, etc.)

UTENSILS:
Small bowl
Wire whisk
Saucepan
2 frying pans
Large saucepan
To serve: 4 heated salad plates

THE VINAIGRETTE:

Place the mustard and a little salt and pepper in a mixing bowl and whisk gently, adding first the sherry vinegar, then the oil. Reserve.

THE LEEKS:

Cut the white of each leek into sections 2 inches long. Cut each section in half lengthwise, then separate the layers from each other. Drop them into a saucepan of rapidly boiling salted water, boil for 3 minutes, drain, cool under running water, and drain again.

THE BACON:

Heat the strips of bacon in a frying pan without any fat, for about 4 minutes to brown lightly, add the red wine vinegar to the pan, remove from the heat, and reserve.

THE LIVER:

Preheat the oven to 250° F. Salt and pepper the calf's liver.

In a frying pan, melt the butter over moderate heat. When very hot, add the liver. Cook for 3 minutes on one side and 2 minutes on the other; the liver should be slightly rare when done. Cover and keep it warm in the oven while preparing the garnish.

THE GARNISH:

Place the leeks on a plate in the oven to warm slightly.

Place the lettuces in a large saucepan, toss with 4 tablespoons of the vinaigrette, and place over very low heat to barely warm the lettuce, tossing constantly; do not allow to wilt.

Place some of the lettuce on each of the warm salad plates. Scatter the leeks over the salad.

Cut the liver into thin slices, dip each slice into the vinaigrette, and arrange on the salad. Lightly salt and pepper, sprinkle the bacon over the salad, and serve. (If necessary, reheat the bacon before serving.)

This salad should be barely warm when served; if need be, place the garnished plates into a hot oven for several seconds before serving.

SUGGESTIONS:
Chicken livers may be used instead of calf's liver; sauté them for about 2 minutes over high heat.

Belgian endive, boiled or sautéed, may be used instead of leeks.

Salade de queue de boeuf
OXTAIL SALAD

Ingredients for 4 to 6 servings:

FOR THE OXTAIL:
2¼ pounds oxtail, cut into pieces
2½ teaspoons coarse salt
1 carrot, quartered
1 large onion, stuck with a clove
1 large stalk celery, quartered
Large *bouquet garni*

FOR THE GARNISH:
1 large or 2 small leeks, white only, cut into julienne strips
1 large or 2 small carrots, cut into julienne strips
1 medium turnip, cut into julienne strips

FOR THE VINAIGRETTE:
2 teaspoons Dijon mustard
2 tablespoons sherry vinegar
2 tablespoons salad oil
Salt, pepper

FOR THE SALAD *(see Note)*:
6 ounces lamb's-lettuce
1 cup lightly pressed *trévise* lettuce
2½ cups tightly packed chickory leaves (measure, then remove rib
    from each leaf)
2 teaspoons finely chopped parsley
2 teaspoons finely chopped chervil
2 teaspoons finely chopped chives
2 shallots, finely chopped
Salt, pepper

UTENSILS:
Large stewing pot
Slotted spoon
Large saucepan
Small mixing bowl
Wire whisk
To serve: 4 to 6 heated salad plates

THE OXTAIL:
Place the oxtail in a large pot, add enough warm water to cover
completely, and bring to a boil. Skim off any foam with a skimmer or
slotted spoon, boil the oxtail for 10 minutes, drain, and cool under
running water. Return the oxtail to the rinsed pot, cover again with
warm water (about 2 quarts), add the salt, and bring to a boil, skimming
off any foam. When boiling, add the vegetables and *bouquet garni*,
skim if necessary, cover the pot, and simmer for 3 hours, or until the
meat detaches easily from the bone.

THE GARNISH:
Bring a large pot of lightly salted water to a boil, add the leeks and boil
for 1 minute, add the carrots and boil 1 minute, then add the turnip and
boil for 1 minute. Drain and cool under running water, drain again, and
reserve.

THE VINAIGRETTE:
Place the mustard in a small bowl, add a little salt and pepper and the
sherry vinegar, whisk to combine, then whisk in the oil. Taste for salt
and pepper and reserve.

TO FINISH AND SERVE:

When the oxtail is cooked, remove from the pot with a slotted spoon and allow to cool enough to handle. Remove the meat from the bones while warm and reserve.

Place the lettuces in a large saucepan with the herbs, shallots, and half of the julienned vegetables. Salt and pepper and place over very low heat to barely warm, tossing constantly; do not allow to wilt. Remove from the heat and toss the salad with 4 tablespoons of the vinaigrette. Place some on each plate.

In the same saucepan, stir the remaining julienne strips and 1½ teaspoons of vinaigrette over low heat to barely warm. Arrange the strips on top of the salad. Pour the remaining vinaigrette over the meat, salt and pepper generously, stir, and place the pieces of oxtail on top of the salad. Serve immediately.

SUGGESTION:

The cooking liquid from the oxtail can be strained and used as stock in many of the recipes in this book, or can be served alone as bouillon, or with vegetables as a soup.

A pressure cooker may be used for cooking the oxtail; proceed as described above, but cook for only 1 hour once the pressure has risen.

NOTE: *If the three lettuces mentioned are not available, use a mixture of spinach, watercress, and a little finely sliced red cabbage.*

The oxtail can be cooked and deboned well ahead of time. Reheat the meat in a little of the cooking liquid to warm, drain, and finish as described above. Ed.

Salade de perdrix au chou
PARTRIDGE AND CABBAGE SALAD
(color picture I)

Ingredients for 2 servings:

FOR THE VINAIGRETTE:
5 teaspoons peanut or walnut oil
1 teaspoon sherry vinegar
Salt, pepper

FOR THE PARTRIDGE:

2 quarts water
2 teaspoons salt
1 carrot, quartered
1 leek
1 turnip, quartered
1 small onion, stuck with a clove
1 stalk celery
Bouquet garni
1 partridge, about ¾ pound (*for substitutions, see Suggestions*)
1 pound loose-leaf cabbage
Salt, pepper
2 thin slices *foie gras* (optional, *for substitution, see Suggestions*)

UTENSILS:

Wire whisk
Medium mixing bowl
Large saucepan
Skimmer or slotted spoon
To serve: 2 heated salad plates

THE VINAIGRETTE:

In a medium mixing bowl whisk the oil, vinegar, salt, and pepper together and reserve.

THE PARTRIDGE:

Bring the water and salt to a boil in a large saucepan. Add the vegetables and the *bouquet garni* and boil gently for 20 minutes. Add the partridge, lower the heat, and poach, skimming off any foam, for 10 minutes. Remove the bird from the pot with a skimmer or slotted spoon and leave to cool on a cutting board. Strain the cooking liquid and pour it back into the pot.

With a sharp knife, cut the legs off the partridge and carefully remove all the breast meat. Cut the carcass into pieces, add it to the cooking liquid, and raise the heat. Boil for 5 minutes, lower the heat, return the legs to the pot, and simmer for 5 minutes more; remove the legs and reserve on a plate with the breast meat.

Strain the liquid once more and pour it back into the saucepan.

THE CABBAGE:

Use a loose-leaf cabbage if possible. Remove the dark outside leaves and use only the light-colored inner ones. Cut the cabbage in half from top to bottom, separate the leaves, and remove the thick central rib from each one.

Bring the partridge cooking liquid to a boil, add the cabbage leaves, and boil slowly for about 4 minutes (the cabbage should be slightly crisp when done). Remove the cabbage from the pot with a skimmer or slotted spoon and drain.

TO FINISH AND SERVE:

Preheat the oven to 425° F.

Place the warm cabbage in the bowl with the vinaigrette and toss to mix.

Quickly reheat the pieces of partridge by dropping them into their hot cooking liquid for 2 minutes to warm through. Drain.

Cut the breast meat into thin slices. Debone the legs and slice them. Lightly season with salt and pepper.

Pile the cabbage in a mound on each salad plate, place the slices of partridge on and around it, and lay a slice of *foie gras* on top.

Place the plates in the oven for 1 minute to warm through and serve immediately.

SUGGESTIONS:

Squab or a rock Cornish game hen could be used instead of partridge (poach either bird for 15 minutes).

An equal weight of leeks or spinach (spinach can be served either raw or cooked) may be used instead of cabbage.

A thin slice of calf's liver may be used instead of *foie gras;* sauté it rapidly in a little butter, sprinkle with salt and pepper, cut it into strips, and arrange it around the salad.

Les entrées
FIRST COURSES

Oeufs pochés au beurre rouge
POACHED EGGS WITH RED BUTTER SAUCE

Ingredients for 4 servings:

FOR THE GARNISH:
¼ pound thick-sliced bacon, cut into short, thick strips *(lardons)*
2 tablespoons butter, in all
16 pearl onions
Salt, pepper
½ teaspoon sugar
½ pound medium mushrooms, halved

FOR THE SAUCE:
1 tablespoon butter
5 shallots, finely chopped
1½ cups red wine
3 tablespoons water
9 tablespoons softened butter, broken into pieces
Salt, pepper

FOR THE EGGS:
1½ quarts water
1½ tablespoons vinegar
1½ teaspoons salt
8 very fresh eggs

UTENSILS:
2 small saucepans
Small frying pan, with cover
Skimmer or slotted spoon
Wire whisk
Large *sauteuse* or high-sided frying pan
Clean cloth
To serve: 4 heated plates

THE GARNISH:
Place the bacon in a small saucepan with cold water to cover, bring to a boil, and drain immediately. Cool under running water, drain again, and reserve.

In a small frying pan, melt a tablespoon of butter, add the onions, salt, pepper, and sugar. Add enough water to almost cover the onions (they should not float), bring to a boil over moderate heat, cover the pan, and cook 10 minutes. Remove the cover and boil to evaporate all the water. Shake the pan to roll the onions around in the butter-sugar syrup, remove them from the pan, and reserve in a clean saucepan.

Rinse the pan used for cooking the onions, place over moderate heat, and melt another tablespoon of butter. Add the mushrooms, salt, and pepper and brown over high heat for about 3 minutes, shaking the pan often. Remove the mushrooms with a skimmer or slotted spoon and place them in the saucepan with the onions. Add the parboiled bacon to the frying pan without cleaning it, brown for about 5 minutes, and drain on a paper towel. Add the bacon to the pan with the onions and mushrooms.

THE RED BUTTER SAUCE:
Melt 1 tablespoon butter in a saucepan, add the shallots, and cook for 2 minutes, or until soft. Add the red wine and boil for about 15 minutes, or until it has evaporated and only the moist shallots are left in the pan. Add 3 tablespoons of water, bring to a boil, and whisk in the remaining butter little by little as described for the foamy butter sauce in the

recipe for **Hot fish terrine** *(see p. 84).* The finished sauce should be smooth and creamy. Taste for salt and pepper, remove from the heat, and reserve.

THE EGGS:
Heat the vinegar in a large pot or frying pan. When simmering, add the vinegar and salt and bring to a gentle boil.

Break each egg first into a small saucer or cup, then slide one by one into the boiling water. Use a spoon to fold as much of the white up over the yolk of each egg as possible. Poach for 3 minutes, lift the eggs out of the water with a skimmer or slotted spoon, and drain on a clean cloth.

TO SERVE:
Reheat the garnish.

Gently reheat the butter sauce if necessary, whisking constantly.

Lift the edge of the cloth to roll an egg onto the slotted spoon, then place it on a plate. Place 2 eggs in the center of each plate, spoon the garnish around them, spoon the sauce over the garnish, and serve.

SUGGESTIONS:
The eggs can be poached in red wine instead of water. If desired, fried croutons and slices of poached bone marrow may be placed over the garnish and sauce just before serving.

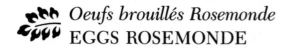

Oeufs brouillés Rosemonde
EGGS ROSEMONDE

Ingredients for 4 servings:
FOR THE HOLLANDAISE:
½ pound smoked salmon, in all
½ pound softened butter
3 egg yolks
3 tablespoons cold water
Salt, pepper
1 tablespoon heavy cream, whipped until stiff

FOR THE TOAST AND EGGS:
1 tablespoon butter
4 slices egg bread or sandwich bread

8 eggs
Salt, pepper
2 tablespoons butter
1 tablespoon *crème fraîche (see p. 331)* or heavy cream
Salt, pepper

UTENSILS:
Blender or food processor
Fine sieve
2 small saucepans
2 medium saucepans
Wire whisk
Large frying pan
2 mixing bowls
To serve: Large ovenproof platter, or 4 plates

THE HOLLANDAISE:

In a blender or food processor purée together half the salmon and the softened butter. Then work the mixture through a sieve with a wooden spoon to eliminate any stringy fibers from the salmon.

Place the salmon butter in a small saucepan and heat gently to boiling, then strain the butter through a fine sieve into another saucepan; stir once or twice, but do not press on the solids. Leave until all the butter has dripped into the saucepan, reserve the butter, and discard the solids left in the sieve.

Place the egg yolks and water in a saucepan, whisk until foamy, then place over low heat and whisk for 2 to 3 minutes, moving the pan on and off the heat to warm the eggs but not cook them. When the eggs begin to thicken, remove the saucepan from the heat and whisk in the melted salmon butter (reheated to warm, but not hot, if necessary) little by little. Season with a little salt and pepper and reserve.

THE TOAST AND EGGS:

Melt the tablespoon of butter in a large frying pan; when very hot, add the slices of bread and brown on both sides (if using sandwich bread, it may be necessary to add more butter). Remove the toasted bread from the pan, cover with a cloth, and keep warm.

Dice the remaining salmon.

Whisk the whole eggs lightly in a bowl with a little salt and pepper.

Melt 1 tablespoon of butter over moderate heat in a medium saucepan; add the beaten eggs and cook for about 4 minutes, stirring constantly with a wire whisk (do not beat). When thick and creamy, add the diced salmon, cream, another tablespoon of butter, salt, and pepper. Cook and stir 1 minute more (the finished eggs will look more like a thick custard than scrambled eggs).

TO SERVE:

Heat the broiler to very hot.

Place the slices of toast on a large ovenproof serving platter or on individual plates. Spoon an equal amount of eggs over each piece of toast.

Fold the whipped cream into the hollandaise and spoon the sauce over the eggs. Place the platter or plates under the broiler to glaze the sauce for a few seconds—watch to see that it browns lightly but does not burn. Serve immediately.

SUGGESTIONS:

Any smoked fish, such as sturgeon, trout, herring, mackerel, and so on may be used instead of salmon.

The finely chopped zest of ½ a lemon can be blanched and added to the hollandaise with the whipped cream.

Feuilleté d'endives
PUFF PASTRY WITH BELGIAN ENDIVES

Ingredients for 4 servings:

FOR THE ENDIVES:
4 small endives (¾ to 1 pound)
1 teaspoon butter
2 medium mushrooms, finely chopped
Salt, pepper

⅔ cup champagne *(or white wine; Ed.)*
⅔ cup *crème fraîche (see p. 331)* or heavy cream

FOR THE MUSHROOMS:
6 ounces (7 medium) mushrooms, chopped
1 teaspoon butter
2 shallots, finely chopped
3 tablespoons *crème fraîche (see p. 331)* or heavy cream
10½ ounces (300 g) **puff pastry** *(see p. 271)*
3 egg yolks (for the sauce)
2 tablespoons softened butter, broken into pieces (for the sauce)
Salt, pepper

UTENSILS:
Large saucepan, with cover
2 small saucepans
Rolling pin
Baking sheet
Wire whisk
To serve: Serving platter and sauceboat

THE ENDIVES:
Cut off the base and remove any wilted or stained leaves from the endives. Use a sharp knife to hollow out a cone in the center of each one, at the base end. Wipe the endives to remove any dirt, then cut off the leafy end, if necessary, so that the endives are no more than 4 inches long.

Melt the teaspoon of butter in a large saucepan, add the mushrooms, season lightly with salt and pepper, and cook slowly for 2 minutes. Stir in the champagne and cream, then add the endives. Season again with salt and pepper, cover the pan, and simmer slowly for 45 minutes to 1 hour, or until the endives are completely tender. Remove the pan from the heat and reserve.

THE MUSHROOMS:
Melt the teaspoon of butter in a small saucepan, add the shallots, and cook slowly 2 to 3 minutes, or until soft, then add the mushrooms, salt, and pepper. Cook 3 minutes, then add the cream, bring to a boil, lower the heat, and simmer for 8 minutes. Remove the pan from the heat and reserve.

57

THE PASTRY:

Roll out the puff pastry on a lightly floured table into a rectangle about 5 × 13 inches. Use a large knife to cut it into 4 rectangles about 4 × 3 inches after the edges have been trimmed. With a pastry brush, brush off any excess flour, then place the pastries upside down on a lightly buttered baking sheet with plenty of space between them. Leave in a cool place 20 to 30 minutes before baking.

Preheat the oven to 425° F.

Just before baking, with the tip of a knife lightly draw a rectangle in each piece of pastry, about ½ inch from the edge. This inner rectangle will form the top of the pastry when it is baked. Bake the pastries for 10 minutes, then lower the heat to 350° F and bake 12 minutes more. Remove from the oven and allow to cool for 3 to 4 minutes.

TO FILL THE PASTRIES:

Run the tip of a knife around the top of each pastry and lift it off and discard it. If necessary, scoop out the centers with a small spoon to make room for the endives.

Reheat the endives and the mushroom garnish.

Lift the endives out of their cooking liquid and slice them in half lengthwise. Season with salt and pepper. Place a quarter of the mushroom garnish on one half of each endive, then place the other half on top, reconstituting each endive with the mushroom filling in the center. Place an endive in each pastry.

TO MAKE THE SAUCE AND SERVE:

Place the egg yolks in a small saucepan, away from the heat. Whisk gently, then strain the endive cooking liquid onto them, whisking constantly. Place the saucepan over low heat and whisk until the mixture becomes foamy and thick (do not allow to boil). Remove from the heat and whisk in the softened butter bit by bit, then taste for salt and pepper.

Preheat the broiler.

Place the filled pastries on a serving platter and spoon some of the sauce into each one. Place the platter under the broiler to lightly glaze the sauce (watch to see that the pastry doesn't burn). Serve with the remaining sauce in a sauceboat.

SUGGESTIONS:

The whites of 4 large or 8 small leeks, or small Bibb lettuces, or escaroles may be used instead of Belgian endives.

If wild mushrooms such as chanterelles or boletus are used instead of ordinary mushrooms, they add a special flavor to this dish.

Feuilletés d'asperges

PUFF PASTRY WITH ASPARAGUS AND FOAMY BUTTER SAUCE

Ingredients for 4 servings:

FOR THE PASTRY:
9 ounces (250 g) **puff pastry** *(see p. 271)*
1 egg
Salt
20 large asparagus (2¾ pounds)

FOR THE SAUCE:
2 teaspoons butter
8 shallots, finely chopped
3 tablespoons wine vinegar
1⅓ cups white wine
1½ sticks (12 tablespoons) softened butter, broken into pieces
Salt, pepper
2 teaspoons finely chopped chervil
2 teaspoons finely chopped parsley
2 teaspoons finely chopped chives

UTENSILS:
Rolling pin
Baking sheet
Mixing bowl
Pastry brush
Kitchen string
Large saucepan
Small saucepan
Wire whisk
To serve: 4 heated plates and sauceboat

THE PASTRY:

Lightly flour a table and roll out the dough into a rectangle about 6½ × 13 inches. Cut the dough into 4 rectangles about 3 × 6 inches after the edges are trimmed and place them on a lightly greased baking sheet with plenty of space between them.

In a small bowl, beat the egg with a pinch of salt and brush it over each rectangle, being careful not to allow the egg to drip over the edges. (This will prevent the dough from rising properly.) With the tip of a pointed knife lightly draw a rectangle in each piece of pastry, about ½ inch from the edge. This central rectangle will form the top of the pastry when it is baked. Leave the dough in a cool place for 15 to 20 minutes.

Preheat the oven to 425° F.

Bake the pastries for 10 minutes, lower the oven to 400° F, and bake 10 minutes more.

THE ASPARAGUS:

Break off the sandy ends of the asparagus, peel them, and cut them off 3½ to 4 inches down from the tips. Cut the stem ends in half lengthwise if the asparagus are large. Tie the tips into three or four bunches. Boil the tips and stems for 10 minutes in rapidly boiling salted water, drain, cover to keep warm, and reserve.

THE SAUCE:

Make the foamy butter sauce as described in the recipe for **Hot fish terrine** *(see p. 84)*, using the measurements given here. When all the butter has been added, taste for salt and pepper, strain the sauce into a sauceboat, and whisk in the chopped herbs.

TO SERVE:

Use the tip of a pointed knife to cut around the tops of the pastries. Lift them off and, if necessary, hollow out the pastries with a small spoon. Place each pastry on a dinner plate. Place the asparagus stems in the pastries, then arrange the tips on top so they stick up above the edge. Replace the tops and serve immediately, with the sauce on the side.

SUGGESTION:

Caviar or truffles may be used instead of herbs in the sauce.

Feuilletés de langouste
SPINY LOBSTER, OYSTERS, AND SCALLOPS IN PASTRY

Ingredients for 4 servings:

FOR THE COURT BOUILLON *(optional, see Note):*
2 quarts water
1 carrot, sliced
1 onion, sliced
Bouquet garni
20 peppercorns
1 generous tablespoon coarse salt
1 live spiny lobster or Maine lobster, weighing about 1¼ pounds

FOR THE SAUCE:
2 tablespoons olive oil
2 tablespoons dry white wine
3 tablespoons cognac
1 medium carrot, diced
1 stalk celery, diced
1 small onion, diced
1 small leek, diced
¼ small fennel bulb, diced
1 medium tomato, diced
1½ cups heavy cream

FOR THE GREENS:
1 tablespoon butter
¼ pound fresh young spinach, stems removed *(see Note)*
⅔ cup tightly packed watercress leaves
Salt, pepper
9 ounces (250 g) **puff pastry** *(p. 271)*

FOR THE SEAFOOD FILLING:
8 oysters
8 small sea scallops (about 4 ounces, *or equal weight of bay scallops. Ed.*)

61

UTENSILS:
3-quart pot (for lobster)
High-sided frying pan or *sauteuse*, 9½ inches in diameter
Skimmer or slotted spoon
2 large saucepans
Rolling pin
Baking sheet
To serve: 4 heated dinner plates and sauceboat

THE COURT BOUILLON *(See Note)* AND LOBSTER:

Place the water, carrot, onion, *bouquet garni,* peppercorns, and salt in a pot and boil for 5 minutes.

Plunge the tip of a large knife into the lobster where the head meets the tail to kill it. Cut off the tail and drop it into the boiling court bouillon. If using a Maine lobster, break off the claws and add them as well. Bring back to a boil and boil gently for 7 minutes, drain, and reserve.

THE LOBSTER SAUCE:

Cut the lobster head into pieces. Heat the olive oil in a high-sided frying pan or *sauteuse*. Add the pieces of head and sauté over moderate heat for about 3 minutes, then add the white wine and cognac; bring to a boil and light with a match. When the flame goes out, add the diced carrot, celery, onion, leek, fennel, and tomato. Sauté for 4 minutes to soften the vegetables and evaporate their water, then add the cream, lower the heat, and simmer for 30 minutes, skimming off any foam that appears. Strain the sauce into a clean saucepan. Use a wooden spoon to press down on the vegetables and shell to extract all the juices; there should be about 1 cup of sauce. Cover the saucepan and reserve.

THE SPINACH AND WATERCRESS:

Melt the butter in a large saucepan, add the spinach and watercress, a little salt and pepper, and allow to melt down. Simmer over low heat for about 5 minutes, stirring frequently. Remove from the heat and reserve.

THE PASTRY:

Roll out and cut the pastry as described in the recipe for **Puff pastry with Belgian endives** *(see p. 56)*. Preheat the oven to 425° F. Bake for 15 to 18 minutes and reserve.

THE FILLING:

Remove the meat from the poached lobster tail (and claws). Cut the tail in half lengthwise and remove the black intestine. Cut the meat it into slices about ½ inch thick. Slice the claw meat as well.

Open the oysters, if necessary, and drain.

Gently heat the lobster sauce, season with salt and pepper if necessary, and add the slices of lobster, the oysters, and scallops. Simmer very slowly for 3 minutes.

TO FILL THE PASTRIES AND SERVE:

With the tip of a knife, detach the tops of the pastries and spoon out the soft centers. Gently reheat the spinach-watercress mixture if it has cooled, then place a spoonful in each pastry.

Use a skimmer or slotted spoon to lift the seafood out of the sauce, and divide it among the pastries. Pour a spoonful of sauce into each pastry, put the top back in place, and serve immediately, with the rest of the sauce in a sauceboat.

SUGGESTION:

A simpler version of this recipe can be made without the pastry by serving the seafood on a bed of spinach and watercress and spooning the sauce over and around it.

NOTE: *It is not absolutely necessary to make a court bouillon. The lobster tail and claws can be simply cooked in boiling salted water.*

If the spinach has thick, very large, dark green leaves, parboil it for 2 minutes in boiling water, drain, cool under running water, and press dry before cooking as described. Ed.

Raie en croûte au cresson
SKATE PÂTÉS WITH WATERCRESS SAUCE

Ingredients for 8 servings:

FOR THE PÂTÉS:
¾ pound skate *(for substitutions, see Suggestions)*
1 cup tightly packed watercress leaves
½ cup *crème fraîche (see p. 331)*

Salt, pepper
18 ounces (500 g) **puff pastry** *(see p. 271)*
1 egg yolk

FOR THE SAUCE:
4 teaspoons butter
4 shallots, finely chopped
1½ cups dry white wine
5 tablespoons wine vinegar
¾ pound minus 3 tablespoons softened butter, broken into pieces
Salt, pepper

UTENSILS:
Filleting knife
Mixing bowl
2 bowls
Baking sheet
Rolling pin
3½-inch round cookie cutter
4-inch round cookie cutter
Pastry brush
Small saucepan
Wire whisk
To serve: Large serving platter and sauceboat

PRELIMINARY PREPARATIONS:
With a filleting knife, remove the skin from the skate. Cut the meat off of the bone, coarsely chop it, and place it in a mixing bowl.

Carefully wash and drain the watercress leaves. Coarsely chop half of them and place them in the bowl with the fish. Cut the remaining leaves into thin strips and reserve in another bowl.

Preheat the oven to 425° F.

Lightly oil or butter a baking sheet.

MAKING THE PÂTÉS:
Add the cream to the mixing bowl with the skate and watercress, stir well, and season generously with salt and pepper.

Roll the puff pastry out to a thickness of about ¹⁄₁₆ inch. Cut out 8 circles with the 3½-inch cookie cutter, then pack the leftover dough into a ball, roll it out again, and cut out 8 circles with the 4-inch cookie cutter.

In a bowl, beat the egg yolk with a pinch of salt, then, using a pastry brush, paint a thin band of egg around the border of each small circle. (Be careful not to let the egg drip over the edge of the circle.)

Place a large spoonful of the fish mixture in the center of each small circle, then cover each one with a large circle, pressing down around the edges to be sure the top and bottom pieces stick together. Brush the top of each pâté with a little beaten egg.

Place the pâtés on the baking sheet, with plenty of space between them, and bake in the oven for 18 minutes or until golden brown.

TO MAKE THE SAUCE AND SERVE:
Make the foamy butter sauce as described in the recipe for a **Hot fish terrine** *(see p. 84)*, using the measurements given here. When all the butter has been added, season the sauce with salt and pepper, strain into a sauceboat, and stir in the strips of watercress.

Serve the pâtés as soon as they come from the oven, with the sauce on the side.

SUGGESTIONS:
Instead of skate, whiting, carp, or pike may be filleted and used in making the pâtés (be sure to remove all the tiny bones from pike).

The watercress may be replaced by an equal amount of spinach, the green of Swiss chard, or parsley.

Tartes de saumon, beurre blanc aux herbes
SALMON TARTS WITH FRESH HERBS
AND BUTTER SAUCE

Ingredients for 4 servings:
   ¾ pound fresh salmon fillets or 1 pound salmon, to be filleted
   9 ounces (250 g) **puff pastry** *(see p. 271)*

   FOR THE SAUCE:
   2 teaspoons butter
   3 shallots, finely chopped

⅔ cup dry white wine
8 teaspoons wine vinegar
¼ pound softened butter, broken into small pieces
Salt, pepper

3 tablespoons melted butter (for the tarts)
2 teaspoons finely chopped parsley
2 teaspoons finely chopped chives
2 teaspoons finely chopped chervil

UTENSILS:
Rolling pin
2 baking sheets
Small saucepan
Wire whisk
Pastry brush
To serve: 4 heated salad plates and sauceboat

THE SALMON:
The salmon fillets should be free of bones and skin. Use a sharp knife to thinly slice the salmon, cutting at a slight angle, as you would smoked salmon.

THE PUFF PASTRY:
Preheat the oven to 425° F.

Roll out the puff pastry on a lightly floured table. Make a sheet about ¹⁄₁₆ inch thick and, with a sharp knife, cut it into 4 circles about 5 inches in diameter. (Cut around a plate. If 4 circles cannot be cut at once, pack the scraps into a ball and roll them out again.)

Lightly butter 2 baking sheets. Place the circles of dough on one baking sheet, then lay the other baking sheet, buttered side down, on top. Bake for 18 minutes; the second baking sheet will keep the dough from rising too much. Remove the top baking sheet and bake for 2 minutes more.

THE FOAMY BUTTER SAUCE:
Make the foamy butter sauce as described in the recipe for a **Hot fish terrine** *(see p. 84)*, using the ingredients listed here. When all the butter has been added, season the sauce with salt and pepper, remove from the heat, and reserve.

TO FINISH AND SERVE:
Preheat the broiler.

Cover each pastry with the salmon, placing the slices so that each one slightly overlaps the preceding one. Brush each tart with a little melted butter and place under the broiler for about 2 minutes (just long enough to heat them through). Watch carefully to see that the salmon does not dry out or burn.

Place a tart on each plate. Gently reheat the sauce, whisking constantly. Place the freshly chopped herbs in a sauceboat and strain the sauce onto them. Stir the sauce, then serve the tarts with the sauce on the side.

SUGGESTIONS:
Any firm-fleshed fish may be used instead of salmon.

Moules d'Espagne au cari
MUSSELS WITH SPINACH AND CURRY
(color picture II)

Ingredients for 4 servings:

2 pounds very large mussels—20 mussels (*for substitution, see Suggestions and Note*)
¾ cup dry white wine
½ teaspoon mild curry powder
¾ pound fresh spinach, stem and rib removed
Salt, pepper

FOR THE SAUCE:
2 teaspoons butter
3 shallots, finely chopped
1 cup dry white wine
2 tablespoons wine vinegar
¼ pound plus 3 tablespoons softened butter, broken into pieces
Generous ½ teaspoon mild curry powder

UTENSILS:
Large saucepan, with cover
Pot
Bowl
2 small saucepans
Wire whisk
Roasting pan
To serve: 4 heated plates

PRELIMINARY PREPARATIONS:
Wash and scrape the mussels clean and remove the "beard" that protrudes from between the shells. Discard any mussel that is not tightly closed.

Place the wine and the curry powder in a large saucepan, bring to a boil, and boil gently, uncovered, for 2 minutes. Remove from the heat, cover the pot, and reserve.

THE SPINACH:
Bring a pot of water to a boil, add the spinach, bring back to a boil, and cook, uncovered, for 1 minute. Drain and cool under running water, then squeeze the spinach leaves to remove any water. Coarsely chop the leaves, place them in a bowl, season with salt and pepper, and reserve.

THE SAUCE:
Make a foamy butter sauce as described in the recipe for **Hot fish terrine** *(see p. 84)*, using the measurements given here. When all the butter has been added, remove the pot from the heat and strain the sauce into another small saucepan, pressing on the shallots with a wooden spoon. Season with salt and pepper, add the curry powder, whisk to make the sauce perfectly smooth, and reserve.

TO COOK THE MUSSELS AND SERVE:
Preheat the oven to its maximum temperature.

Place the mussels in the saucepan with the white wine-curry mixture. Cover the pot, place over high heat, and boil rapidly for about 5 minutes, or until all the mussels have opened, shaking the pot occasionally. Remove the mussels from their shells and reserve. Reserve one shell from each mussel as well and place it in a large roasting pan.

Place a little spinach in each mussel shell and place a mussel on top. When all the shells are filled, cover the roasting pan with a sheet of aluminum foil and place it in the oven for about 5 minutes, just long enough to warm the mussels.

Over low heat, reheat the sauce to warm, whisking constantly. Arrange five mussels on each plate, spoon a little of the sauce over them, and serve immediately.

SUGGESTIONS:

Oysters may be used instead of mussels. In this case, open the oysters with an oyster knife and poach them for 2 minutes in the wine-curry infusion.

The green of Swiss chard leaves or watercress may be used instead of spinach.

Paprika may be used instead of curry powder, but in this case (keep this in mind whenever paprika is used) add a little sugar or chopped onion to both the sauce and the wine-paprika infusion.

NOTE: *If very large mussels, or oysters in their shells, are unavailable, large clam shells or small porcelain dishes may be used instead. If using small mussels, go by the weight rather than the number when purchasing them, and place 2 in each clam shell or dish rather than one.*

In his restaurant, Alain Senderens does not chop the spinach when he makes this dish. Instead, he boils it as described, then drains it, carefully separates the leaves, and spreads them out on a towel to dry. He then garnishes each shell with a folded spinach leaf. We found it very difficult to keep the leaves intact once they were cooked and have therefore proposed this simplified version, since only the presentation, not the taste, is affected, and the dish takes much less time to make. Ed.

Moules au basilic et à la tomate
MUSSELS WITH TOMATOES AND BASIL

Ingredients for 4 servings:

FOR THE TOMATO SAUCE:
1 tablespoon butter
3 shallots, finely chopped
5 tomatoes, peeled, seeded, and chopped
1 small clove garlic, crushed
Bouquet garni
Salt, pepper

FOR THE MUSSELS:
2¼ pounds mussels
1 tablespoon butter
3 shallots, finely chopped
¾ cup dry white wine
1 small clove garlic, crushed
Pepper

12 large or 24 small basil leaves, cut into thin strips
1 tablespoon chopped parsley

UTENSILS:
2 large saucepans, with covers
To serve: Large serving bowl (optional)

THE TOMATO SAUCE:
Melt the butter in a large saucepan, add the shallots, and cook over low heat about 2 minutes, or until soft and transparent. Add the tomatoes, garlic, *bouquet garni*, salt, and pepper, simmer for 15 minutes, stirring frequently, and remove the pot from the heat. Remove the *bouquet garni* and discard. Cover the sauce and reserve.

THE MUSSELS:
Wash the mussels and scrape them clean with a knife; pull out the stringy "beard" that protrudes from between the shells. Discard any mussels that are not tightly closed.

Heat the butter in a large saucepan, add the shallots, and cook until soft and transparent. Add the white wine and boil for 2 minutes. Add the garlic, mussels, a little pepper, stir, raise the heat, and cover the pot. Boil very rapidly for 3 to 5 minutes, or until all the mussels have opened, shaking the pot occasionally.

TO FINISH AND SERVE:

Add the tomato sauce to the pan with the mussels and continue cooking, covered, over high heat for 4 minutes.

Serve the mussels either in the pot they cooked in or in a large serving bowl. Just before serving, sprinkle with the strips of basil and the chopped parsley.

SUGGESTION:

Clams may be used instead of mussels.

Soufflé aux moules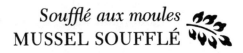
MUSSEL SOUFFLÉ

Ingredients for 4 servings:

FOR THE MUSSELS:
3 pounds mussels
1 tablespoon butter
2 shallots, finely chopped
4 mushrooms, finely chopped
Bouquet garni
1 cup dry white wine
½ teaspoon mild curry powder (optional)
Pepper

FOR THE FOAMY BUTTER SAUCE:
2 teaspoons butter
2 shallots, finely chopped
1 cup dry white wine
3 tablespoons wine vinegar
6 tablespoons softened butter, broken into pieces
Salt, pepper

FOR THE SOUFFLÉS:
4 egg yolks
1½ tablespoons softened butter
6 egg whites
Pinch salt

UTENSILS:
5-quart pot, with cover
Clean cloth
2 small saucepans
Wire whisk
4 individual soufflé molds, 4 inches in diameter
Mixing bowl
2 large mixing bowls
Large roasting pan

THE MUSSELS AND STOCK:
Clean and cook the mussels as described in the recipe for **Mussels with tomatoes and basil** *(see p. 70)*, using the ingredients listed here (cook the mushrooms with the shallots). Once the mussels have opened, remove 20 of them from the pot, remove them from their shells, and reserve, covered.

Add the curry to the pot and boil the cooking liquid and the rest of the mussels for about 10 minutes, or until the liquid has reduced to about 1 cup, strain it through a clean cloth, and reserve *(see Note)*.

THE SAUCE:
Make the foamy butter sauce as described in the recipe for **Hot fish terrine** *(see p. 84)*, using the measurements given here. When all the butter has been added, remove from the heat, season the sauce with salt and pepper, and reserve.

THE SOUFFLÉS:
Preheat the oven to 425° F. Butter the molds.

Place the egg yolks in a mixing bowl, beat lightly, and pour the hot cooking liquid from the mussels onto them, whisking vigorously. Pour the mixture into a saucepan and heat gently, still whisking, until it becomes thick, opaque, and foamy (do not allow to boil). Whisk in 1½ tablespoons of butter, pour into a large bowl, and allow to cool.

Place the egg whites in a large bowl with a pinch of salt and whisk until very stiff, then fold them into the egg yolk mixture with a wooden spatula. When smooth, fold in the reserved mussels.

Pour this mixture into the soufflé molds, distributing the mussels evenly among them. Fill the molds to within ¼ inch of the rim and wipe the edge clean with your finger.

Place the molds in the roasting pan, pour in enough boiling water to come halfway up the sides of the molds, and bake 15 minutes, or until a straw plunged into the center of a soufflé comes out clean.

TO SERVE:

Over low heat, reheat the sauce, whisking constantly.

Remove the soufflés from the oven, cut a little hole in the center of each one with the tip of a knife, and pour in some of the sauce. Serve immediately.

SUGGESTION:

Clams may be used instead of mussels.

NOTE: *The leftover mussels used in making the stock may be removed from their shells, mixed with a homemade mayonnaise made with the leftover egg yolks, and chilled. Serve on lettuce as an appetizer. Ed.*

Belons chaudes à la julienne de poireaux
OYSTERS WITH LEEK SAUCE

Ingredients for 4 servings:

    2 medium leeks, white only
    1 tablespoon butter
    Salt, pepper
    ⅓ cup water

    FOR THE SAUCE:

    2 teaspoons butter
    5 shallots, finely chopped
    ⅔ cup dry white wine (or champagne)
    3 tablespoons vinegar
    6½ tablespoons softened butter, broken into pieces
    Salt, pepper

FOR THE OYSTERS:
24 very large oysters in their shells
3 tablespoons white wine
Salt, pepper

UTENSILS:
Large frying pan, with cover
2 small saucepans
Wire whisk
Oyster knife
Mixing bowl
Clean cloth
Baking sheet
Skimmer or slotted spoon
To serve: 4 dinner plates

THE LEEKS:
Cut the leeks into pieces about 2 inches long. Cut in half lengthwise, then into julienne strips. Wash carefully under cold running water and drain.

Melt the tablespoon of butter in a large frying pan, add the leeks, and spread them out in a single layer. Cook for 3 minutes to soften, but do not allow to brown. Season with salt and pepper, add the water, and bring to a boil. Lower the heat, cover, and simmer very slowly for 15 minutes, or until all the liquid has evaporated. Reserve.

THE SAUCE:
Make the foamy butter sauce as described in the recipe for a **Hot fish terrine** *(see p. 84)*, but using the ingredients listed here. Remove the pan from the heat and reserve.

TO COOK THE OYSTERS AND SERVE:
Preheat the broiler to moderate.

Open the oysters over a mixing bowl in order to catch all of their liquid. Place the oysters in a small saucepan, then strain their liquid onto them through a clean cloth.

Save the bottom (concave) shell of each oyster. Rinse the shells, place them on a baking sheet, and heat them under the broiler while cooking the oysters.

74

Add 3 tablespoons of white wine to the oysters and heat them slowly until almost boiling; at the first bubble, remove the pan from the heat. Use a skimmer or slotted spoon to lift the oysters out of the liquid and place them on a towel to drain.

Boil the oyster liquid for about 3 minutes. Add 1 tablespoon of the liquid and the foamy butter sauce to the leeks. Stir gently over low heat to reheat the leeks. Add a little salt and pepper if needed.

Remove the oyster shells from the broiler and place 6 on each plate. Place an oyster in each shell. Lightly whisk the leek sauce; using a fork, lift a few strips of leek out of the sauce and place them on each oyster, spoon a little sauce over each one, and serve.

Grenouilles cressonière
FROGS' LEGS WITH WATERCRESS

Ingredients for 4 servings:

FOR THE FROGS' LEGS:
12 ounces frogs' legs (*see Note*)
2 cups water
½ bay leaf
½ sprig thyme (or pinch whole thyme leaves)

FOR THE VEGETABLES:
4 teaspoons butter, in all
1 carrot, cut into julienne strips
1 pinch sugar
5 cups tightly packed watercress leaves (2 to 3 large bunches)
Salt, pepper

FOR THE SAUCE:
2 teaspoons butter
6 shallots, finely chopped
1⅔ cups dry white wine
¼ pound plus 2½ tablespoons softened butter, broken into pieces
Salt, pepper

75

UTENSILS:
2 medium saucepans
Skimmer or slotted spoon
Frying pan
Blender or food processor
Small saucepan
Wire whisk
Small baking dish
To serve: 4 heated dinner plates and a sauceboat, warm but not hot

THE STOCK:

Cut the frogs' legs off of the back at the hip joint, then cut the lower leg at the knee. Reserve the meaty thighs; place the backs and lower legs in a medium saucepan. Add 2 cups of water, place over low heat, and bring slowly to a boil. Boil gently, uncovered, for 5 minutes, then skim off any foam. Add the bay leaf and thyme and cook 5 minutes more.

THE VEGETABLES:

In a frying pan, melt 2 teaspoons of butter, add the strips of carrot, salt, pepper, and a pinch of sugar, and cook over low heat for 3 to 5 minutes, stirring frequently (the carrots should barely begin to color).

In a medium saucepan, melt 2 teaspoons of butter and add the watercress leaves. Stir, turning the leaves over until they have melted down, season with a little salt and pepper, and simmer for 4 minutes.

Purée the cooked watercress in a blender or food processor, return the purée to the saucepan, taste for seasoning, and reserve.

THE SAUCE:

Using the measurements given here, make the foamy butter sauce as described in the recipe for **Hot fish terrine** *(see p. 84)*. When all the butter has been added, season the sauce with salt and pepper and strain it into a sauceboat.

TO COOK THE FROGS' LEGS AND SERVE:

Preheat the oven to 425° F.

While the shallots and wine are reducing for the sauce, arrange the reserved frogs' leg thighs in a baking dish just large enough to hold them in one layer.

Season the legs with salt and pepper, strain the hot stock over them, and bake for 5 minutes.

Reheat the carrots and watercress purée.

When the frogs' legs have finished cooking, lift them carefully from the baking dish with a skimmer or slotted spoon and drain on a cloth.

Place some watercress purée in the center of each dinner plate and arrange the frogs' legs on top. Spoon a little sauce around the watercress, sprinkle the carrots over each serving and serve, with the rest of the sauce on the side.

SUGGESTIONS:

An equal amount of lettuce or spinach leaves may be used instead of the watercress.

A little curry powder or freshly chopped herbs may be added to the sauce.

If you don't have time to make the stock, the frogs' legs may be left whole and simply sautéed in a frying pan with a little butter, salt, and pepper for about 5 minutes.

NOTE: *In the U.S. the size of frogs' legs can vary enormously. If very large, debone the thighs and cut the meat into pieces before serving. Ed.*

"Soupe" de grenouilles 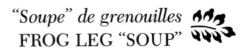
 FROG LEG "SOUP"

Ingredients for 4 servings:

   ¼ pound snow peas, strings and stems removed

   1 tablespoon butter

   1 medium tomato, peeled, seeded, and chopped

     FOR THE FROGS' LEGS:

   24 frogs' legs, weighing about 1¼ pounds *(see Note* to **Frogs' legs with watercress** *[see p. 75])*

   2 teaspoons butter

   1 cup water

   1 clove garlic, sliced

   1½-inch piece fresh ginger

FOR THE SAUCE:

2 teaspoons butter
2 shallots, finely chopped
¾ cup white wine
3 tablespoons vinegar
¼ pound softened butter, broken into pieces
Salt, pepper

TO FINISH:

1 tablespoon butter (for the frogs' legs)
Salt, pepper
4 small canned or poached artichoke bottoms, sliced
Pinch cayenne pepper
6 small or 3 large fresh basil leaves, cut into thin strips

UTENSILS:

2 medium saucepans
Small frying pan
Bowl
Small saucepan
Wire whisk
Large frying pan
To serve: 4 heated soup plates

PRELIMINARY PREPARATIONS:

Cook the snow peas in a saucepan of lightly salted water for 6 to 8 minutes, cool under running water, drain, and reserve.

Melt a tablespoon of butter in a small frying pan, add the tomato, salt and pepper lightly, and simmer for 10 minutes. Reserve.

THE STOCK:

Cut the backs off of the frogs' legs and cut off the lower leg at the knee. Separate the thighs from each other and reserve.

Melt 2 teaspoons of butter in a saucepan, add the backs and lower legs, and sauté for about 3 minutes to brown lightly. Add the water, bring to a boil, and skim off any foam that appears. Add the garlic and ginger and boil slowly for about 40 minutes, or until there is only ⅔ cup of liquid left. Strain the stock into a bowl and reserve.

78

THE SAUCE:

Make the foamy butter sauce as described in the recipe for **Hot fish terrine** *(see p. 84)*, using the measurements given here. Once all the butter has been added, season with salt and pepper and strain the sauce into the bowl with the stock. Whisk together and reserve.

THE FROGS' LEGS:

Heat a tablespoon of butter in a large frying pan until nearly smoking. Generously salt and pepper the reserved thighs and add them to the hot butter. Brown over moderate heat for about 5 minutes, shaking the pan often to roll the frogs' legs in the butter, remove from the pan, and drain the thighs for a few seconds on a paper towel. Cover and keep warm.

TO FINISH AND SERVE:

Place the snow peas, tomato, and sliced artichoke bottoms in a saucepan. Add the mixture of stock and butter sauce, taste for salt and pepper, add the cayenne pepper, and heat for 1 to 2 minutes, stirring occasionally. The "soup" should be very hot, but do not allow to boil.

Ladle the liquid and vegetables into the soup plates, place the frogs' legs on top, sprinkle with the strips of basil, and serve immediately.

Feuilletés de grenouilles au beurre de cerfeuil FROGS' LEGS IN PASTRY WITH CHERVIL BUTTER SAUCE

Ingredients for 4 servings:
    9 ounces (250 g) **puff pastry** *(see p. 271)*
    24 frogs' legs, weighing about 1¼ pounds *(see Note)*
    2 cups water
    1 large clove garlic, crushed
    1-inch piece fresh ginger, finely chopped
    Bouquet garni
    Salt, pepper

FOR THE BUTTER SAUCE:

2 teaspoons butter
5 shallots, finely chopped
¾ cup white wine
3 tablespoons wine vinegar
½ pound less 2 tablespoons softened butter, broken into pieces
Salt, pepper
1 heaping tablespoon whole chervil leaves *(see Note)*

FOR THE GARNISH:

2 teaspoons butter
½ pound young fresh spinach, stems and ribs removed
½ cup tightly packed watercress leaves

UTENSILS:

Rolling pin
Baking sheet
3 small saucepans
Slotted spoon
Wire whisk
Small frying pan
To serve: Serving platter, or 4 plates and a sauceboat

TO ROLL AND CUT THE DOUGH:

Roll out the dough, cut it into 4 rectangles, and make an incision to form a top as described for **Puff pastry with Belgian endives** *(see p. 56)*. Place the pastry on a baking sheet and leave in a cool place for 30 minutes before baking.

THE FROGS' LEGS:

Cut the frogs' legs from the back at the hip. Cut the lower leg from the thigh at the knee. Place the backs and lower legs in a small saucepan and reserve.

Using a small sharp knife, carefully debone the thighs, trying to keep the meat as whole as possible. Place the meat on a plate, salt and pepper, and reserve.

Place the bones from the thighs in the saucepan with the backs and lower legs, add just enough water to cover them (2 to 2½ cups), bring to a boil, skim off any foam, and add the garlic, ginger, and *bouquet garni*. Lower the heat and simmer slowly for 15 minutes, then strain the liquid into a small saucepan and season lightly with salt and pepper. Bring to a boil, add the meat from the thighs, and simmer for 4 minutes. Lift the meat out with a slotted spoon and drain on a towel.

THE BUTTER SAUCE:

Make the foamy butter sauce as described in the recipe for **Hot fish terrine** *(see p. 84)*, using the ingredients listed here. When all the butter has been added, season the sauce with salt and pepper and reserve.

BAKING THE PASTRIES:

Preheat the oven to 425° F.

Place the pastries in the oven and bake 11 minutes, lower the heat to 400° F, and bake 15 minutes more.

Remove the pastries from the oven. With the tip of a knife, lift off the top of each pastry; hollow out the middles with a small spoon. Leave the oven on 400° F.

TO FINISH AND SERVE:

Melt 2 teaspoons of butter in a small frying pan, add the spinach leaves and watercress, stir until melted down, then simmer, uncovered, for 4 minutes. Season with salt and pepper, then place a little of this garnish inside each pastry shell. Divide the meat from the frogs' legs among the pastries, then put the tops back in place. Place the filled pastries back into the oven for a minute or two to warm through.

Gently reheat the butter sauce, whisking constantly. Place the fresh chervil leaves in a sauceboat, strain the butter sauce over them and stir.

Remove the pastries from the oven, place them on a serving platter or plates, and serve, with the sauceboat of sauce on the side.

NOTE: *Fresh basil, parsley, or chives, coarsely chopped, may be used instead of chervil leaves.*

Because the size of frogs' legs can vary a great deal in the U.S., buy by the weight, not by the piece. Ed.

Ragoût malin
FROGS' LEG, OYSTER, AND LANGOUSTINE STEW

Ingredients for 4 servings:

2 teaspoons butter
5 shallots, finely chopped
1⅔ cups red wine
6 tablespoons red wine vinegar
1½ cups heavy cream

12 pairs of frogs' legs (10 ounces) *(for substitutions, see Suggestions)*

12 shelled *langoustines (for substitutions, see Note)*
12 shelled oysters
Salt, pepper
8 basil leaves, cut into thin strips

UTENSILS:
Saucepan
To serve: Serving platter, or 4 heated dinner plates

THE SAUCE:
Melt the butter in a saucepan, add the shallots, and simmer until soft and transparent. Add the wine and vinegar and boil rapidly for about 10 to 15 minutes, or until all the liquid has evaporated. Stir in the cream and boil gently for 10 minutes to allow it to thicken slightly.

TO MAKE THE STEW AND SERVE:
Season the frogs' legs, *langoustines*, and oysters with salt and pepper.

Add the frogs' legs to the sauce and simmer for 2 minutes. (If an absolutely smooth sauce is desired, place the frogs' legs in a clean saucepan and strain the sauce over them.) Add the *langoustines*, simmer for 1 minute, add the oysters, and simmer for 2 minutes more.

Either serve on a platter or on individual plates; if using plates, arrange 3 *langoustines*, 3 oysters, and 3 pairs of frogs' legs on each one. Spoon the sauce over them, sprinkle with the basil, and serve immediately.

SUGGESTIONS:
The red wine vinegar and red wine may be replaced by equal amounts, respectively, of cider vinegar and hard cider, or by white wine and tarragon-flavored vinegar.

About 6 ounces of shelled scallops (4 large sea scallops) may be used instead of the frogs' legs.

Instead of basil, a julienne of green beans, or a mixture of a julienne of truffles and carrots, sautéed in butter with a little salt and pepper, or some boiled asparagus tips, may be used.

NOTE: *A pound of large shrimp or a lobster tail, poached separately, and reheated in the sauce, may be used instead of the langoustines. Ed.*

Fricassée d'escargots à la crème
SNAILS WITH CREAM AND HERBS

Ingredients for 4 servings:

   1 large can (5 dozen snails) of *escargots au naturel (for substitutions, see Suggestion)*
   1½ tablespoons butter
   ½ pound medium mushrooms, cut into 8 pieces each
   8 shallots, finely chopped
   ¼ cup white wine vinegar
   Salt, pepper
   Nutmeg
   ¼ cup dry white wine
   1½ cups heavy cream
   2 teaspoons finely chopped parsley
   2 teaspoons finely chopped chervil
   2 teaspoons finely chopped chives
   2 basil leaves, finely chopped
   1 mint leaf, finely chopped

   UTENSILS:
   Large frying pan
   To serve: 4 heated dinner plates, or ramekins (1-cup capacity)

TO COOK AND SERVE:
Wash and drain the snails.

    Melt the butter in a large frying pan. Add the mushrooms and cook 5 minutes, stirring often, until the mushroom juices have evaporated. The mushrooms should begin to brown. Add the shallots and cook 1 minute. Add the vinegar, stir, and boil until it has almost completely evaporated. Add the snails, salt, pepper, a little nutmeg, and the wine. Boil until almost all the wine has evaporated. Stir in the cream and boil for 5 minutes, or until the sauce is thick and creamy. Stir in the fresh herbs and serve immediately on plates or in individual ramekins.

SUGGESTION:
Cooked shrimp, crayfish, or even chicken livers may be prepared and served in the same way as the snails. (Brown the chicken livers in a little butter for about 1 minute before following the above recipe.)

Terrine de poisson chaude
HOT FISH TERRINE

Ingredients for 1 *terrine,* serving 6 to 8:

FOR THE TERRINE:
2 teaspoons butter
1 medium mushroom, finely chopped
2 shallots, finely chopped
½ pound hake fillets *(for substitution, see Note)*
¼ pound pike or trout fillets *(for substitution, see Note)*
2 cups *crème fraîche (see p. 331)*
1 egg
¼ pound plus 2 tablespoons softened butter
1 generous teaspoon finely chopped chives
1 generous teaspoon finely chopped chervil or parsley
1 teaspoon salt
¾ teaspoon pepper
Pinch cayenne pepper

FOR THE FOAMY BUTTER SAUCE:
4 teaspoons butter
6 shallots, finely chopped
1 cup dry white wine
3 tablespoons vinegar
½ pound softened butter, broken into pieces
Salt, pepper

UTENSILS:
Large pot
Porcelain or earthenware terrine (1-quart capacity), preferably rectangular
Small saucepan
Food processor or heavy-duty blender
2 mixing bowls
Roasting pan
Large roasting pan
Wire whisk
To serve: 6 to 8 heated plates and warm sauceboat

PRELIMINARY PREPARATIONS:
Preheat the oven to 400° F.
Bring a large pot of water to a boil for baking the terrine.
Lightly butter the inside of the terrine.

MAKING THE TERRINE:
In a small saucepan, melt 2 teaspoons of butter. Add the mushroom, simmer gently for about 2 minutes, or until it has melted down and its juice has evaporated. Add the shallots and simmer, stirring occasionally, for 2 minutes more, or until soft and transparent. Remove from the heat and allow to cool.

Place the fish fillets and the cream in a food processor or heavy-duty blender and blend to a smooth purée. Transfer this mixure to a mixing bowl and stir in the shallots and mushrooms and the egg.

In another mixing bowl, beat the butter with a wooden spoon until creamy. Add several spoonfuls of the fish mixture and stir it in. Stir in the rest of the fish mixture to the butter, little by little. Stir in the herbs, salt, pepper, and cayenne pepper. Pour the mixture into the buttered *terrine* and cover (if the *terrine* has no cover, use aluminum foil).

85

Pour enough boiling water into a roasting pan to half fill it, place the *terrine* in the roasting pan, and bake for 45 minutes, or until a trussing needle or a knife blade stuck into the center of the *terrine,* and held there for 5 seconds, comes out hot (touch it to the inside of your wrist).

Allow the *terrine* to cool, uncovered. When cool, replace the cover and refrigerate until the next day.

THE SAUCE:

Melt 2 teaspoons of butter in a small saucepan, add the shallots, and simmer until soft and transparent. Add the white wine and the vinegar and cook at a moderate boil, uncovered, for about 10 minutes, or until only about 1 tablespoon of liquid is left. Over moderate heat, add a piece of softened butter, then lift the pan off the heat and whisk it in. Continue to add butter in this way, setting the pan down on the heat, then lifting it off to maintain even heat. Test the temperature of the sauce by touching it with the back of a finger; the sauce should feel hot, but not burn. When all the butter has been added, taste for salt and pepper, and reserve away from the heat.

TO SERVE:

Preheat the oven to 425° F.

Remove the *terrine* from the refrigerator, run the blade of a knife around the inside of the mold, and turn the *terrine* out onto a cutting board. Cut it into 6 to 8 slices.

Place 2 tablespoons of water in a large roasting pan, lay the slices of *terrine* in the pan, and cover with a buttered sheet of aluminum foil, buttered side down. Bake about 4 to 5 minutes, or until the slices are warm to the touch.

Reheat the sauce over low heat, whisking constantly, then strain it into a warm (not hot) sauceboat.

Place a slice of *terrine* on each plate, spoon a little sauce around it, and serve immediately, with the rest of the sauce in a sauceboat.

NOTE: *Other fish fillets of your choice may be used, but try to respect the proportions of ½ pound of saltwater fish to ¼ pound of freshwater fish. Ed.*

Terrine de poissons fumés
SMOKED FISH TERRINE WITH WHIPPED
CREAM SAUCE

Ingredients for 1 *terrine*, serving 4 to 6:

FOR THE FISH JELLY:
1½ pounds fish bones
1 small carrot, sliced
1 small onion, sliced
½ bay leaf
1 small sprig thyme
6 parsley stems
Pinch salt
1 large mushroom, chopped
3 peppercorns
4 cups water

1 tablespoon gelatin
3 tablespoons cold water
1 egg white (for clarifying)

FOR THE TERRINE:
½ pound smoked salmon, thinly sliced
½ pound smoked sturgeon, thinly sliced
¾ cup *crème fraîche (see p. 331)* or heavy cream
1 tablespoon coarsely chopped parsley leaves
1 tablespoon coarsely chopped chervil
1 tablespoon finely chopped chives
Salt, pepper

FOR THE SAUCE:
¾ teaspoon finely chopped lemon zest
¾ cup heavy cream, whipped
Salt, pepper
Pinch cayenne pepper
¼ teaspoon lemon juice
1 large or 2 small tomatoes, peeled, seeded, and diced
2 tablespoons whole chervil leaves
2 tablespoons whole parsley leaves

87

2 tablespoons finely chopped chives
Slices of toast, for serving

UTENSILS:

Medium pot
Small bowl
Large bowl
Wire whisk
Muslin cloth
Saucepan
Weight
Earthenware or porcelain *terrine* (1-quart capacity)
Blender or food processor
Small saucepan
4 mixing bowls
To serve: Sauceboat, serving platter, and plates

THE FISH JELLY:

Place all of the ingredients for the fish jelly, except the peppercorns, in a pot. Bring to a slow boil and cook, uncovered, for 50 minutes. Add the peppercorns and cook for 10 minutes more.

Moisten the gelatin with the water.

Strain the fish stock and whisk in the gelatin.

Clarify the jelly by lightly beating an egg white in a saucepan. Pour the fish stock slowly on to the egg white, whisking vigorously, then place over moderate heat and bring almost to a boil, whisking constantly. Lower the heat and simmer, uncovered, for 12 to 15 minutes.

Moisten a thin (muslin) cloth and line a bowl with it. Pour in the hot jelly and gather up the corners of the cloth to form a bag. Suspend the bag from a shelf or a chair over the bowl, holding it in place with a heavy weight, and allow the jelly to drip into the bowl—do not press on the cloth. When the jelly has been strained once, strain it again through the same cloth (the egg white acts as a filter). When done, measure the jelly; you will need 1 cup for making this recipe. Reserve. (The jelly may be made 1 to several days in advance and stored in the refrigerator.) Ed.

THE TERRINE:

Place the empty *terrine* in the refrigerator for at least 1 hour to chill it.

If the jelly has set, place it in a saucepan and heat, stirring, until it is liquid again. Remove from the heat.

Reserve one third of each fish. Purée the remaining salmon with 6 tablespoons of the cream in a blender or food processor until smooth. Reserve in a bowl.

Purée the remaining sturgeon, using the rest of the cream. Reserve in another bowl.

Set the saucepan of jelly into a bowl filled with ice cubes and water and stir constantly until cool (but not cold) to the touch.

Pour 5 tablespoons of the jelly into the bowl with the salmon purée, add half of the herbs, and stir to combine. Season lightly with salt and pepper.

Add the remaining herbs and 5 tablespoons of the jelly to the sturgeon purée, mix well, and season with salt and pepper.

Place the remaining jelly back over the ice and stir until cold and the consistency of olive oil. At this point it will be on the verge of setting. Remove the *terrine* from the refrigerator and pour the remaining jelly into it. Tip and turn the *terrine* so that the sides and bottom are coated with jelly—a pastry brush may be used to paint the sides with jelly if preferred. Refrigerate the *terrine* for about 5 minutes, or until the jelly is set.

Pour half of the salmon purée into the *terrine*, smooth the surface with the back of a spoon dipped in warm water, and lay half of the sturgeon slices on top (they should cover the purée). Pour half of the sturgeon purée on top of this, smooth the surface, and top with half of the salmon slices. Finish filling the *terrine* with the remaining fish purées and slices, in the same order as before, ending with slices of salmon.

Cover the *terrine* tightly with aluminum foil and refrigerate for 24 hours before serving.

TO MAKE THE SAUCE AND SERVE:

Place the lemon peel in a saucepan, cover with cold water, and bring to a boil; boil for 5 minutes and drain.

Season the whipped cream with salt, pepper, cayenne pepper and lemon juice. Delicately fold in the diced tomato pulp, herbs, and lemon peel. Pour the sauce into a sauceboat and chill.

Just before serving, quickly dip the *terrine* into a bowl of hot water, run the blade of a knife around the inside of the mold, and turn the *terrine* out onto a serving platter. Serve with the sauce in the sauceboat and slices of hot toast on a plate.

Fricassée d'écrevisses aux asperges
CRAYFISH FRICASSEE WITH ASPARAGUS

Ingredients for 4 servings:

 32 live crayfish, weighing about 3¼ pounds *(for substitution, see Note)*
 2 tablespoons olive oil
 6 shallots, coarsely chopped
 1 medium tomato, sliced
 1 medium carrot, coarsely chopped
 ¼ bulb fennel, coarsely chopped
 1 stalk celery, coarsely chopped
 2 tablespoons white wine
 3 tablespoons cognac
 1⅔ cups heavy cream

 16 medium asparagus (about 1½ pounds)
 2 quarts water
 2 teaspoons coarse salt
 Salt, pepper
 1 tablespoon freshly chopped *fines herbes* (parsley, chives, chervil, and so on—optional)

 UTENSILS:
 High-sided frying pan or *sauteuse*, 11 inches in diameter, with cover
 Small saucepan
 Kitchen string
 Large saucepan
 Skimmer or slotted spoon
 To serve: 4 heated dinner plates

 THE CRAYFISH:
Remove the central fin from the tail of each crayfish as described in **Lamb with crayfish** *(see p. 177)*.

 In a high-sided frying pan or *sauteuse* heat the olive oil until it almost smokes, then add enough of the crayfish to cover the bottom of the pan in a single layer. Cover the pan and cook over high heat, shaking the pan often, until all of the crayfish are red, about 6 minutes.

Remove them from the pot and reserve in a colander. Cook the rest of the crayfish in the same way.

Detach the tails from the heads of the crayfish and peel them. Reserve the heads in the colander and the tail meat on a plate.

Place the pan back over high heat and add the crayfish heads, shallots, tomato, carrot, fennel, and celery. Stir together and cook, uncovered, for 5 minutes. Add the wine and cognac and light with a match. When the flame has died down, add the cream, and lower the heat. Stir, pressing on the crayfish heads to extract their juices, then simmer gently, uncovered, for 20 minutes. Skim off any foam that appears.

Strain the sauce into a small saucepan, pressing on the shells and vegetables to extract all the liquid. There should be 1 to 1⅓ cups of strained sauce.

THE ASPARAGUS:

Peel the asparagus, cut them off about 5 inches below the tip, and tie them into 3 bunches. Bring the water to a boil in a large saucepan, add the asparagus, bring back to a boil, add the salt, and boil for 7 minutes, or until tender.

TO FINISH AND SERVE:

Season the crayfish sauce with salt and pepper to taste, bring almost to a boil, add the crayfish tails, and heat gently for 3 minutes. Do not allow to boil.

Drain the asparagus, untie them, and place 4 of them on each plate. With a skimmer or slotted spoon, lift the crayfish tails out of the sauce and place 8 of them on each plate, on and around the asparagus. Spoon the sauce over them, sprinkle with the chopped herbs, and serve.

NOTE: *32 raw (live, fresh, or frozen) shrimp with heads, if possible, weighing about 1¼ pounds, may be used instead of crayfish. Cook as described for the crayfish, but turn each one over halfway through the cooking time. All the shrimp may be sautéed at the same time. Use both the heads and the shells from the tails for making the sauce. Ed.*

Ecrevisses aux cèpes
CRAYFISH WITH BOLETUS MUSHROOMS

Ingredients for 4 servings:

½ pound fresh boletus mushrooms *(for substitution, see Suggestion)*
1½ pounds live crayfish *(for substitution, see Note)*
2 teaspoons butter
8 shallots, finely chopped
1 cup dry white wine
2 cups heavy cream
Salt, pepper
1 tablespoon butter (for the mushrooms)
1 teaspoon each chopped parsley, chervil, and chives

UTENSILS:
Pastry brush
Sauteuse or high-sided frying pan, 9 to 10 inches in diameter, with
   cover
Skimmer or slotted spoon
Frying pan
To serve: Serving platter, or 4 plates

PRELIMINARY PREPARATIONS:

Cut off the sandy end of the mushrooms. Rather than cutting the stems straight off, cut around the tip to form a point—this way none of the edible part of the stem is wasted. If the caps are clean, simply brush the mushrooms off. If they are very dirty, or if there are little cracks in the top, scrape them clean with a paring knife—in any case, don't wash them.

Cut each mushroom in half. The flesh of both cap and stem should be white and firm. Discard any mushrooms that have holes through them, as they have been attacked by parasites.

Separate the caps from the stems and cut everything into slices about ⅛ inch thick and then into strips about ⅛ inch wide.

Place the crayfish in a colander, rinse under cold running water, then remove the intestine as described in the recipe for **Lamb with crayfish** *(see p. 177)*. Reserve.

THE SAUCE AND THE CRAYFISH:

In a *sauteuse* or high-sided frying pan, melt 2 teaspoons of butter, add the shallots, and simmer for about 2 minutes, or until soft and transparent. Add the white wine, bring to a boil, and boil rapidly for 4 to 5 minutes, or until about 2 tablespoons of liquid is left.

Stir in the cream and boil gently for 3 minutes. Season with salt and pepper and add the crayfish, pushing them down into the cream as much as possible. Cover the pan, bring to a boil, and boil gently for 5 minutes, or until the crayfish have turned completely red, stirring once or twice.

Lift the crayfish out of the sauce with a skimmer or slotted spoon and place them upside down on a cutting board. With a large sharp knife, cut each one in half lengthwise, place them on a serving platter or on individual plates with the cut side (inside) facing up. Cover with aluminum foil and keep warm.

THE MUSHROOMS:

In a frying pan, melt a tablespoon of butter. When it is very hot, add the mushrooms and cook over high heat for 4 to 5 minutes, stirring constantly, so that they brown lightly on all sides. Season with salt and pepper.

TO SERVE:

Place the sauce over high heat and boil rapidly until reduced to 1⅓ cups. Taste for seasoning, spoon the sauce over the crayfish, place the mushrooms on top, sprinkle with the fresh herbs, and serve immediately.

SUGGESTION:

Other wild mushrooms, such as chanterelles or morels, or even ordinary mushrooms, may be used instead of the boletus.

NOTE: *Instead of crayfish, shrimp may be used. Buy 1½ pounds of uncooked shrimp with heads, if possible, peel them, and poach them in the cream as described for the crayfish. Since they are peeled, it is unnecessary to cut them in half. Ed.*

Fricassée de homard au concombre et à la menthe fraîche LOBSTER FRICASSEE WITH CUCUMBERS AND MINT

Ingredients for 4 servings:

FOR THE LOBSTER:
3 quarts water
4 teaspoons coarse salt
1 medium carrot, thinly sliced
1 small onion, thinly sliced
1 clove garlic
1 medium tomato, cut into 8 wedges
Bouquet garni
12 peppercorns
2¾-pound live lobster

FOR THE SAUCE:
2 tablespoons olive oil
1 small carrot, diced
1 stalk celery, diced
½ medium onion, diced
¼ bulb fennel, diced
1 medium tomato, coarsely chopped
⅓ cup cognac
3 tablespoons white wine
1⅓ cups heavy cream

1 tablespoon butter
2 tablespoons finely chopped shallot
2 medium cucumbers (1 pound), peeled, seeded, and scooped into
    balls or cut into ½-inch cubes
Salt, pepper
10 fresh mint leaves, cut into thin strips

UTENSILS:
Large pot, with cover
Scissors

Hammer or cleaver

Large high-sided frying pan or *sauteuse*, 11 to 12 inches in diameter

Small, high-sided frying pan *or sauteuse*, 9½ inches in diameter

To serve: Heated serving platter, or 4 heated dinner plates

THE LOBSTER:

In a large pot, bring the water and salt to a boil. Add the carrot, onion, garlic, tomato, *bouquet garni,* and peppercorns, bring back to a boil, and cook gently for 10 minutes.

Raise the heat and when the liquid is rapidly boiling, drop the lobster into the pot. Cover the pot until the water comes back to a boil, remove the top, and boil the lobster, uncovered, for 9 minutes.

Remove the lobster from the court bouillon and place it on paper towels to drain.

Reserve 2 cups of the court bouillon, strained.

When the lobster has cooled enough to handle, separate the tail from the head. With a pair of scissors, cut the shell on the underside of the tail in half lengthwise and remove the meat. Crack each claw with a hammer or the blunt edge of a cleaver and remove the meat. Reserve all of the lobster meat on a plate.

THE SAUCE:

With a cleaver or large knife, split the lobster head in half lengthwise. With a small spoon, scoop out the greenish matter along the top of each half, then chop the head into small pieces.

In a large high-sided frying pan or *sauteuse* heat the olive oil over high heat until it is nearly smoking. Add the pieces of lobster head, stirring well to coat them. Add the carrot, celery, onion, fennel, and tomato. Stir well, add the cognac and white wine, and light with a match. When the flame has died down, stir in the cream, bring to a boil, and boil gently, uncovered, for 20 minutes, skimming off the foam when necessary, until the sauce is reduced by half and thickened.

THE CUCUMBERS:

While the sauce is cooking, melt the butter in a small high-sided frying pan or *sauteuse,* add the shallot, and simmer until soft and transparent, stirring occasionally. Add the cucumber balls, stir to coat them with the butter, and spread them out in a single layer.

Pour just enough of the reserved court bouillon over the cucumbers to almost cover them. Boil, uncovered, for 12 minutes, or until almost all of the liquid has evaporated.

TO FINISH THE SAUCE AND SERVE:
While the sauce and cucumbers are cooking, cut the lobster tail in half lengthwise and carefully remove the blackish intestine, then cut the meat into slices ¼ inch thick. Cut the meat from the claws into small cubes.

Season the cucumbers with salt and pepper, stir, then strain the lobster sauce over them. Press on the vegetables and shells with a wooden spoon to extract any liquid and taste for seasoning. Be sure the sauce is hot (it should not boil), add the lobster meat, and heat over very low heat, stirring occasionally, for 3 minutes.

Place the lobster meat on a serving platter, or divide it among the dinner plates. Arrange the cucumber balls around the lobster, spoon over the sauce, sprinkle with the strips of mint, and serve immediately.

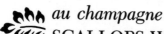

Coquilles Saint-Jacques, julienne de légumes, au champagne
SCALLOPS WITH VEGETABLES AND CHAMPAGNE CREAM SAUCE
(color picture III)

Ingredients for 4 servings:

12 large sea scallops (6 pounds) in their shells (*see Note under* **Scallop salad with fried celery leaves,** *p. 31)*

FOR THE STOCK:
1½ tablespoons butter
1⅔ cups water
Salt, pepper

FOR THE VEGETABLES:
1 medium leek, white only
2-inch piece cucumber, seeded and cut into julienne strips
1 small carrot, cut into julienne strips
2 large mushrooms, cut into julienne strips *(see Suggestions)*

FOR THE SAUCE:
1½ tablespoons butter
8 shallots, finely chopped
1⅓ cup champagne *(or dry white wine. Ed.)*
1 cup heavy cream
Salt, pepper
3 tablespoons softened butter, broken into pieces

UTENSILS:
Saucepan
2 small saucepans
Wire whisk
Small frying pan or medium saucepan
Skimmer or slotted spoon
To serve: 4 heated salad plates

THE STOCK:
Make scallop stock as described in the recipe for **Scallop salad with fried celery leaves** *(see p. 31)*, using the measurements given here (there is neither wine nor dill in this recipe).

THE VEGETABLES:
Cut the white of the leek into sections about 2 inches long, cut each in half lengthwise, then into julienne strips. Rinse under cold running water, drain, and reserve.

Bring 4 cups of lightly salted water to a boil and add the carrots and leek. Boil for 1 minute, then add the cucumber and mushrooms, and boil for 30 seconds more. Drain, cool under running water, drain well, and reserve in a clean saucepan.

THE SAUCE:
Melt 1½ tablespoons of butter in a small saucepan, add the shallots, and simmer for 2 to 3 minutes to soften. Add the champagne and boil until it has almost completely evaporated. Add the cream and continue

boiling rapidly for about 3 minutes, or until thick and creamy, then remove the pan from the heat and whisk in the softened butter bit by bit. Season with salt and pepper and strain the sauce into the saucepan with the cooked vegetables.

TO COOK THE SCALLOPS AND SERVE:

Heat the stock in a saucepan just large enough to hold the scallops in a single layer. Simmer, covered, for 3 minutes, lift them out, and drain on paper towels.

Reheat the vegetables and sauce if necessary (do not allow to boil). Place 3 scallops on each dinner plate. Lift the vegetables out of the saucepan with a slotted spoon and place them on top of the scallops, then spoon the sauce over and around the scallops and serve.

SUGGESTIONS:

A teaspoon each of lemon and lime zest, cut into julienne strips, may be cooked with the vegetables. Or, a fine julienne of truffles may be substituted for the mushrooms; add the truffles to the sauce after whisking in the butter.

Coquilles Saint-Jacques au fenouil et au Ricard STEAMED SCALLOPS WITH FENNEL AND RICARD

Ingredients for 4 servings:

    1 pound scallops (12 sea scallops)
    Salt, pepper
    1 tablespoon chopped fresh dillweed
    2 tablespoons Ricard or Pernod (or other anise-flavored alcohol)

    1 tablespoon butter
    2 medium bulbs fennel (1 pound), cut into julienne strips
    Salt, pepper
    ¾ teaspoon curry powder
    6½ tablespoons softened butter, broken into pieces

98

UTENSILS:
Steamer, or large pot and steaming basket, with cover
Saucepan
Slotted spoon
Wire whisk
To serve: Heated serving platter

THE SCALLOPS:
Place the scallops on one half of a large sheet of aluminum foil. Season with salt, pepper, dillweed, and the Ricard or Pernod. Fold the other half of the foil over the scallops, and roll the edges together, pressing on them to seal the scallops inside, *en papillote*.

Bring some water to a boil in the bottom of a steamer (or a large pot with a steaming basket set in it), place the *papillote* in the basket, cover the pot, and steam for 9 minutes.

THE FENNEL:
While the scallops are steaming, melt 1 tablespoon of butter in a saucepan over moderate heat. Add the fennel, season with salt, pepper, and curry, stir, then add just enough water to almost cover (about ½ cup); boil gently for 3 minutes.

Lift the fennel out of the saucepan with a slotted spoon and place it on a serving platter. Keep warm while making the sauce.

THE SAUCE:
Boil the fennel cooking liquid until there are about 2 tablespoons left, then whisk in the softened butter, little by little, as described for the foamy butter sauce in **Hot fish terrine** *(see p. 84)*. When all the butter has been added, remove the sauce from the heat and taste for seasoning.

TO SERVE:
When the scallops are cooked, remove the *papillote* from the steamer and place on a plate. Open it carefully and place the scallops on the bed of fennel. Whisk the cooking juices from the scallops into the sauce, pour over the scallops, and serve.

SUGGESTIONS:
The scallops can be replaced by mussels, fish fillets such as sea bass or turbot or other firm-fleshed fish, or even by salmon.

The fennel can be replaced by celery, but in this case do not use curry or Ricard. Instead add 2 tablespoons of white wine or dry sherry to the envelope.

Coquilles Saint-Jacques aux petits pois SCALLOPS WITH GREEN PEAS

Ingredients for 4 servings:

> ½ pound fresh peas, in all
> 2 tablespoons softened butter, broken into pieces

> FOR THE GARNISH:
> 1 tablespoon butter
> ½ small onion, thinly sliced
> 2 lettuce leaves, cut into thick strips
> Salt, pepper
> 3 tablespoons water

> FOR THE SCALLOPS:
> 1 tablespoon butter
> 2 shallots, finely chopped
> Salt, pepper
> 1 pound sea scallops (*or bay scallops. Ed.*)
> ⅓ cup white wine

> FOR THE SAUCE:
> ¾ cup heavy cream
> Salt, pepper

> UTENSILS:
> Blender or food processor
> Bowl
> Large frying pan, with cover
> Oval or rectangular roasting pan, 12 inches long

Skimmer or slotted spoon
Wire whisk
To serve: 4 heated dinner plates

THE PEA BUTTER:
Shell the peas; measure out ⅓ cup for making the pea butter and save the rest for the garnish.

Purée the peas for the pea butter in a blender or food processor. Add the butter, blend, place in a sieve, and rub the mixture through with a wooden spoon. Place the pea butter in a bowl and reserve.

THE GARNISH:
Melt 1 tablespoon of butter in a large frying pan. Add the onion and cook until soft; do not allow to brown. Add the reserved peas, lettuce, salt, and pepper, stir, and cover the pan. Simmer very slowly for 5 to 6 minutes, then add the water and simmer, covered, for 5 minutes, or until all the water has been absorbed. Remove from the heat and reserve.

THE SCALLOPS:
Preheat the oven to 425° F.

Melt a tablespoon of butter in a roasting pan, add the shallots, and cook over moderate heat until soft.

Generously salt and pepper the scallops, place them in the roasting pan in a single layer, add the white wine, bring just to a boil, then place the pan in the oven, and cook for 5 minutes (*cook bay scallops 3 minutes. Ed.*). Lift out the scallops with a skimmer or slotted spoon and place them in the pan with the vegetables for the garnish.

THE SAUCE:
Boil the liquid in the roasting pan over high heat for about 3 minutes, or until there are about 2 tablespoons left. Add the cream and boil for 3 minutes, or until the sauce is thick and creamy. Taste for salt and pepper, remove the pan from the heat, and whisk in the pea butter.

TO FINISH AND SERVE:
Strain the sauce into the pan with the vegetables and scallops. Reheat over moderate heat, shaking the pan to mix the vegetables and sauce together. When hot (do not allow to boil), serve immediately.

Fricassée aux asperges, coquilles Saint-Jacques, et huîtres
FRICASSEE OF ASPARAGUS, SCALLOPS, AND OYSTERS

Ingredients for 4 servings:

2¼ pounds large asparagus

FOR THE SAUCE:
2 teaspoons butter
2 large shallots, finely chopped
3 tablespoons wine vinegar
¾ cup white wine
¾ cup *crème fraîche (see p. 331)* or heavy cream
5 tablespoons softened butter, broken into pieces

FOR THE SHELLFISH:
8 large sea scallops, each cut into 3 slices (*or 24 bay scallops. Ed.*)
Salt, pepper
Pinch cayenne pepper
8 large oysters, shelled

UTENSILS:
Large pot
2 medium saucepans
Wire whisk
Skimmer or slotted spoon
To serve: 4 heated dinner plates

THE ASPARAGUS:
Cut off each asparagus about 3½ to 4 inches from the tip. Peel them, being careful not to damage the tips, then drop them into a large pot of boiling salted water. Bring back to a boil and boil for 10 minutes. Lift the asparagus out of the pot and drain on a cloth or towel.

THE SAUCE:
Melt 2 teaspoons of butter in a saucepan, add the shallots, and cook for about 2 minutes, or until soft and transparent. Add the vinegar and wine, and boil rapidly for 10 minutes, or until about 2 tablespoons of

liquid are left. Add the cream and boil rapidly for 2 minutes, or until thick and creamy, stirring occasionally.

TO COOK THE SHELLFISH AND SERVE:

Sprinkle the scallops generously with salt and pepper, add a pinch of cayenne, then place them with the oysters in a saucepan. Strain the sauce onto them and heat for about 3 minutes. As soon as the sauce begins to simmer, but before it boils, the shellfish are cooked.

Divide the asparagus tips, the scallops, and oysters among the dinner plates. If necessary, boil the sauce rapidly until a creamy consistency is obtained, then away from the heat, whisk in the softened butter, little by little. Taste for seasoning, spoon over asparagus tips and shellfish, and serve.

Asperges et morilles meunière
ASPARAGUS AND MORELS MEUNIÈRE

(color picture IV)

Ingredients for 4 servings:
    About 5 ounces fresh morels, or 1⅓ cup drained canned morels, or
        ⅔ cup dried morels (*for substitutions, see Suggestion*)
    2 tablespoons vinegar
    16 large asparagus (about 2 pounds)
    4 tablespoons butter, in all
    Salt, pepper
    6 shallots, finely chopped
    4 teaspoons lemon juice
    1 tablespoon finely chopped chives
    1 tablespoon finely chopped parsley
    1 tablespoon finely chopped chervil

    UTENSILS:
    Mixing bowl
    Kitchen string
    Large pot

Large frying pan (preferably nonstick)
Skimmer or slotted spoon
To serve: Large serving platter

PRELIMINARY PREPARATIONS:

If using fresh mushrooms, cut off the dirt end and cut large ones in half lengthwise. Place the mushrooms in a large bowl of cold water, add the vinegar, and soak for 3 to 4 minutes. Drain, rinse thoroughly in cold water, and allow to drain completely on paper towels before cooking.

Canned morels should be rinsed off and drained on a towel.

Dried morels should be soaked as described on their package (generally about 30 minutes in warm water). If necessary, cut off the base of the stems and drain them on a towel.

Break off the bottom 2 to 3 inches of each asparagus. Peel the asparagus, being careful not to damage the tips. Tie them in 2 or 3 bunches, according to thickness.

TO COOK AND SERVE:

Drop the asparagus into a large pot of boiling salted water. When the water comes back to a boil, cook them for 7 minutes, then remove the thin asparagus and continue cooking the thicker ones 2 to 3 minutes more. Lift them carefully out of the water, untie them, and drain on a towel. Cut each asparagus in half crosswise.

Heat a tablespoon of butter in a large (preferably nonstick) frying pan. Add the asparagus and cook over moderate heat about 4 minutes, shaking the pan to roll them around and brown lightly. Season with salt and pepper, remove them with a skimmer or slotted spoon, and keep warm on the serving platter while cooking the mushrooms.

Add another tablespoon of butter to the frying pan; when hot, add the mushrooms, salt and pepper. Cook over moderate heat, covered, 6 to 10 minutes, or until tender, shaking the pan occasionally. Remove the mushrooms from the pan with the slotted spoon and place on the platter with the asparagus.

Melt the remaining 2 tablespoons of butter in the same pan, add the shallots, salt, and pepper, and cook for 2 to 3 minutes or until soft, but not brown.

Sprinkle the asparagus with the lemon juice, the butter and shallots, and finally with the chopped herbs, and serve immediately.

104

SUGGESTION:
Fresh chanterelles or any other fresh wild mushroom can be used instead of morels—even ordinary mushrooms may be used.

Navets farcis
STUFFED TURNIPS

Ingredients for 4 servings:
    4 large turnips (1½ pounds) as round and regular as possible
    1 pound duck breast or legs (or ¾ pound boneless breast meat)
    1 shallot, finely chopped
    2 teaspoons finely chopped parsley
    2 teaspoons finely chopped chives
    2 teaspoons finely chopped chervil
    Salt, pepper
    Pinch thyme
    3¼ cups (1 large bottle) hard cider
    1 tablespoon butter, in all
    ¾ cup heavy cream
    Salt, pepper

UTENSILS:
Melon-ball cutter
Large pot
Slotted spoon
Blender or food mill
2 mixing bowls
Large frying pan
Wire whisk
Large baking dish
To serve: 4 heated dinner plates

THE TURNIPS:
Peel, wash, and dry the turnips. Slice a little off the bases so that they will stand upright. Use a melon-ball cutter to hollow out each turnip,

forming a round cup with walls and a bottom a little more than ⅛ inch thick. Reserve the pulp.

Bring a large pot of lightly salted water to a boil, drop in the turnips, and cook for 3 minutes. Remove with a slotted spoon and drain on a cloth or paper towels. Drop the turnip pulp into the same water, cook for 10 minutes, drain, purée in a blender or food mill, and reserve in a mixing bowl.

THE STUFFING:

Bone the duck and remove all the skin and fat. Dice the meat and place it in a bowl with the shallot, herbs, salt, pepper, and a pinch of thyme (the stuffing can take a lot of salt and pepper). Mix well, then form the stuffing into 4 little balls and reserve.

TO COOK AND STUFF THE TURNIPS:

Heat the cider in a large pot and boil for 20 minutes, or until reduced by half. Reserve.

Heat 2 teaspoons of butter in a large frying pan. Add the hollowed-out turnips over moderate heat, rolling them around to brown on all sides for 5 minutes; remove and drain on a cloth.

Heat the reduced cider until boiling, add the turnips, and boil gently for 10 to 12 minutes to finish cooking. Lift the turnips out and drain on a cloth. Measure the remaining cider—there should be ½ cup left; if not, boil to reduce to this amount, remove from the heat, and reserve.

Add 1 teaspoon of butter to the pan used to brown the turnips and brown the 4 balls of stuffing in it, turning frequently to brown on all sides (about 5 minutes). Drain the stuffing on a cloth, then place a ball inside each turnip.

TO FINISH AND MAKE THE SAUCE AND SERVE:

Preheat the oven to 425° F.

Whisk the cider and cream into the reserved turnip purée. Pour this sauce into a baking dish, place the stuffed turnips in the dish, and heat to just below the boiling point; place in the oven and bake for 9 minutes.

Carefully lift out each turnip and place it on a dinner plate. Whisk the sauce, add salt and pepper if needed, and spoon it around the turnips. Serve immediately.

SUGGESTIONS:
A less refined version of this dish can be made using sausage meat or chicken livers instead of duck.

Gâteaux de foies de volaille à la crème de bacon
CHICKEN LIVER MOUSSE WITH BACON
CREAM SAUCE

Ingredients for 4 servings:

FOR THE MOUSSE:
½ pound chicken livers
4 shallots, finely chopped
3 eggs
2 cups *crème fraîche (see p. 331)* or heavy cream
4 generous tablespoons chopped parsley
1 teaspoon salt
Pinch pepper

FOR THE SAUCE:
1 cup (about 5 ounces) finely diced Canadian bacon
1 shallot, finely chopped
2 tablespoons red wine vinegar
1 cup heavy cream
Pepper
1 teaspoon butter (for the parsley)
Whole leaves from 2 sprigs parsley
1 generous teaspoon Dijon mustard

FOR THE TOMATO GARNISH:
1 teaspoon butter
1 shallot, finely chopped
2 medium tomatoes, peeled, seeded, and chopped
Salt, pepper

UTENSILS:

Roasting pan
4 ramekins (1-cup capacity)
Food processor or heavy-duty blender
Large frying pan
Small frying pan
Slotted spoon
To serve: 4 heated dinner plates and sauceboat

PRELIMINARY PREPARATIONS:

Preheat the oven to 425° F.

Pour water ½ inch deep into a roasting pan and place the pan in the oven.

Lightly butter each ramekin.

THE MOUSSE:

Purée the chicken livers, shallots, eggs, cream, and parsley in a food processor or blender until smooth. Add the salt and pepper and pour the mixture into the ramekins. Place in the roasting pan and immediately lower the oven to 350° F. Bake for 10 minutes, reset the oven to 425° F, and bake 30 minutes more.

THE SAUCE:

Heat the bacon and shallot in a frying pan over moderate heat, to melt the fat in the bacon. Stir frequently and cook until the shallots are soft and transparent. Add the vinegar, stirring constantly, until it has completely evaporated, then stir in the cream and a pinch of pepper (no salt is needed because of the bacon). Lower the heat and simmer the sauce for 10 minutes, cover, and keep warm over very low heat.

Melt a teaspoon of butter in a small frying pan, add the parsley leaves, and simmer slowly for 2 minutes. Remove the parsley from the pan and reserve.

THE TOMATO GARNISH:

In the same small frying pan, melt another teaspoon of butter and add the shallots. Simmer until soft and transparent, then add the tomato. Season with a little salt and pepper, stir, then simmer for 4 to 5 minutes, stirring occasionally.

Just before the mousse is done, taste the sauce for seasoning and add pepper if needed. Stir in the mustard and strain the sauce into a sauceboat, stirring so that all the liquid goes through; discard the solids. Stir in the cooked parsley.

Check the ramekins. Insert the blade of a knife into one; if it comes out clean, the mousse is done—if not, cook 5 to 10 minutes longer and check again. Remove the ramekins from the roasting pan and turn each one out onto a dinner plate (if necessary, run the blade of a knife around the inside of the ramekins). Garnish each plate with a little tomato, spoon a little of the sauce over each mousse, and serve immediately, with the sauceboat on the side.

SUGGESTIONS:
Individual soufflé molds of the same capacity (4 inches in diameter) may be used instead of ramekins, or a 1-quart soufflé mold, or an earthenware baking dish may be used instead of individual molds. Cooking times will be longer; be sure to test before serving.

Calf's liver may be used instead of chicken livers.

The cooked mousse can also be served cold, with a cold tomato sauce flavored with finely chopped fresh herbs, and a green salad.

Leftover mousse may be served spread on toast as an appetizer.

Les poissons, coquillages & crustacés
FISH & SHELLFISH

Filets de dorade sur lit d'épinards, maïs, et tomates
SALAD OF SEA BREAM WITH SPINACH, CORN, AND TOMATOES

Ingredients for 4 servings:
  1 sea bream or porgy, weighing 2¾ pounds *(see Suggestions)*
  1 pound fresh spinach, stems and ribs removed
  2 medium tomatoes, peeled, seeded, and coarsely chopped
  4 ounce can corn, drained

  1 teaspoon melted butter
  ⅔ cup dry white wine
  6 tablespoons olive oil, in all
  2 tablespoons sherry vinegar
  Salt, pepper

  UTENSILS:
  Filleting knife
  Pastry brush
  Oval or rectangular baking dish, 13 to 14 inches long
  Spatula
  To serve: 4 dinner plates

110

PRELIMINARY PREPARATIONS:

Ask the fish seller to scale and fillet the fish, but to leave the skin on. If he removes each side of the fish in one piece, ask him to cut each one in half lengthwise so that there will be 4 fillets.

Preheat the oven to 425° F.

Cut the spinach leaves into thin strips with a large knife and reserve in a salad bowl.

Add the tomatoes and corn to the bowl with the spinach.

THE FISH:

Brush the baking dish with the melted butter. Salt and pepper the fish fillets, place them skin side up in the baking dish, add the white wine, and bake for 7 minutes.

TO FINISH AND SERVE:

While the fish is cooking, season the spinach, corn, and tomatoes with 5 tablespoons of olive oil and the sherry vinegar; salt and pepper generously. Toss the salad and place some on each plate.

When the fillets are done, remove them from the pan with a spatula and place them on a clean cloth to drain. Remove the skin with a filleting knife and place each fillet on a bed of spinach. Pour a tiny bit of olive oil over each fillet (use only 1 tablespoon in all), and serve immediately.

SUGGESTIONS:

Almost any fish can be used in making this recipe.

Watercress, or a mixture of salad greens may be used instead of spinach, if desired. A little fennel may also be coarsely chopped and added to the salad with the corn and tomatoes.

The zest of one-half a lemon, parboiled for 2 minutes, then finely chopped, or a tablespoon of finely chopped fresh herbs may be added to the salad dressing.

Bar aux courgettes
SEA BASS WITH ZUCCHINI
(color picture V)

Ingredients for 4 servings:

FOR THE FISH:
3-pound sea bass
1 tablespoon butter
3 shallots, finely chopped
3 medium mushrooms, finely chopped
Salt, pepper
¾ cup dry white wine
3 tablespoons water
2 teaspoons thyme leaves
1 cup heavy cream

FOR THE ZUCCHINI:
2 tablespoons olive oil
1 pound zucchini, cut into julienne strips (do not peel)
Salt, pepper
4 teaspoons thyme leaves
1 tablespoon butter (to finish the sauce)

UTENSILS:
Oval or rectangular roasting pan, 13 to 14 inches long
Spatula
Saucepan
Frying pan
Wire whisk
To serve: Serving platter

THE FISH:
Ask the fish seller to scale and fillet the fish, but to leave the skin on the fillets.

Melt the butter in a roasting pan, add the shallots and mushrooms, season with salt and pepper, and simmer for 5 minutes, stirring occasionally.

Preheat the oven to 425° F.

Salt and pepper the fish fillets, then place them skin side up on the bed of vegetables; add the wine, water, and thyme. Cover with aluminum foil and bake in the oven for 5 minutes.

Remove the fish from the pan with a spatula, drain on a clean cloth, lift off the skin with a knife, and place the fillets on a serving platter. Keep warm.

Place the roasting pan over high heat, stir in the cream, and boil rapidly for 6 to 8 minutes, or until thick and creamy. Strain into a saucepan, pressing on the shallots and mushrooms with a wooden spoon.

THE ZUCCHINI:

While the cream is reducing, heat the olive oil in a frying pan until very hot and add the strips of zucchini, salt, and pepper. Sauté, stirring constantly, for 3 to 4 minutes, then sprinkle with the thyme, and sauté for 1 to 2 minutes more. The zucchini should just begin to color.

TO FINISH THE SAUCE AND SERVE:

Heat the sauce if necessary, then whisk in a tablespoon of butter. Taste for salt and pepper, spoon the sauce over the fish, sprinkle the strips of zucchini on top, and serve immediately.

SUGGESTIONS:

Any fish fillets may be prepared this way.

A pound of green or red bell peppers, mushrooms, carrots, or spinach may be cut into julienne strips and prepared as described for the zucchini.

Bar au beurre rouge au Bouzy
SEA BASS WITH RED BUTTER SAUCE

Ingredients for 4 servings:

FOR THE BUTTER SAUCE:
1 tablespoon butter
2 shallots, finely chopped
Salt, pepper
1½ cups (½ bottle) red wine
1 tablespoon water
9 tablespoons softened butter, broken into pieces

FOR THE FISH:

1½ tablespoons butter
1 shallot, finely chopped
Salt, pepper
1½ pounds sea bass fillets (from a 3-pound fish) *(for substitution, see Suggestions)*
6 tablespoons red wine

UTENSILS:

Saucepan
Oval or rectangular roasting pan, 13 to 14 inches long
Wire whisk
Spatula
To serve: 4 dinner plates or a heated serving platter

THE REDUCTION FOR THE SAUCE:

Melt 1 tablespoon of butter in a saucepan, add the shallots, and simmer gently, stirring occasionally, for 2 to 3 minutes, or until soft and transparent.

Sprinkle the shallots with salt and pepper, add the red wine, and cook, uncovered, at a moderate boil for 30 to 45 minutes, or until all but about a tablespoon of wine has evaporated.

THE FISH:

Preheat the oven to 425° F.

Melt the butter in a roasting pan over moderate heat, add the shallot, salt and pepper lightly, and simmer, stirring occasionally, until soft and transparent.

Salt and pepper the fish fillets, lay them on the bed of shallots, skin side down, add the wine, cover with aluminum foil, and bake for 6 minutes.

TO FINISH THE SAUCE AND SERVE:

Add 1 tablespoon of water to the saucepan with the shallots, heat, then whisk in the softened butter as described in the recipe for **Hot fish terrine** *(see p. 84).* Taste for salt and pepper.

Carefully lift the fish fillets out of the roasting pan with a spatula and drain for a few seconds on a clean cloth. Place them on the dinner plates or serving platter, spoon the sauce over them, and serve with a julienne of vegetables cooked as described for the **Turbot with five-vegetable** sauce *(see p. 125)*, or with spinach prepared as for the **Turbot with curry sauce and spinach** *(see p. 128)*.

SUGGESTIONS:
Any fish with firm, white flesh may be used for this recipe.

White wine may be used instead of red wine. In this case, a few chopped herbs, or a little curry or paprika may be added to the sauce reduction with the wine.

The reduction may also be made with 3 tablespoons of Ricard, Pernod, or ouzo, and so on instead of wine.

Saumon aux poireaux
SALMON WITH LEEK SAUCE

Ingredients for 4 servings:
   1½ pounds fresh salmon

   FOR THE LEEKS:
1½ tablespoons butter
3 medium leeks (1 pound), white part only, cut into julienne strips
      (for substitutions, see Suggestions)
Salt, pepper
½ cup water

   FOR THE FISH:
Salt, pepper
1 cup white wine

   FOR THE SAUCE:
2 teaspoons butter
2 shallots, finely chopped
¾ cup white wine
3 tablespoons wine vinegar
½ pound less 2 tablespoons softened butter, broken into pieces
Salt, pepper

UTENSILS:
Medium high-sided frying pan or *sauteuse,* with cover
Roasting pan
Spatula
Filleting knife
Bowl
Small saucepan
Wire whisk
To serve: 4 heated dinner plates

PRELIMINARY PREPARATIONS:
Ask the fish seller to scale and fillet the salmon, but to leave the skin on the fillets.
Preheat the oven to 425° F.

THE LEEKS:
In a high-sided frying pan or *sauteuse,* melt the butter over moderate heat. Add the leeks, salt and pepper lightly, and cook gently for 3 minutes without allowing to brown. Add the water, cover, and simmer for 20 minutes more; the water should have completely evaporated. Reserve.

THE SALMON:
Lightly grease a roasting pan with butter and sprinkle it with salt and pepper. Place the salmon fillets in the pan skin side down, season with salt and pepper, add the white wine, and bake for 12 minutes.
Using a spatula, lift the salmon fillets carefully out of the roasting pan and place them skin side up on a clean cloth to drain for a few seconds. Remove the skin with a filleting knife, then place the fillets on a plate, cover with aluminum foil, and keep warm while making the sauce.
Strain the salmon cooking liquid into a bowl and reserve.

THE SAUCE:
Make the foamy butter sauce as described in the recipe for **Hot fish terrine** *(see p. 84),* using the measurements listed here. When all the butter has been added, strain the sauce, taste for salt and pepper, and whisk in the reserved salmon cooking liquid.

TO SERVE:
Place the leeks back over low heat until warm, then pour the sauce over

them, stirring constantly. Remove from the heat, taste for seasoning, and stir to mix everything well together (the pan should be on the heat just long enough to warm the sauce).

Cut each salmon fillet in half and place a piece on each of the dinner plates. Spoon the sauce over the fish and serve immediately.

SUGGESTIONS:
The leeks can be replaced by an equal weight of broccoli, fennel, or tomatoes, or by a ½ pound of green or red bell peppers. Broccoli, fennel, or peppers should be prepared exactly as described for the leeks. Tomatoes should be prepared as for **Turbot fillets with tomato** *(see p. 134).*

Instead of making a foamy butter sauce and mixing it with the leeks, the leek sauce can be made as follows:

Cook the leeks with the butter as described, then instead of adding water, add 1 cup of heavy cream, cover, and simmer for 20 minutes. At the end of this time, the cream should have reduced to a creamy consistency. If not, remove the cover, and boil gently until a creamy consistency is obtained. Taste for salt and pepper, spoon over the fish, and serve.

Saumon au caviar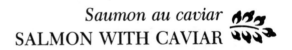
SALMON WITH CAVIAR

Ingredients for 4 servings:
    1½ pounds fresh salmon, in one piece
    Zest of 1 small lemon, finely chopped
    Salt, pepper
    1 tablespoon butter
    5 shallots, finely chopped
    3 medium mushrooms, finely chopped
    ⅔ cup dry white wine
    ½ cup water
    1⅓ cups heavy cream
    3 tablespoons (1¾ ounce) caviar *(for substitutions, see Suggestion)*

UTENSILS:

Filleting knife

Small saucepan

Oval or rectangular roasting pan, 13 to 14 inches long

Spatula

Wire whisk

To serve: Serving platter, or 4 heated dinner plates

PRELIMINARY PREPARATIONS:

Using a filleting knife, cut the salmon from the bone into 2 fillets, but leave the skin and scales on. Remove any small bones left in the flesh.

Preheat the oven to 425° F.

Place the chopped lemon zest in a small saucepan, cover with cold water, and bring to a boil. Boil for 1 minute, drain, cool under running water, and drain again. Return the zest to the dry saucepan and reserve.

THE FISH:

Season the salmon fillets with salt and pepper.

In a roasting pan, melt the butter over low heat. Add the shallots and simmer for about 2 minutes, or until soft, add the mushrooms, and simmer for another 3 minutes.

Place the fillets skin side down on top of the shallots and mushrooms, add the wine and water, and bake for 8 minutes.

TO MAKE THE SAUCE AND SERVE:

Remove the fish from the roasting pan with a spatula and place it on a clean cloth for a few seconds to drain. Carefully remove the skin with a filleting knife, then either place the fillets on a serving platter, or cut each one in half and place a piece on each dinner plate. Keep warm while making the sauce.

Place the roasting pan over high heat and boil the cooking liquid until the pan is nearly dry. Whisk in the cream, mixing in any juices caramelized on the bottom of the pan, and boil rapidly for 2 to 3 minutes, or until thick and creamy. Taste for seasoning, then strain into the saucepan containing the lemon peel, pressing the vegetables. Make sure the sauce is very hot, but do not allow to boil.

Spoon the sauce over the salmon fillets, sprinkle some of the caviar over each one, and serve immediately.

Boiled broccoli or potatoes, served with a little butter, are excellent with this dish. Or the salmon fillets can be served on a bed of buttered spinach.

SUGGESTIONS:
The caviar may be replaced by lumpfish or salmon roe or by a few finely diced mixed vegetables (carrots, turnips, celery, green beans, for example), cooked for about 3 minutes in boiling salted water.

Barbue aux endives
BRILL WITH ENDIVE SAUCE

Ingredients for 4 servings:

FOR THE ENDIVES:
1 pound Belgian endives
1 tablespoon butter
Salt, pepper
Juice of ½ lemon
Large pinch sugar

FOR THE FISH:
1 tablespoon butter
5 shallots, finely chopped
Salt, pepper
4 fillets of brill, weighing about 1½ pounds (from a 3-pound fish)
6 tablespoons dry white wine
1 cup heavy cream
2 teaspoons Dijon mustard
2 teaspoons softened butter

UTENSILS:
Medium saucepan, with cover
Oval or rectangular roasting pan, 13 to 14 inches long
Spatula
To serve: Heated serving platter and sauceboat

THE ENDIVES:

Cut off the base of each endive, wipe clean (do not wash), and cut in half lengthwise. Cut out the central section near the base, separate the leaves, and cut them into julienne strips.

In a saucepan, melt the butter, add the strips of endive, and season with salt and pepper. Stir in the lemon juice and sugar, cover, and simmer, stirring occasionally, for 10 minutes. Reserve.

THE FISH:

Preheat the oven to 400° F.

In a roasting pan, melt the butter, add the shallots and mushrooms, season with salt and pepper, stir, then remove from the heat.

Salt and pepper the brill fillets, lay them in the pan, skin side down, add the white wine, place the pan back over moderate heat, and bring the wine to a boil. Cover the pan with aluminum foil and bake the fish for 5 minutes, remove the foil, and bake for 5 minutes more.

TO MAKE THE SAUCE AND SERVE:

Remove the fish from the pan with a spatula and place the fillets on a serving platter. Cover with aluminum foil and keep warm.

Place the roasting pan over high heat and boil the cooking liquid until the pan is almost dry; if the fish gives out liquid during this time, add it to the roasting pan.

Whisk the cream into the reduced liquid, bring to a boil, and boil rapidly over high heat for 4 minutes, or until thick and creamy. Taste for seasoning, then strain the sauce into the saucepan with the endives, pressing on the shallots and mushrooms.

Heat the endives and the sauce over moderate heat, stirring constantly. When the sauce is hot, but not boiling, remove from the heat and whisk in the mustard, then the butter, a teaspoon at a time. Taste for seasoning and add salt and pepper if necessary.

Spoon the sauce over the fish and serve immediately.

SUGGESTIONS:

Virtually any fish can be used to make this recipe: turbot, sole, or any other flatfish, as well as whiting, sea bass, salmon, etc.

The zest of 1 lemon or ½ an orange, cut into julienne strips and parboiled, may be used instead of mustard.

Beer may be used instead of white wine. In this case, serve beer with the fish as well.

Barbue au cidre sec et aux pointes d'asperges
BRILL WITH CIDER AND ASPARAGUS

Ingredients for 4 servings:
  20 medium fresh asparagus (about 2 pounds)
  6 cups water
  1½ teaspoons coarse salt
  4 brill fillets or other flatfish, weighing about 1½ pounds (from a 3-pound fish)
  2 teaspoons butter
  3 shallots, finely chopped
  2 mushrooms, finely chopped
  ¾ cup hard cider
  1½ cups heavy cream
  Salt, pepper

  UTENSILS:
  Saucepan
  Skimmer or slotted spoon
  Oval roasting pan, about 16 inches long
  Spatula
  To serve: Heated serving platter

  THE ASPARAGUS:
Cut off the tough, stringy ends of the asparagus; the remaining asparagus should be about 4 to 5 inches long. Peel them, rinse under running water, and drain.

Bring the water and coarse salt to a boil in a saucepan, add the asparagus, and boil for 5 minutes, or until tender. Lift the asparagus out of the pot with a skimmer or slotted spoon to avoid damaging the tips, drain on a cloth, and reserve.

  THE FISH:
Preheat the oven to 425° F.

Salt and pepper the fish fillets on both sides.

Melt the butter in a roasting pan, add the shallots, and simmer, stirring frequently, until soft and transparent. Stir in the mushrooms, lay the fish on the bed of vegetables, add the cider, and bake for 8 minutes.

TO MAKE THE SAUCE AND SERVE:

When the fish fillets are done, lift them out of the roasting pan with a spatula and drain on a cloth. Place on a serving platter, cover with aluminum foil, and keep warm.

Place the roasting pan over high heat and boil rapidly until there are about 2 tablespoons of liquid left. Stir in the cream, add salt and pepper, and boil for 4 minutes more, or until thick and creamy.

Strain the sauce into a saucepan, pressing on the vegetables, taste for seasoning, add the asparagus, and heat for about 2 minutes, without boiling, to warm the asparagus.

Place the asparagus on top of the fish, spoon over the sauce, and serve immediately.

Suprême de turbot à la carotte et au persil
TURBOT FILLETS WITH CARROTS AND PARSLEY

Ingredients for 4 servings:

FOR THE COLORING:
8 medium carrots, peeled and sliced
3⅓ cups water, in all
1 cup tightly packed parsley leaves

FOR THE GARNISH:
1 tablespoon butter
4 medium carrots, cut into julienne strips
Salt, pepper
½ cup tightly packed parsley leaves

FOR THE FISH:
4 turbot fillets, weighing about 1½ pounds (from a 3-pound fish) *(see Suggestions and Note)*
Salt, pepper
1 tablespoon butter
7 shallots, finely chopped
4 medium mushrooms, chopped

1 cup dry white wine
1½ cups heavy cream
2 teaspoons softened butter

UTENSILS:
Food processor or blender
2 saucepans
2 clean cloths
Fine sieve
Small bowl
Large frying pan
Oval or rectangular roasting pan, 16 inches long
Spatula
Small saucepan
Wire whisk
To serve: Heated serving platter and sauceboat

THE CARROT AND PARSLEY COLORINGS:

Place the sliced carrots in a food processor or blender with 1 cup of the water and grind to a pulp. Add another cup of water and blend.

Line a saucepan with a clean cloth and pour the contents of the processor into it. Twist the ends of the cloth together as hard as possible to squeeze out all the liquid. Discard the solids in the cloth.

Bring the carrot juice to a boil; a thick foam will rise to the surface. Boil gently for 45 seconds, then strain the juice through a fine sieve. With a spoon, scoop everything out of the sieve and place it in a small bowl; this is the carrot coloring.

Rinse out the cloth used for the carrots and line the rinsed saucepan with it. Make the parsley coloring exactly as described for the carrot coloring (use only 1⅓ cups total water) and add it to the bowl with the carrot coloring.

THE VEGETABLE GARNISH:

In a large frying pan, melt a tablespoon of butter and add the julienne of carrots. Salt and pepper, stir, and cook over moderate heat, stirring occasionally. The carrots should become shiny and color lightly. Reserve.

Bring a saucepan of water to a boil and add the parsley leaves. Boil for 1 minute, drain, cool under running water, and drain again. Place the parsley leaves in a small saucepan and reserve.

123

THE FISH:

Preheat the oven to 425° F.

Season the fish on both sides with salt and pepper.

In a roasting pan, melt a tablespoon of butter, add the shallots, and simmer until soft and transparent. Add the mushrooms, salt, and pepper, stir together, and simmer, stirring occasionally, for 2 minutes more. Place the fish fillets on top of the vegetables, add the white wine, cover with aluminum foil, and bake for 6 minutes.

When the fish is done, lift the fillets out of the pan with a spatula, drain on a clean cloth, place them on a serving platter, cover with foil, and keep warm while making the sauce.

TO MAKE THE SAUCE AND SERVE:

Place the roasting pan over high heat and boil the cooking liquid rapidly until it has almost completely evaporated. Stir in the cream and boil rapidly 4 minutes more, or until thick and creamy.

Strain the sauce into a saucepan, pressing on the vegetables to extract all their liquids. Taste for seasoning.

Add 2 tablespoons of the sauce to the parsley leaves and reheat them over low heat. Add salt and pepper if necessary.

Reheat the carrots.

Whisk the carrot and parsley colorings into the sauce—it will be speckled with orange and green flecks. Heat gently for about 2 minutes, whisking occasionally until the sauce is hot (do not boil). Away from the heat, whisk in the butter, a teaspoon at a time, then pour into a sauceboat.

Place four mounds each of carrots and parsley around the fish, alternating them, and serve immediately, with the sauceboat on the side.

SUGGESTIONS:

Sea bass may be used instead of turbot, and the parsley may be replaced by an equal amount of watercress leaves.

NOTE: *An equal weight of fillets of flounder or halibut, or other fish with firm white flesh such as snapper, may also be used. Ed.*

Turbot aux cinq légumes
TURBOT WITH FIVE-VEGETABLE SAUCE

Ingredients for 4 servings:

FOR THE VEGETABLES:
¼ pound very thin green beans, strings removed, cut into 2-inch pieces
1 tablespoon butter
2 medium carrots, cut into julienne strips
1⅓ cups water
1 teaspoon curry powder
1 small zucchini, unpeeled, cut into julienne strips
4-inch piece cucumber, peeled, seeded, and cut into julienne strips
¼ pound large mushrooms, caps cut into julienne strips, stems chopped

FOR THE FISH:
1 tablespoon butter
5 shallots, finely chopped
4 turbot fillets, weighing about 1½ pounds (from a 3-pound fish)
1⅓ cups white wine
1½ cups heavy cream
Salt, pepper

UTENSILS:
Medium saucepan
Sauteuse or high-sided frying pan, 9½ inches in diameter
Oval or rectangular roasting pan, 13 to 14 inches long
Spatula
Clean cloth
Wire whisk
Slotted spoon
To serve: Heated serving platter

THE VEGETABLES:
Boil the green beans in salted water for 6 minutes, drain, cool under running water, drain again, and reserve.

In a *sauteuse* or high-sided frying pan, melt the butter, add the carrots, stir for a few seconds to coat them, and add the water and curry

125

powder. Stir again and boil, uncovered, for 7 minutes. Add the zucchini and cucumber, and cook for 1 minute longer, add the julienne of mushroom caps, and cook for 1 minute more. Add the green beans, sprinkle with salt and pepper, stir all the vegetables together, then remove the pan from the heat. Reserve.

THE FISH:

Preheat the oven to 425° F.

In the roasting pan, melt the butter over moderate heat, add the shallots, and simmer until soft and transparent. Add the chopped mushroom stems, salt, and pepper and cook, stirring occasionally, for 1 minute.

Salt and pepper the fish fillets, lay them on top of the vegetables, add the white wine, cover with aluminum foil, and bake for 6 minutes.

When the fish is cooked, lift the fillets out of the roasting pan with a spatula and drain on a clean cloth. Place on a serving platter, cover with aluminum foil, and keep warm.

TO MAKE THE SAUCE AND SERVE:

Place the roasting pan over high heat, boil rapidly until almost all the liquid has evaporated, then whisk in the cream. Bring back to a boil and boil for 2 to 3 minutes, or until creamy.

Heat the vegetables over low heat, then strain the sauce over them, pressing on the shallots and mushrooms with a wooden spoon. Stir and taste the sauce for seasoning. Lift the vegetables out of the sauce with a slotted spoon, arrange them around the fish, then pour the sauce over the fish, and serve immediately.

SUGGESTIONS:

Almost any fish fillets may be used in making this dish, but if using fish other than flatfish (such as salmon, sea bass, etc.) count 7 minutes cooking time rather than 6.

Turbotin aux raisins et au thé
TURBOT FILLETS WITH GRAPES AND TEA

Ingredients for 4 servings:
    20 large, sweet white grapes, or 40 small ones
    1 tablespoon butter (for the fish)
    5 shallots, finely chopped
    2 medium mushrooms, finely chopped
    Salt, pepper
    4 turbot fillets weighing about 1½ pounds (from a 3-pound fish)
    ⅔ cup dry white wine
    1½ cups heavy cream
    4½ teaspoons Ceylon tea
    3 teaspoons softened butter

UTENSILS:
Toothpick or small, pointed knife
Oval or rectangular roasting pan, 13 to 14 inches long
Spatula
Small saucepan
Wire whisk
To serve: Heated serving platter and sauceboat

PRELIMINARY PREPARATIONS:
Preheat the oven to 425° F.

Remove the seeds from each grape, using a toothpick or a small pointed knife *(see Note)*. Carefully peel the skin off each grape and reserve.

THE FISH:
In a roasting pan, melt the butter, add the shallots, and cook for 1 minute over moderate heat, stirring constantly. Add the mushrooms, season with salt and pepper, and cook for 1 minute more. Salt and pepper the fish fillets, place them on top of the vegetables, add the wine, cover the pan with aluminum foil, and bake for 6 minutes.

When the fillets are done, lift them out of the pan with a spatula and place them on a serving platter. Keep warm in the oven with the door ajar while making the sauce.

TO MAKE THE SAUCE AND SERVE:

Place the roasting pan over moderate heat and boil the cooking liquid for 2 minutes, or until there are about 3 tablespoons left, then add the cream. Raise the heat and boil rapidly for 4 to 5 minutes, or until the cream has thickened slightly, then stir in the tea. Lower the heat and allow to infuse for 1 minute at a very gentle boil, then strain the sauce into a small saucepan. Away from the heat, whisk in the butter a teaspoon at a time, then add the grapes. Taste for seasoning and heat the sauce for 1 minute over low heat, stirring very gently.

Remove the fish from the warming oven and pour off any liquid it has given out. Spoon a little of the sauce over the fish and serve immediately, with the rest of the sauce in a sauceboat.

SUGGESTIONS:

The flavor of the sauce can be varied according to the kind of tea used; even flavored teas (apple, rose, and so on) may be experimented with.

Other fish may be used instead of turbot, but it is preferable to use those with firm, white flesh.

NOTE: *Removing the seeds from the whole grapes is quite painstaking. To make it easier, the grapes may be peeled, then slit down one side, or cut in half, to remove the seeds. Ed.*

Turbot aux épinards et au cari
TURBOT WITH CURRY SAUCE AND SPINACH

Ingredients for 4 servings:

2 teaspoons butter (for the spinach)
1½ pounds fresh young spinach (*see Note and Suggestions*)

1 tablespoon butter (for the fish)
6 shallots, finely chopped
3 medium mushrooms, finely chopped
Salt, pepper
1 teaspoon mild curry powder
4 turbot fillets weighing about 1½ pounds (from a 3-pound fish)

½ cup dry white wine
1⅔ cups heavy cream
2 teaspoons softened butter (for the sauce)

UTENSILS:
Large pot
Oval or rectangular roasting pan, 13 to 14 inches long
Spatula
Small saucepan
Wire whisk
To serve: Heated serving platter and sauceboat

THE SPINACH:
In a large pot, melt the butter. Add the spinach, stirring until it has melted down, season with salt and pepper, and cook over low heat, uncovered, for 4 minutes, stirring occasionally.

THE FISH:
Preheat the oven to 425° F.

In a roasting pan, melt the butter for the fish and add the shallots. Stir for a few seconds, add the mushrooms, and season with salt, pepper, and curry. Stir, then simmer for 3 minutes.

Salt and pepper the fish fillets, place them on the bed of vegetables, and add the wine. Bring the liquid to a boil, cover with aluminum foil, and bake for 6 minutes.

When the fillets are done, lift them out of the baking dish with a spatula and place on a cloth for a few seconds to drain.

Place the spinach on a serving platter, arrange the fillets on top, cover with foil, and keep warm in the oven with the door ajar while making the sauce.

TO MAKE THE SAUCE AND SERVE:
Place the roasting pan over high heat and boil the cooking liquid rapidly until the pan is nearly dry. Add the cream and boil for 3 to 4 minutes, or until thick and creamy.

Strain the sauce into a small saucepan, taste for seasoning, and bring back to a boil. Remove from the heat and whisk in the butter, a teaspoon at a time.

Remove the fish from the oven, spoon a little of the sauce over it, and serve immediately, with the rest of the sauce in a sauceboat.

SUGGESTIONS:
Instead of the spinach, 4 bunches of watercress, or 4 heads of lettuce may be used in making this recipe (prepare exactly as described for the spinach).

Or the greens can be eliminated altogether and cucumber balls, boiled for 5 minutes in salted water, may be added to the sauce instead.

NOTE: *Spinach with large, very dark green leaves should be parboiled in unsalted water for 2 minutes, drained, cooled under cold running water, and squeezed dry before preparing as described. Ed.*

Turbot aux fèves et au chou
TURBOT WITH FAVA BEANS AND CABBAGE

Ingredients for 4 servings:

2¾ pounds turbot
2 pounds fresh fava (broad) beans
8 cabbage leaves (preferably loose-leaf cabbage)
3½ tablespoons softened butter

Salt, pepper
2 teaspoons butter
3 shallots, finely chopped
2 medium mushrooms, finely chopped
⅔ cup white wine
1⅓ cups heavy cream

UTENSILS:
Food processor or blender
Oval or rectangular roasting pan, 13 to 14 inches long
Large pot
Spatula
Medium saucepan
Wire whisk
Skimmer or slotted spoon
To serve: Heated serving platter, or 4 heated dinner plates

PRELIMINARY PREPARATIONS:

Ask the fish seller to fillet the fish for you, but to leave the skin on.

Shell the fava beans and remove the skin that surrounds each bean. Set aside a quarter of the beans for the sauce. Reserve the rest for the garnish.

Cut out the central rib from each cabbage leaf, then wash, and drain them. Set aside 2 leaves for the sauce.

Take the remaining 6 leaves, pile them on top of each other, and cut them lengthwise into thin strips. Reserve for the garnish.

Preheat the oven to 425° F.

THE VEGETABLE BUTTER:

Place the beans and cabbage leaves to be used in the sauce in a food processor or blender and blend until the vegetables are finely chopped. Add the softened butter, blend to mix well, then rub the vegetable butter through a sieve and into a bowl, using a wooden spoon.

THE FISH:

Salt and pepper the fish fillets.

In a roasting pan, melt 2 teaspoons of butter, add the shallots, and simmer until soft and transparent. Add the mushrooms, season with salt and pepper, stir, and cook for 1 minute longer. Place the fish on top of the shallots and mushrooms, skin side up, add the white wine, cover with aluminum foil, and bake for 7 minutes.

THE VEGETABLES:

Bring a large pot of salted water to a boil and add the fava beans. Boil for 3 minutes, add the strips of cabbage, and boil for 2 minutes more. Drain, cool under running water, and drain again.

TO MAKE THE SAUCE AND SERVE:

When the fish is done, remove it from the pan with a spatula and place the fillets on a cloth to drain. With a knife, remove the skin, place the fillets on a serving platter or dinner plates, and keep warm.

Place the roasting pan over high heat and reduce the cooking liquids until the pan is almost dry. Add the cream, stir, and boil gently for 2 minutes, then strain it into a saucepan.

Over low heat, whisk the vegetable butter into the sauce, little by little, taste for seasoning, and add the cooked beans and strips of cabbage. Stir until the vegetables are hot, but do not allow to boil.

With a skimmer or slotted spoon, lift the vegetables out of the sauce and arrange them around the fish. Spoon the sauce over the fish and serve immediately.

SUGGESTION:
The turbot can be replaced by virtually any fish with firm white flesh.

Turbot aux cinq champignons
TURBOT WITH WILD MUSHROOMS

Ingredients for 4 servings:

FOR THE MUSHROOMS:
10½ ounces wild mushrooms—ideally equal amounts of chanterelles, morels, fairy-ring mushrooms, horn-of-plenty, and boletus (*see Suggestions and Note*)
2 teaspoons butter

FOR THE FISH:
4 fillets of turbot, weighing about 1½ pounds (from a 3-pound fish)
2 teaspoons butter
2 shallots, finely chopped
2 large mushrooms, chopped
¾ cup dry white wine
1½ cups heavy cream
Salt, pepper

UTENSILS:
Frying pan
Oval or rectangular roasting pan, 13 to 14 inches long
Spatula
Wire whisk
To serve: Heated serving platter

THE MUSHROOMS:
Cut the sandy base of the stem off each mushroom, carefully wash, and drain them.

132

In a frying pan, melt the butter over moderate heat. When it is very hot, add the mushrooms, stir, and sprinkle with salt and pepper. Sauté lightly for 2 to 3 minutes, stirring frequently, lower the heat, and cook very slowly, uncovered, for 8 minutes more, stirring occasionally. Reserve.

THE FISH:

Preheat the oven to 425° F.

Sprinkle the fish fillets with salt and pepper.

Melt the butter in the roasting pan, add the chopped shallots and mushrooms, salt, and pepper, and simmer for 3 minutes, stirring occasionally; do not allow to brown.

Place the fish on the bed of vegetables, add the wine, cover with aluminum foil, and bake for 6 minutes.

TO MAKE THE SAUCE AND SERVE:

When the fish is done, lift it out of the roasting pan with a spatula, drain on a clean cloth for a few seconds, place it on a serving platter, cover with aluminum foil, and keep warm.

Place the roasting pan over high heat and boil the cooking liquid until the pan is nearly dry, add the cream, and boil for about 3 minutes, or until thick and creamy.

Place the wild mushrooms back over low heat to warm up. When hot, strain the sauce over them, stir together, and taste for salt and pepper.

Remove the fish from the oven, spoon the mushrooms and sauce over it, and serve immediately.

SUGGESTIONS:

Dried wild mushrooms may be used instead of fresh ones. In this case, use about ¼ cup of each kind, or a total of about 1¼ cups of dried mushrooms. Allow to soak for about 20 minutes in warm water (or follow the directions on the package) before cleaning and using them as you would fresh ones.

NOTE: *Any kind of wild mushrooms may be used, and if only one kind is available, either fresh or dried, use it. In any case, do not use ordinary mushrooms, as this would completely change the character of the dish. Ed.*

Suprême de turbot à la tomate
TURBOT FILLETS WITH TOMATO

Ingredients for 4 servings:

FOR THE TOMATOES:
1 tablespoon butter
6 shallots, finely chopped
2 pounds tomatoes, peeled, seeded, and coarsely chopped
Salt, pepper

FOR THE FISH:
1 tablespoon butter
6 shallots, finely chopped
3 medium mushrooms, finely chopped
4 fillets of turbot, weighing about 1½ pounds (from a 3-pound fish)
1⅓ cups dry white wine
1½ cups heavy cream
Salt, pepper

UTENSILS:
Medium saucepan
Food mill
Oval or rectangular roasting pan, 13 to 14 inches long
Spatula
Wire whisk
Small saucepan
To serve: Heated serving platter

THE TOMATOES:
Melt the butter in a medium saucepan. Add the shallots, stir, and simmer for 2 to 3 minutes, or until soft and transparent. Add the tomatoes, salt, and pepper, and cook over low heat, uncovered, for 25 minutes, stirring occasionally.

Purée half of the tomato mixture in a food mill. Reserve separately from the rest of the tomatoes (still in pieces).

THE FISH:
Preheat the oven to 425° F.

Salt and pepper the fish fillets.

134

In a roasting pan, melt the butter, add the shallots, and cook gently until soft, then add the mushrooms. Salt and pepper, stir, and spread the mixture over the bottom of the pan. Lay the fillets on top, add the wine, cover the pan with aluminum foil, and bake for 7 minutes.

TO MAKE THE SAUCE AND SERVE:

When the fillets are done, remove them from the pan with a spatula and place on a cloth to drain for a few seconds. Place them on a serving platter, cover with foil, and keep warm in the oven with the door ajar while making the sauce.

Place the roasting pan over moderate heat and boil the cooking liquid until it has almost completely evaporated. Add the cream, then boil rapidly for 2 to 3 minutes, or until thick and creamy, whisking occasionally. Strain the sauce into a small saucepan, pressing on the shallots and mushrooms with a wooden spoon. Add the tomato purée, whisk to combine, taste for salt and pepper, and heat without allowing to boil.

Reheat the pieces of tomato.

Remove the fish from the oven, pour the sauce around it, and spoon some of the tomato over each fillet. Serve immediately.

SUGGESTIONS:

A mixture of chopped fresh herbs (parsley, chervil, chives, tarragon, etc.) or freshly chopped basil may be added to the tomatoes.

This dish can be made with all kinds of fish fillets.

Lotte aux blancs de poireaux, sauce au coriandre frais, et safran
ANGLERFISH WITH LEEK, CORIANDER, AND SAFFRON SAUCE

Ingredients for 4 servings:

2¼ pounds anglerfish (goosefish or monkfish), filleted
    and cut into 4 pieces *(see Note)*.
4 large leeks, white only, cut into 2-inch pieces
2 sprigs fresh coriander (cilantro), leaves only
Pinch powdered saffron

Salt, pepper
2 teaspoons butter
2 shallots, finely chopped
1 large mushroom, finely chopped
⅔ cup white wine
1½ cups heavy cream

UTENSILS:

Pot
Medium saucepan
Oval or rectangular roasting pan, 13 to 14 inches long
Spatula
Skimmer or slotted spoon
To serve: 4 heated dinner plates, or a heated serving platter

PRELIMINARY PREPARATIONS:

If the pieces of fish are very thick, flatten them slightly with the flat side of a cleaver.
Preheat the oven to 425° F.

THE LEEKS:

In a pot of boiling salted water, cook the leeks at a moderate boil, uncovered, for 10 minutes, then drain. Place them in a saucepan with the coriander and saffron and reserve.

THE FISH:

Season the fish with salt and pepper.
Melt the butter in a roasting pan, add the shallots, and simmer for about 1 minute, or until soft and transparent. Stir in the mushroom, place the pieces of fish on top, and add the white wine. Bring to a boil, then bake for 6 minutes.
Remove the fish from the pan with a spatula and drain for a few seconds on a cloth. Place on dinner plates or a serving platter and keep warm while making the sauce.

TO MAKE THE SAUCE AND SERVE:

Over high heat, reduce the liquid in the roasting pan until there are only about 3 tablespoons. Whisk in the cream and boil rapidly for 2 to 3 minutes, or until creamy.
Place the leeks over moderate heat and strain the sauce over them,

pressing on the shallots and mushroom with a wooden spoon. Bring the sauce to a boil, stir, and simmer for 3 to 4 minutes; salt and pepper generously.

With a skimmer or slotted spoon, lift the leeks out of the saucepan and place next to the fish, pour over the sauce, and serve.

SUGGESTIONS:
Any fish with firm white flesh can be used instead of anglerfish.

Instead of using leeks, cucumbers (peeled, seeded, cut into finger-sized pieces, and boiled for 5 minutes) may be used, and mint and curry may be used to flavor the sauce instead of coriander and saffron.

Homard à la coque
ROAST LOBSTER WITH FENNEL

Ingredients for 2 servings:
   1 live lobster, weighing about 2¼ pounds
   1 tablespoon olive oil

   FOR THE SAUCE:
2 teaspoons butter
4 shallots, finely chopped
½ cup dry white wine
1½ tablespoons wine vinegar
6 tablespoons softened butter, broken into pieces
Salt, pepper
1 tablespoon chopped parsley, chives, and chervil, mixed

   FOR THE FENNEL:
1 tablespoon butter
1 pound fennel, thinly sliced
Salt, pepper
1 tablespoon water
2 tablespoons heavy cream
¼ teaspoon mild curry powder

UTENSILS:

Cleaver or hammer
Large rectangular roasting pan, 14 inches long
Scissors
Aluminum foil
2 saucepans
Wire whisk
High-sided frying pan or *sauteuse*, with cover
To serve: 2 warm dinner plates

THE LOBSTER:

Preheat the oven to 500° F; place the roasting pan in the oven.

With the blunt edge of a cleaver or a hammer, crack the lobster claws. Place the lobster in the hot roasting pan, pour the oil over it, and roast for 15 minutes. The lobster is done when it has turned red.

When the lobster is cool enough to handle, remove the meat from the claws and detach the tail from the head with a twisting motion. With a pair of scissors, cut the shell on the underside of the tail in half lengthwise and remove the meat. With the tip of a knife, scrape out any blackish matter near the top of the tail, then cut the tail and claw meat into slices about ¼ inch thick. Place the lobster meat on a plate, cover with aluminum foil, and keep warm.

THE SAUCE:

Make the foamy butter sauce as described in the recipe for **Hot fish terrine** *(see p. 84)*, using the measurements given here. When all of the butter has been added, strain the sauce into a clean saucepan, taste for salt and pepper, and reserve.

THE FENNEL:

In a high-sided frying pan or *sauteuse*, melt the butter, add the fennel, salt, pepper, water, cream, and curry, stir together, cover, and simmer for 7 minutes.

TO SERVE:

Gently reheat the sauce to warm, whisking constantly, then stir in the chopped herbs.

Place a bed of fennel on each plate, arrange the lobster meat on top, spoon the sauce over the lobster, and serve immediately.

Homard à la vanille

ROAST LOBSTER WITH VANILLA BUTTER SAUCE

Ingredients for 4 servings:
    2 live lobsters, weighing about 2¼ pounds each
    2 tablespoons olive oil

FOR THE SAUCE:
2 teaspoons butter
5 shallots, finely chopped
1 cup white wine
3 tablespoons wine vinegar
1½ sticks softened butter, broken into pieces
1 vanilla bean, split in half lengthwise

FOR THE GARNISH:
1 tablespoon butter
1½ pounds fresh young spinach, stems and ribs removed
2 large bunches (about 2 pounds) watercress, leaves only (1¾ cups,
    packed down)
Salt, pepper

UTENSILS:
Cleaver or hammer
Oven roasting pan
Scissors
2 saucepans
Wire whisk
Large pot
To serve: 4 heated dinner plates

THE LOBSTER:
Place the roasting pan that comes with the oven on the middle shelf and
preheat the oven to 500° F.

With the blunt edge of a cleaver or a hammer, crack the lobster
claws. Place the lobsters in the hot roasting pan, pour a tablespoon of
olive oil over each one, and roast for 15 minutes, or until red.

When the lobsters are cool enough to handle, remove the meat from
the claws and detach the tails from the heads with a twisting motion.

With a pair of scissors, cut the shell on the underside of each tail in half lengthwise and remove the meat. With the tip of a knife, scrape out any blackish matter near the top of the tails, then cut the tail and claw meat into slices about ¼ inch thick. Place the lobster meat on a plate, cover with aluminum foil, and keep warm.

THE SAUCE:

Make the foamy butter sauce as described in the recipe for **Hot fish terrine** *(see p. 84)*, using the measurements given here. When all of the butter has been added, taste for salt and pepper, then scrape the pulp from the vanilla bean into it with the tip of a knife. Stir the sauce, then strain it into a clean saucepan, rubbing on the shallots with a wooden spoon to make sure all the sauce and vanilla goes through. Reserve.

THE GARNISH:

Melt a tablespoon of butter in a large pot and add the spinach and watercress. Stir until the vegetables have melted down, then simmer, uncovered, for 5 minutes, stirring occasionally.

TO SERVE:

Over low heat, reheat the sauce to warm, whisking constantly.

Place a bed of spinach and watercress on each plate, arrange the pieces of lobster on top, spoon the sauce over the lobster, and serve immediately.

NOTE: *Only young pale-green spinach should be prepared as described. If the spinach you use has large, thick, dark green leaves, boil it for 2 minutes once the water comes back to a boil in rapidly boiling unsalted water. Drain the spinach, cool it under running water, and squeeze out all the water with your hands. To prepare the garnish, first melt down the watercress in a pot with the butter as described, then add the parboiled spinach, and cook for the remaining 5 minutes. Ed.*

Fricassée de homard aux petits pois frais
LOBSTER FRICASSEE WITH FRESH PEAS

Ingredients for 4 servings:

FOR THE COURT BOUILLON:
6 quarts water
6 teaspoons coarse salt
1 large carrot, sliced
1 small onion, sliced
1 medium tomato, cut into 8 wedges
1 stalk celery, diced
Leaves of 1 small leek, sliced
1 slice lemon
1 bay leaf
3 sprigs parsley
1 sprig thyme
15 peppercorns
2 cloves garlic
2 live lobsters, weighing about 2½ pounds each

FOR THE SAUCE:
2 tablespoons olive oil
1 medium carrot, diced
5 shallots, finely chopped
White of 1 small leek, sliced
1 tomato, diced
1 stalk celery, diced
¼ bulb fennel, diced
3 tablespoons dry white wine
⅓ cup cognac
1⅔ cups heavy cream

FOR THE PEAS:
1 tablespoon butter
2 shallots, finely chopped
1¼ pounds fresh peas, shelled
Salt, pepper

UTENSILS:
Large pot, with cover
Cleaver or hammer
2 bowls
Scissors
Large *sauteuse* or high-sided frying pan
Medium *sauteuse* or high-sided frying pan
Wire whisk
To serve: 4 heated dinner plates

THE LOBSTER:

Place the water and coarse salt in a large pot and bring to a boil. Add all the ingredients for the court bouillon, except the lobsters, and cook at a slow boil, uncovered, for 25 minutes.

Bring the court bouillon to a rapid boil and drop the lobsters into it. Cover the pot until the liquid comes back to a boil, then boil rapidly, uncovered, for 9 minutes. Lift the lobsters out of the court bouillon and drain, head down, in a colander until cool enough to handle.

Break off the claws and crack the shells with a hammer or the blunt edge of a cleaver. Remove the meat, cut it into ½-inch cubes, and place in a bowl.

With a twisting motion, separate the tails from the heads. Reserve the heads. Cut the underside of each tail shell in half lengthwise with a pair of scissors and remove the meat. Cut the tail in half lengthwise, remove the grainy, blackish intestine, then cut each half tail into ½-inch slices. Place the tail meat in the bowl with the claw meat, cover, and reserve.

Strain 1 cup of the court bouillon and reserve in a bowl.

THE LOBSTER SAUCE:

With a spoon, scoop out the inside of each head and discard. Cut each head in half lengthwise, then into several pieces with a large knife.

In a large *sauteuse* or high-sided frying pan, heat the olive oil until almost smoking, add the pieces of lobster head, and cook for 3 minutes, stirring frequently. Add the carrot, shallots, leek, tomato, fennel, and celery and cook for about 4 minutes, or until the water they give out has evaporated. Add the white wine and cognac, light with a match, and boil over high heat until the flame goes out.

Stir in the cream, lower the heat, and simmer, uncovered, for 20 minutes, stirring occasionally. Strain the sauce into a bowl, pressing on the lobster heads with a small ladle or wooden spoon to extract all the juices. There should be about 1⅓ cups of strained sauce. Reserve.

THE PEAS:

In a medium *sauteuse* or high-sided frying pan, melt a tablespoon of butter. Add the shallots and simmer, stirring occasionally, until soft and transparent. Add the peas, sprinkle with salt and pepper, stir gently for 2 minutes, then add the reserved court bouillon. Cook at a gentle boil for 5 to 6 minutes, or until there are only about 5 tablespoons of liquid left, then remove from the heat. Add the lobster meat to the peas and reserve.

TO FINISH AND SERVE:

Place the lobster sauce over moderate heat and simmer for 6 to 7 minutes, whisking occasionally. Season with salt and pepper, then add the sauce to the lobster and peas. Heat at a gentle boil for 1 to 2 minutes, or until the lobster is hot, then divide among the dinner plates, and serve immediately.

Fricassée de langouste aux morilles et asperges
SPINY LOBSTER FRICASSEE WITH MORELS AND ASPARAGUS

Ingredients for 4 servings:
   About 6 ounces fresh morels or other wild mushrooms *(see Note)*
   3 tablespoons vinegar
   2 pounds very thin asparagus
   1 live spiny lobster, weighing 3 pounds *(for substitution see Suggestion)*

FOR THE COURT BOUILLON:

4 quarts water
4 teaspoons coarse salt
1 bay leaf
1 sprig thyme
3 sprigs parsley

143

15 peppercorns
2 cloves garlic, crushed
1 large carrot, sliced
1 onion, sliced
3 stalks celery, diced
1 tomato, cut into 8 wedges
Green leaves of 1 small leek, sliced
1 slice lemon

FOR THE LOBSTER SAUCE:
2 tablespoons olive oil
1 medium carrot, diced
5 shallots, finely chopped
White of 1 small leek, sliced
1 tomato, diced
1 stalk celery, diced
¼ bulb fennel, diced
5 tablespoons cognac
2 tablespoons white wine
1⅔ cups heavy cream
Salt, pepper
1 tablespoon butter (for the morels)

UTENSILS:
Pastry brush
Large basin
Kitchen string
Large pot
Scissors
Bowl
Large pot or *sauteuse*, 11½ inches in diameter
Medium *sauteuse* or high-sided frying pan, 9½ inches in diameter
Frying pan
Skimmer or slotted spoon
Large saucepan
To serve: 4 heated dinner plates

PRELIMINARY PREPARATIONS:
Cut off the sandy end of the stems and remove any damaged parts of the morels, then cut them in half lengthwise. With a pastry brush, brush the morels gently to remove as much dirt as possible from the

crevices, drop them into a large bowl of water laced with 2 tablespoons of vinegar, and allow to soak for 5 to 6 minutes. Drain, then wash the mushrooms very carefully in a large basin of water, changing the water 2 to 3 times. Drain and pat dry in a cloth.

Break off the woody ends of the asparagus, peel them, then cut into 4-inch lengths. Wash and tie them together in 3 to 4 bunches with kitchen string and reserve.

THE SPINY LOBSTER:

The spiny lobster may simply be cooked in salted water (4 quarts water and 4 teaspoons coarse salt), but it is preferable to make a court bouillon as follows:

Place the water and coarse salt in a large pot, add the bay leaf, thyme, parsley, and peppercorns and bring to a boil. Add all the other ingredients for the court bouillon and boil gently for 15 minutes.

Bring to a rapid boil and drop in the lobster. Cover the pot until the liquid comes back to a boil, then boil, uncovered, for 13 minutes. Lift the lobster out of the liquid and drain, head down, in a colander until cool enough to handle.

With a twisting motion, separate the tail from the head. Using a pair of scissors, cut the underside of the tail shell in half lengthwise and remove the meat. Cut the tail in half lengthwise and remove the blackish intestine that runs along the top, then cut the meat into pieces about ½ inch thick and reserve in a bowl.

With a large knife, cut the head in half lengthwise. Remove any meat, place it in the bowl with the tail meat, and sprinkle with salt and pepper. Cover and reserve.

THE LOBSTER SAUCE:

Using a large knife, cut the head and legs into several pieces.

In a large pot or *sauteuse,* heat the olive oil until almost smoking, add the pieces of head and legs, and sauté for 6 to 7 minutes, stirring often.

Add the carrot, shallots, leek, tomato, celery, and fennel and cook over moderate to high heat for 3 to 5 minutes, or until the water the vegetables have given out evaporates completely. Add the cognac and white wine, light with a match, and boil rapidly for about 4 minutes, or until almost all of the liquid has evaporated. Stir in the cream, lower the heat, and boil gently for 20 minutes, skimming off any foam that surfaces.

Strain the finished sauce into a smaller *sauteuse* or high-sided frying pan, pressing on the vegetables and pieces of lobster to extract as much liquid as possible; there should be about 1⅓ cups of strained sauce. Season with salt and pepper and reserve.

THE MORELS:

Melt a tablespoon of butter in a frying pan, add the morels, and sprinkle with salt and pepper. Sauté over moderate heat for 5 to 10 minutes, or until tender, stirring often to brown them lightly on all sides. Remove from the heat and reserve.

THE ASPARAGUS:

Bring a large saucepan of salted water to a boil, drop in the bunches of asparagus, and boil for 5 to 7 minutes, or until tender. Lift the asparagus out of the water with a skimmer or slotted spoon, untie them, and drain for a few seconds on a cloth.

TO SERVE:

Heat the lobster sauce until almost boiling, then add the pieces of lobster and morels. Simmer for about 1 minute to heat them through, then divide the lobster, mushrooms, and sauce among the dinner plates, decorate each serving with asparagus, and serve immediately.

SUGGESTION:

Maine lobster may be used and prepared as described for the spiny lobster. Use a lobster of the same weight, be sure not to overcook, and cut the meat from the claws and tail into ½-inch slices.

NOTE: *Canned (bottled) or dried morels may be used instead of fresh ones. Use 1½ cups drained canned morels or ¾ cup dried ones. Canned morels should be rinsed off and drained on a cloth before cooking. Dried morels should be soaked as described on their package (generally about 30 minutes in warm water) and drained on a cloth. Canned and dried morels cook much more quickly than fresh ones—as soon as they begin to brown, in about 2 to 3 minutes, they are done. Ed.*

Fricassée de langoustes, langoustines, truffes, et chou nouveau
SPINY LOBSTER AND LANGOUSTINE FRICASSEE WITH BABY CABBAGE AND TRUFFLES

Ingredients for 4 servings:

FOR THE COURT BOUILLON:

3 quarts water
3 teaspoons coarse salt
2 carrots, sliced
1 medium onion, sliced
1½ bay leaves
2 sprigs thyme
3 sprigs parsley
10 peppercorns
1 live spiny lobster or Maine lobster, weighing 2¾ pounds
12 large *langoustines* (3 pounds) or 16 live crayfish (*for substitution, see Note*)

FOR THE SAUCE:

2 tablespoons olive oil
1 medium carrot, diced
¼ bulb fennel, diced
1 small onion, diced
1 stalk celery, diced
White of 1 medium leek, diced
2 small tomatoes, peeled, seeded, and diced
8 teaspoons cognac
8 teaspoons dry white wine
1⅓ cups *crème fraîche (see p. 331)* or heavy cream
3 leaves from a baby cabbage (or from the heart of an ordinary loose-leaf cabbage)
1 large truffle (about 1¼ ounces), drained and cut into julienne strips
Salt, pepper

UTENSILS:

Large pot
Cleaver or hammer

Scissors
Bowl
Large pot or *sauteuse*
Saucepan or small *sauteuse*
Medium pot
To serve: 4 heated dinner plates

THE LOBSTER:

Bring the water and coarse salt to a boil, add all the ingredients for the court bouillon, except the shellfish, and boil gently for 20 minutes.

Kill the lobster by plunging the tip of a large knife into the slit where the head meets the tail. Cut the head from the tail. If using a Maine lobster, break off the claws with a quick wrenching movement and crack them with the blunt edge of a cleaver or a hammer. Reserve the head for making the sauce.

Drop the lobster tail (and claws) into the boiling court bouillon. Bring back to a boil and boil gently for 5 minutes, add the *langoustines* or crayfish, and cook for 8 minutes more.

With a skimmer or slotted spoon, lift the shellfish out of the court bouillon and drain in a colander until cool enough to handle. Cut open the underside of the lobster tail shell with a pair of scissors and remove the meat. Cut the tail in half lengthwise and remove the blackish intestine, then cut the tail into slices about ½ inch thick. (Remove the meat from the claws and slice it as well.) Separate the tails from the heads of the *langoustines* or crayfish and peel them. Place all the meat from the shellfish in a bowl, cover, and reserve.

THE SAUCE:

Cut the lobster head into small pieces with a large knife.

Heat the olive oil in a large pot or *sauteuse* until it is nearly smoking, then add the pieces of head. Stir over high heat for 3 to 4 minutes, add the carrot, fennel, onion, celery, leek, and tomatoes, stir to mix well, add the cognac, and light. When the flame dies down, add the white wine and boil rapidly for 1 to 2 minutes, or until the bottom of the pot is nearly dry.

Add the cream, stirring and scraping the bottom of the pot to dissolve all the juices, and simmer, uncovered, for 16 minutes. Strain the sauce into a saucepan or smaller *sauteuse*, rubbing and pressing on the lobster and vegetables with a wooden spoon to extract all the liquid. Reserve.

148

THE CABBAGE:

Wash and drain the cabbage leaves, then cut them lengthwise into strips about ¼ inch wide.

Bring a pot of salted water to a boil, add the cabbage strips, and boil for 2 minutes, from the time the water comes back to a boil. Drain and cool under running water, drain again, and reserve.

TO FINISH AND SERVE:

Heat the sauce over moderate heat until simmering and add the reserved meat from the shellfish and the strips of cabbage. Stir gently and taste for seasoning.

When hot, add the julienne of truffle, heat for a few seconds more, then serve immediately on individual dinner plates.

SUGGESTIONS:

The cabbage may be replaced by a julienne of carrots, leeks, or Belgian endives, prepared in the same way. Use 1½ medium carrots, the white of 2 medium leeks, or 1 large endive.

NOTE: *If* langoustines *or crayfish are unavailable, two 2-pound lobsters may be used instead of the combination of shellfish used above. Since they are slightly smaller than the lobster used in this recipe, reduce the total cooking time to 10 minutes. Ed.*

Assiette de poissons, sauce vin blanc
FISH FILLETS WITH CREAM SAUCE

Ingredients for 4 servings:

½ pound fresh salmon

1 pound sea bass (*or porgy. Ed.*)

1½ pounds flatfish, or ¾ pound flatfish fillets (preferably turbot or brill)

FOR THE VEGETABLES:
2 tablespoons butter, in all
5 medium carrots, cut into julienne strips
Salt, pepper
½ teaspoon mild curry powder
6 tablespoons water
1 pound fresh spinach, ribs and stems removed

FOR THE FISH:
1 tablespoon butter
5 shallots, finely chopped
4 medium mushrooms, finely chopped
Salt, pepper
1⅓ cups dry white wine
1⅓ cups heavy cream

UTENSILS:
2 medium saucepans, with covers
Oval or rectangular roasting pan, 15 to 16 inches long
Spatula
Wire whisk
Sieve
To serve: 4 heated dinner plates

PRELIMINARY PREPARATIONS:
Ask the fish seller to fillet the fish for you. Ask him to scale the sea bass or porgy, but to leave the skin on the fillets.
Preheat the oven to 425° F.

THE VEGETABLES:
In a saucepan, melt 1 tablespoon of butter and add the strips of carrot. Season with salt, pepper, and the curry powder and simmer over low heat for 1 minute. Add the water and simmer, uncovered, for 7 minutes more, or until the carrots are tender and the water has evaporated. Reserve.

In another saucepan, melt 1 tablespoon of butter, add the spinach, and season with salt and pepper. Stir and toss the spinach until it has melted down, lower the heat, and simmer for 3 minutes, uncovered, stirring occasionally. Reserve.

THE FISH:

Melt the butter for the fish in the roasting pan over low heat; add the shallots, and simmer for 1 minute to soften. Do not allow to brown.

Season the fish fillets with salt and pepper.

Add the chopped mushrooms to the shallots, stir gently, and cook for 2 minutes, then place the fish on top of the vegetables (place the sea bass or porgy skin side up), add the white wine, cover with aluminum foil, and bake for 7 minutes.

Just before the fish has finished cooking, heat the spinach, if necessary.

Remove the fish from the pan with a spatula and place the fillets on a cloth for a few seconds to drain. With a knife, remove the skin from the bass or porgy fillets.

Place a bed of spinach on each dinner plate, arrange the fish on top, and keep warm in the oven with the door ajar while making the sauce.

TO MAKE THE SAUCE AND SERVE:

Place the roasting pan over moderate heat and boil the cooking liquids until the pan is nearly dry. Whisk in the cream and boil for about 4 minutes, or until thick and creamy, then strain the sauce pressing on the vegetables.

Reheat the carrots if necessary.

Remove the plates from the oven, spoon the sauce over the fish, arrange the carrots around them, and serve immediately.

SUGGESTIONS:

The spinach may be replaced by 6 cups tightly packed watercress leaves, lettuce leaves, or the green of Swiss chard, all prepared in the same way.

A little mustard or horseradish may be added to the sauce; the mustard or horseradish taste should be identifiable, but not overpowering.

Aïoli garni
MIXED FISH DINNER WITH GARLIC MAYONNAISE

Ingredients for 6 servings:

1¼ pounds salt cod fillet, cut into 6 pieces
6 very large mussels (about ½ pound if using smaller mussels)
6 eggs

FOR THE COURT BOUILLON:
4 quarts water
4 teaspoons coarse salt
20 whole peppercorns
2 medium onions, sliced
6 shallots, sliced
1 bulb fennel, sliced
2 tomatoes, quartered
3 cloves garlic, cut in half
1 bell pepper, seeded and sliced
Bouquet garni (4 sprigs parsley, 1½ bay leaves, 2 sprigs thyme)
2 cloves

FOR THE SAUCE:
8 cloves garlic
2 egg yolks
Juice of 1 lemon
¼ teaspoon salt
2 cups olive oil

FOR THE VEGETABLES:
3 medium carrots
6 artichoke bottoms, cooked or canned
¾ pound broccoli (thick stems removed)
½ pound green beans, strings removed
1 pound new potatoes
3 small turnips (about ¾ pound), cut into 4 pieces each

FOR THE FRESH FISH AND SHELLFISH (*see Suggestion and Note*):

2 tablespoons melted butter
Salt, pepper
1½ pound porgy, filleted
1½ pound sea bass, filleted
1½ pound turbot, filleted (or ¾ pound flatfish fillets)
6 large sea scallops, or 18 bay scallops
6 *langoustines* (*for substitution, see Note*)
2½ dozen canned snails, drained

UTENSILS:

Steaming basket or colander
Large bowl or basin
Small saucepan
Large pot
2 bowls
Small square of muslin
Wire whisk
2 pots or large saucepans
Large steaming basket and pot, or steamer
Skimmer or slotted spoon
Pastry brush
Large bowl
3 large roasting pans, each about 14 inches long
2 saucepans, 1 with cover
1 small saucepan
Spatula
To serve: Large heated serving platter, or 6 heated dinner plates, and sauceboat

PRELIMINARY PREPARATIONS:

The day before making the meal: Soak the salt cod in a steaming basket or colander set in a large bowl or basin of water. It is important that the cod does not touch the bottom of the bowl so that it can desalt properly. Soak it for 24 hours, changing the water at least 3 times.

The day of the meal: Clean the mussels by scraping the shells clean with a knife and remove the beards that protrude from the shells. Rinse the mussels under running water and reserve in the refrigerator.

Boil the eggs for 10 minutes, drain, and cool under running water. Peel them, cover, and reserve.

THE COURT BOUILLON:

Place the water in a large pot, add the coarse salt and peppercorns, and bring to a boil. Add all of the other ingredients for the court bouillon, return to a moderate boil, and cook, uncovered, for 1 hour, or until the liquid has reduced by ¼. Strain into a bowl and reserve.

THE GARLIC MAYONNAISE:

Peel the garlic, cut the cloves in half lengthwise, and remove the central green sprouts. Chop the garlic as fine as possible and place it on a little piece of muslin. Gather the corners of the cloth together to form a ball. Hold the ball of garlic under cold running water, then squeeze it completely; do this twice (to eliminate the acrid taste of raw garlic).

When it has been squeezed as dry as possible, empty the garlic into a bowl. Stir in the egg yolks, lemon juice, and salt. Slowly begin whisking in the olive oil, about a tablespoon at a time; make sure each spoonful of oil is incorporated before adding the next. When the sauce begins to thicken, the oil may be added more quickly. The finished sauce should be golden yellow and the consistency of mayonnaise. Taste for salt and pepper, place in the sauceboat, cover tightly with plastic wrap, and reserve in a cool place, but *not* in the refrigerator.

THE VEGETABLES:

Bring two pots of salted water to a boil.

Peel the carrots, cut them into quarters lengthwise, cut out the light-colored central core, then cut each quarter into pieces about 1½ inches long.

Place the artichoke bottoms in a steaming basket or the top of a steamer (make a little pile) and reserve.

When the water boils in one of the pots, add the broccoli and boil for 7 minutes. Lift the broccoli out of the water with a skimmer or slotted spoon, drain, cool under running water, drain, then place in a pile next to the artichoke bottoms in the steamer.

Boil the green beans for 4 minutes in the pot the broccoli cooked in. Lift out of the water, drain, cool under running water and place in a third pile in the steaming basket.

In the same pot, boil the potatoes for 12 minutes, or until tender. Drain the potatoes and place in the steaming basket.

In the second pot of boiling salted water, boil the carrot sticks for 4 minutes, add the turnips, and boil for 4 minutes more. Remove the pot from the heat (keep the vegetables in their cooking liquid) and reserve.

THE FISH:
Preheat the oven to 425° F.

With a pastry brush, grease 3 roasting pans with the melted butter. Sprinkle 2 of the pans with salt and pepper.

Drain the pieces of salt cod and pat them dry on a cloth, then place them in the unseasoned roasting pan. All the pieces should lie flat.

In one of the seasoned roasting pans, place the fillets of porgy and sea bass; do not allow the fillets to overlap.

In the other seasoned pan, place the fillets of turbot and the scallops.

Add ¾ cup of the strained court bouillon to each of the roasting pans and bake for 10 minutes.

THE SHELLFISH:
Place the mussels in a saucepan with ½ cup of the court bouillon, cover the pot, and bring to a rapid boil over high heat. Cook the mussels for 3 to 5 minutes, or until they have all opened, shaking the pot occasionally.

Bring 2½ cups of the court bouillon to a boil, add the *langoustines*, bring back to a boil, and cook, covered, for 3 minutes; drain.

Place the drained snails in a small saucepan with ½ cup of court bouillon, bring almost to a boil, and simmer for 1 minute.

TO HEAT THE VEGETABLES AND SERVE:
Reheat the carrots and turnips in the liquid they cooked in.

Bring a little water to a boil in a large pot or the bottom of a steamer, place the steaming basket with the vegetables in place, cover, and steam for 1 to 2 minutes, or until hot to the touch.

Cut the hard-boiled eggs in half.

On a large serving platter, or on individual plates, arrange the different vegetables in little piles around the edge. Inside the circle of vegetables, arrange the mussels and *langoustines*. Lift the fish out of their cooking liquid with a spatula or skimmer and place them toward the center; place the drained scallops and the hard-boiled eggs in the very middle, sprinkle the drained snails over the top, and serve immediately, with the sauce in a sauceboat on the side.

SUGGESTION:

A simpler version of this recipe can be made with only salt cod and shellfish; in this case, double the weight of salt cod.

NOTE: *Before serving, cut each fish fillet into 3 pieces so that everyone has a taste of each kind of fish.*

Instead of langoustines, *large shrimp may be used.*

The mussels and langoustines *or shrimp may be cooked in advance and heated up in the steamer with the vegetables. Ed.*

Les viandes & abats
MEATS & VARIETY MEATS

Côte de boeuf beaujolaise
RIB STEAK WITH RED WINE SAUCE

Ingredients for 4 servings:

FOR THE BEEF:

1 rib steak, weighing 2¼ to 2½ pounds, including the curved rib bone, but without the flat end bone (*for substitutions, see Suggestions*)

Salt, pepper

1 tablespoon cooking oil

1 tablespoon butter

FOR THE SAUCE:

1 tablespoon butter

4 shallots, finely chopped

1 stalk celery, finely chopped

15 peppercorns, coarsely crushed

⅓ cup red wine vinegar

⅔ cup red wine (preferably Beaujolais)

¼ pound plus 1 tablespoon softened butter, broken into pieces

¼ cup, in all, chopped parsley, chervil, and chives, mixed

UTENSILS:
Large frying pan
Wire whisk
Large nonstick frying pan
To serve: Heated serving platter and sauceboat

THE BEEF:

Salt and pepper the steak on both sides.

In a large frying pan, heat the oil until very hot, add the butter, and when it has melted, place the steak in the pan. Brown over moderate to high heat for 7 minutes, then lower the heat, and cook for 1 minute more. Turn the meat over and cook over low heat for 14 minutes. Place on a plate, cover with aluminum foil, and allow to rest for 10 to 15 minutes.

THE SAUCE:

Pour off the fat in the frying pan and pat the bottom dry with a paper towel. Place the pan back over moderate heat, melt a tablespoon of butter, add the shallots, celery, and peppercorns, and cook for about 1 minute, stirring constantly, to soften the vegetables. Add the vinegar, stir, scraping the bottom of the pan to dissolve the meat juices, and boil rapidly until the pan is almost dry. Add the wine, stir, and boil for about 5 to 6 minutes, or until the liquid has almost evaporated.

Remove the pan from the heat and begin adding the softened butter as described for the foamy butter sauce in the recipe for **Hot fish terrine** *(see p. 84)*. When all the butter has been added, taste for salt and pepper, stir in the chopped herbs, and pour into a sauceboat.

TO SERVE:

Place the steak in a nonstick frying pan and reheat it for 2 minutes on each side over moderate to high heat.

Lay the meat on a cutting board and cut it into slices, parallel to the bone, ¼ to ½ inch thick. Sprinkle with salt and pepper, place the slices of meat on a serving platter, and serve with the sauce on the side.

SUGGESTIONS:

Homemade pasta *(see p. 256)* makes an excellent accompaniment to this dish.

Other cuts of beef, such as sirloin steaks, or fillet steaks may be used instead of a rib steak. Cooking times for the meat will be shorter than those given here, but the sauce is made in exactly the same way.

NOTE: *If you don't have a nonstick frying pan, clean the pan the sauce was made in and heat a teaspoon of cooking oil before reheating the beef in it. Ed.*

Filet de boeuf à la ficelle
BOILED BEEF TENDERLOIN WITH BÉARNAISE SAUCE

Ingredients for 6 servings:
  2¼ pounds beef tenderloin
  2 teaspoons coarse salt
  3 quarts water
  4 teaspoons coarse salt
  Bouquet garni (including the green leaves of 1 leek)
  18 small carrots
  6 small leeks, (use the white plus about 1 inch of green)
  1 green cabbage (2 pounds), cut into 6 wedges, each tied to hold its
      shape
  6 small turnips
  1 large onion, stuck with 2 cloves
  3 stalks celery, cut in half

  FOR THE SAUCE:
  ½ pound plus 1½ tablespoons butter
  2 shallots, finely chopped
  15 peppercorns, coarsely ground or crushed
  4 teaspoons fresh tarragon, chopped, in all
  6 tablespoons white wine
  6 tablespoons wine vinegar
  3 egg yolks
  Salt

UTENSILS:
Earthenware or glass dish
Large pot
3 small saucepans
Wire whisk
Skimmer or slotted spoon
To serve: Heated serving platter, and sauceboat

PRELIMINARY PREPARATIONS:

Place the meat in an earthenware or glass dish, rub it all over with 2 teaspoons of coarse salt, and place it in the refrigerator for 2 hours before cooking.

THE MEAT:

Remove the meat from the refrigerator, wipe off any traces of salt, and reserve while preparing the vegetable stock.

Bring 3 quarts of water to a boil in a large pot, add the coarse salt, *bouquet garni,* and all the vegetables. Bring back to a boil, lower the heat, and boil very gently for 20 minutes.

Preheat the oven to 275° F.

Bring the liquid to a rapid boil, add the tenderloin, and cook at a moderate boil for 15 minutes. Remove the meat and vegetables from the liquid, place on a serving platter, and cover with aluminum foil. Place in the oven for 15 minutes, while preparing the sauce.

THE BÉARNAISE SAUCE:

Melt ½ pound of butter in a saucepan and clarify it by skimming off the foam that surfaces when the butter comes to a boil. Remove from the heat and reserve.

Melt 1½ tablespoons of butter in another saucepan and add the shallots, peppercorns, half the tarragon, the wine, and the vinegar. Boil for 9 to 10 minutes, or until the liquid is reduced by half, remove from the heat, and allow to cool for 3 to 4 minutes.

Place the egg yolks in a small heavy saucepan and strain the cooled liquid onto them, pressing on the shallots to extract all their juices. Place the saucepan over low heat and whisk constantly until the mixture foams and starts to thicken (allow 3 to 4 minutes). Remove the pan from the heat and add the butter little by little, whisking in each addition completely before adding the next. The finished sauce should be

Previous page: I Partridge and cabbage salad

Above: II Mussels with spinach and curry

Opposite: III Scallops with vegetables and champagne cream sauce

Above: V Sea bass with zucchini

Opposite: IV Asparagus and morels meunière

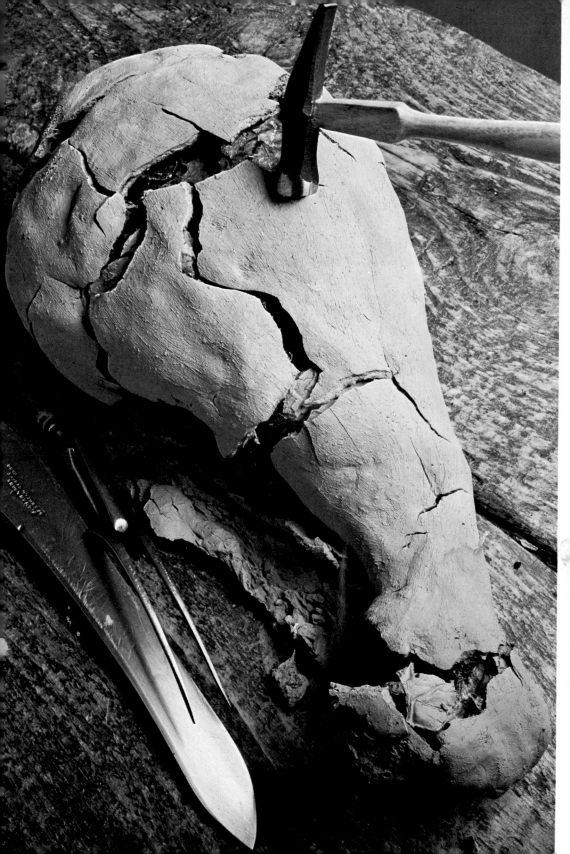

Above: VII Apple tart

Opposite: VI Haunch of venison baked in clay

Next page: VIII Chocolate truffles

smooth and as thick as a mayonnaise. Add a little salt, whisk in the remaining tarragon, and pour the sauce into a sauceboat.

TO SERVE:
Remove the serving platter from the oven; serve the meat either whole or in slices, surrounded by the vegetables, with the sauce on the side.

SUGGESTIONS:
The meat can be served without the sauce, accompanied simply by pickled gherkins (*cornichons*), different mustards, and a small bowl of coarse salt.

NOTE: *In French, tenderloin cooked this way is called* à la ficelle *(on a string) because traditionally the meat would be tied with a string, suspended in the boiling liquid to cook, and pulled out with the same string. Only the finest and most tender cut of beef can be cooked this way; it is always served quite rare. Ed.*

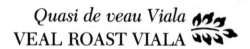

Quasi de veau Viala
VEAL ROAST VIALA

Ingredients for 4 servings:
    2 medium onions
    1¾ pounds veal rump roast
    Salt, pepper
    2 tablespoons cooking oil
    2 tomatoes, peeled and cut into wedges
    6 tablespoons white wine
    Bouquet garni
    5 tablespoons water
    ⅓ cup *crème fraîche (see p. 331)* or heavy cream (optional, *see Suggestions*)

    UTENSILS:
    Small stewing pot, with cover
    Skimmer or slotted spoon
    To serve: Heated serving platter and sauceboat

TO COOK:

Cut each onion in half and cut each half into 5 wedges. Reserve.

Salt and pepper the veal generously. Heat the oil in a small stewing pot; when very hot, add the veal and brown over high heat for 3 to 4 minutes, turning frequently. Lower the heat, add the onions, cook for 8 to 10 minutes to brown them lightly. Add the tomatoes and white wine, scraping the bottom of the pot with a wooden spoon to detach any caramelized meat juices. Add the *bouquet garni*, water, salt, and pepper and bring to a boil. Cover and simmer for 20 minutes; turn the veal over and cook 25 minutes more.

TO SERVE:

Remove the meat from the pot. Discard the *bouquet garni* and boil the cooking liquid rapidly, uncovered, while carving the veal.

Cut the veal into relatively thin slices and place them on a warm serving platter. Salt and pepper the veal lightly, then, using a skimmer or slotted spoon, lift the onions and tomatoes out of the pot, place them on top of the slices of veal. Pour the cooking liquid into a sauceboat and serve.

SUGGESTIONS:

The veal can be served garnished with **homemade pasta** *(see p. 256)* or a mixture of green peas, glazed carrots, and turnips, or simply boiled broccoli with butter.

The sauce can be made richer by the addition of ⅓ cup cream for the last 15 minutes of the cooking time. (You may have to add a bit more salt and pepper.)

Noisettes de veau aux capres et au raifort
VEAL STEAKS WITH CAPERS AND HORSERADISH

Ingredients for 4 servings:

    ½ medium fresh horseradish root *(for substitutions, see Suggestions)*
    ¾ cup water
    1 tablespoon sugar

4 veal loin steaks, about 8 ounces each
Salt, pepper
1 tablespoon cooking oil
2 teaspoons butter
5 shallots, chopped
1 medium tomato, cut into wedges
3 tablespoons madeira
¾ cup water
⅔ cup *crème fraîche (see p. 331)* or heavy cream

2 teaspoons butter
2½ tablespoons capers, washed and drained
Salt, pepper
Freshly chopped parsley, chervil, or chives (optional)

UTENSILS:
Food processor, blender, or vegetable grater
2 small saucepans
Very large frying pan
Wire whisk
Small frying pan
To serve: Serving platter

THE HORSERADISH:
Peel the horseradish and either chop it fine in a food processor or blender, or grate it with a vegetable grater. There should be ¼ cup tightly packed, grated (chopped) horseradish. Rinse the grated horseradish in cold water, drain well, then place it in a small saucepan with the water and sugar. Simmer, uncovered, over very low heat for 1 hour, then allow to cool for 2 hours.

THE VEAL:
Preheat the oven to 425° F.

Season the veal with salt and pepper. Heat the oil in a very large frying pan (or two smaller ones) and brown the veal rapidly on both sides. Lower the heat and cook 7 minutes more, then add the butter, shallots, and tomatoes, turn the veal over, and cook another 6 minutes.

Place the veal on a serving platter, cover with aluminum foil, and keep warm in the oven while making the sauce.

163

TO MAKE THE SAUCE AND SERVE:

Add the madeira to the pan the veal cooked in and cook for 2 minutes over moderate heat, stirring frequently, then add the water and boil 2 minutes more. Add the cream and whatever juices the veal has given out during this time. Season with salt and pepper, whisk, and boil gently a final 2 minutes. Strain the sauce into a clean saucepan, pressing on the vegetables to extract the juices. Keep the sauce warm over low heat.

Heat 2 teaspoons of butter in a small frying pan and quickly sauté the capers over moderate heat to color lightly, then add them to the sauce. Add the horseradish, season with salt and pepper, and stir gently.

Remove the serving platter from the oven, spoon the sauce over the veal, sprinkle with freshly chopped herbs, and serve with **homemade pasta** *(see p. 256)*.

SUGGESTIONS:

Three tablespoons of bottled horseradish may be used instead of the fresh horseradish. Wash and drain the bottled horseradish, but do not cook it, simply add it to the sauce when called for.

Fresh ginger may be grated and cooked as described for the fresh horseradish, or the peel of a lemon, cut into julienne strips and parboiled for 2 minutes, may be added to the sauce instead of either horseradish or ginger.

Côtes de veau à la crème de poivrons rouges
VEAL CUTLETS WITH BELL PEPPER SAUCE

Ingredients for 4 servings:
    2 very large red bell peppers *(see Suggestions)*
    4 veal cutlets, about 8 ounces each
    Salt, pepper
    3 tablespoons cooking oil
    ⅔ cup white wine
    1½ cups *crème fraîche (see p. 331)* or heavy cream
    ¼ cup chopped parsley, chives, and chervil, mixed

UTENSILS:
Baking dish
Blender
Very large frying pan
To serve: 4 heated dinner plates

THE PEPPER PURÉE:

Cut each pepper in half lengthwise; remove the seeds and stems.

Preheat the oven to 425° F.

Place the peppers in a baking dish skin side up and bake for 20 minutes, or until the skin has dried out and colored; peel off the skin. Cut 1½ pepper halves into lengthwise strips about ⅛ inch thick; reserve.

Purée the rest of the peppers in a blender and reserve.

Lower the oven to 250° F.

THE MEAT AND SAUCE:

Lightly salt and pepper each cutlet.

Over moderate heat, heat the oil in a very large frying pan (or 2 small ones) until very hot. Add the cutlets and brown one side for about 5 minutes, turn them and brown the other side for 3 minutes. Place on a plate, cover with aluminum foil, and keep warm in the oven.

Pour off any fat in the frying pan and add the white wine. Scrape the bottom of the pan and boil the wine for about 2 minutes, add the pepper purée, boil for 2 minutes more, then add the cream and any juices given out by the cutlets. Boil the sauce for 4 to 5 minutes, or until thick and creamy, taste for salt and pepper, then add the strips of pepper, stir, and simmer for 1 minute.

TO SERVE:

Place the cutlets on individual dinner plates, spoon the pepper sauce over them, sprinkle with the herbs, and serve.

SUGGESTIONS:
Either red or green bell peppers may be used in this recipe.

The cutlets and their sauce are excellent with a garnish of **homemade pasta** (*see p. 256*), a vegetable purée, or a wild-mushroom purée.

Pork chops, lamb chops, or chicken can be prepared in the same way.

Côtes de veau au gingembre et au citron vert
VEAL CUTLETS WITH LIME AND GINGER CREAM SAUCE

Ingredients for 4 servings:
>   Zest of 1 lime, finely chopped
>   3-inch piece fresh ginger, peeled and finely chopped
>   ⅓ cup water
>   1 tablespoon sugar
>
>   4 veal cutlets, about 8 ounces each
>   Salt, pepper
>   2 tablespoons cooking oil
>   1 medium tomato, chopped
>   1⅓ cups *crème frâiche (see p. 331)* or heavy cream

>   UTENSILS:
>   Small saucepan
>   Very large frying pan
>   Skimmer or slotted spoon
>   *To serve:* 4 heated dinner plates

THE LIME AND GINGER:

Place the lime zest in a sieve and rinse under cold running water, then put it into a small saucepan, and add enough cold water to cover. Boil over high heat for 2 minutes, drain, cool under running water, drain again, and reserve.

Place the ginger in the same saucepan, add the water and sugar, bring to a boil, lower the heat, and simmer until all the water has evaporated. Add the lime zest and reserve.

THE VEAL AND SAUCE:

Salt and pepper the cutlets. Heat the oil in a very large frying pan (or 2 smaller ones), add the cutlets, and brown over moderate heat for 5 minutes on each side. Remove the cutlets from the pan with a skimmer or slotted spoon, place on a plate, cover with aluminum foil, and keep warm.

Pour off any fat in the pan and pat the pan dry with a paper towel. Place the pan back over low heat and add the tomato, scraping the bottom of the pan with a wooden spoon to dissolve any meat juices. Boil to evaporate almost all the liquid given out by the tomato, then add the cream and any juices the cutlets have given out. Boil for 4 minutes, or until the sauce is thick and creamy.

TO FINISH THE SAUCE AND SERVE:
Taste the sauce, season with a little salt and pepper, then strain it into the saucepan with the lime zest and ginger, and reheat it.

Place the cutlets on the dinner plates, spoon over the sauce, and serve immediately.

SUGGESTIONS:
A julienne of mixed red and green bell peppers may be used instead of the lime zest and ginger. Parboil the peppers for 1 minute, drain, cool under running water, drain, and add to the sauce before serving. Or cook and purée the green pepper and serve it with the strips of parboiled red pepper on top.

NOTE: *Pork chops may be used instead of veal cutlets; cook them for about 7 to 8 minutes on a side. Ed.*

Côtes de veau à l'estragon et à la badiane
VEAL CUTLETS WITH TARRAGON AND STAR ANISE

Ingredients for 4 servings:

FOR THE INFUSION:
1 branch fresh tarragon (or 1 teaspoon dried)
10 whole star anise *(see Note)*
1½ cups water

FOR THE CUTLETS:
2 tablespoons cooking oil
Salt, pepper
4 veal cutlets, about 8 ounces each

167

1½ cups heavy cream
8 whole star anise (for serving)
8 whole tarragon leaves (for serving)

UTENSILS:
Small mixing bowl
Small saucepan
Very large frying pan
Wire whisk
To serve: 4 heated dinner plates

THE INFUSION:

Place the tarragon in a small mixing bowl with the star anise. Bring the water to a boil, pour it over the herbs, cover the bowl, and leave to infuse for 10 minutes.

THE VEAL:

In a very large frying pan (or 2 smaller ones), heat the oil until very hot. Salt and pepper the cutlets and cook them 5 minutes on each side over moderate heat. Place on a plate, cover with aluminum foil, and keep warm.

Pour off any fat in the pan and pat the pan dry with a paper towel. Pour the herb infusion and herbs into the pan and place it back over moderate heat, stirring to detach any meat juices stuck to the bottom of the pan. Simmer the liquid for about 10 minutes, or until there is about ¼ cup left. Add any juices the cutlets have given out, as well as the cream, and boil for 7 minutes, or until the sauce is thick and creamy.

TO SERVE:

Place a cutlet on each dinner plate; decorate each one with 2 whole star anise and 2 tarragon leaves. Salt and pepper lightly.

Whisk the sauce and strain it over the cutlets. Serve with a vegetable purée, **homemade pasta** *(see p. 256)*, **Spinach au gratin** *(see p. 248)*, or **Potatoes au gratin** *(see p. 251)*.

SUGGESTIONS:

Pork chops may be used instead of veal, and a little lemon juice may be added before serving.

NOTE: *Star anise is sometimes called Chinese anise; it can be found in fine food shops and in Chinese groceries. Ed.*

Côtes de veau au thé et concombres
VEAL CUTLETS WITH CUCUMBERS AND TEA SAUCE

Ingredients for 4 servings:
  1 medium cucumber (about ½ pound)
  2 tablespoons butter
  Salt, pepper
  2 teaspoons tea leaves (preferably Ceylon)
  ¾ cup boiling water

  2 tablespoons cooking oil
  4 veal cutlets, about 8 ounces each
  Salt, pepper
  1½ cups *crème fraîche (see p. 331)* or heavy cream
  1 teaspoon tea leaves

  UTENSILS:
  Vegetable peeler
  Medium frying pan
  Very large frying pan
  Slotted spoon
  Small teapot
  Large platter
  Wire whisk
  To serve: 4 heated dinner plates

THE CUCUMBER AND THE TEA:

Peel the cucumber and cut it in half lengthwise. Scoop out the seeds with a spoon and cut each half into pieces about 3 inches long. Cut the pieces into sticks ½ inch thick, then cut the sticks diagonally into 4 to 5 pieces each.

Heat the butter in a medium frying pan, add the cucumber, salt, and pepper. Sauté over moderate heat to brown lightly (about 5 minutes) and drain on paper towels. Reserve.

Place 2 teaspoons of tea in a teapot, adding the boiling water, cover, and steep for 8 minutes.

THE VEAL AND SAUCE:

Heat the oil in a very large frying pan. Season the cutlets with salt and

169

pepper and brown over moderate heat for 5 minutes on one side and 3 on the other. Place on a platter, cover with aluminum foil, and place in a 250° F oven while making the sauce.

Pour all the fat from the pan, replace over moderate heat, and strain the tea into the pan. Stir to detach all the juices stuck to the bottom of the pan and boil the liquid rapidly for 5 minutes, or until there are about 1½ tablespoons of syrupy liquid left. Add the cream and any juices the cutlets have given out, whisk lightly, and boil for 5 minutes more, or until creamy.

TO FINISH THE SAUCE AND SERVE:

Place the cucumbers over low heat to warm up.

Add 1 teaspoon of new tea leaves to the cream sauce, remove from the heat, and leave to infuse for 1 minute. Strain the tea sauce into the pan with the cucumbers and season with salt and pepper.

Place the cutlets on dinner plates, spoon the cucumbers and sauce over them, and serve.

SUGGESTIONS:

The plates can be garnished with **homemade pasta** *(see p. 256).*

One tablespoon of lemon or orange juice, or the parboiled zest of ½ a lemon or ¼ orange, may be added to the sauce before serving.

This dish can also be made with either veal sweetbreads or chicken.

NOTE: *Everything can be done ahead of time. Keep the meat on the platter covered with aluminum foil and the cucumbers in the sauce. Five minutes before serving, uncover the meat and reheat in a preheated oven (350° F), reheat the cucumbers and sauce, and serve. Ed.*

Navarin aux petits légumes
LAMB STEW WITH VEGETABLES

Ingredients for 4 servings:

FOR THE LAMB:

2¼ pounds boneless lamb shoulder or neck, fat removed and cut into 8 pieces

Salt, pepper
3 tablespoons cooking oil
1 tablespoon butter
2 large tomatoes, peeled, seeded, and chopped
2 cloves garlic, crushed
Bouquet garni
1⅔ cups chicken stock
½ teaspoon tomato paste

FOR THE VEGETABLES:
2 medium carrots, cut into sticks 1½ inches long and ½ inch thick
2 medium turnips, prepared like the carrots
20 pearl onions, peeled
¼ pound snow peas, strings removed
1 pound broad (fava) beans or limas, shelled
½ pound fresh peas, shelled
Salt, pepper
2 tablespoons chervil or parsley leaves, whole

UTENSILS:
Large *sauteuse* or high-sided frying pan, 10 inches in diameter, with
    cover
Skimmer or slotted spoon
Bowl
To serve: Large heated serving dish

THE LAMB:
Season the lamb with salt and pepper. Heat the oil in a high-sided frying pan or *sauteuse*. When very hot, add the meat, and brown over moderate heat for 3 minutes, turning frequently. Add the butter and continue browning 3 minutes more, then remove the meat with a skimmer or slotted spoon, and drain on paper towels. Pour all the fat from the pan and pat the pan dry with a paper towel.

Place the meat back in the pan with the tomatoes, garlic, *bouquet garni*, stock, and tomato paste. Season lightly with salt and pepper, bring to a boil, cover the pan, lower the heat, and simmer for 40 minutes.

TO COOK THE VEGETABLES AND SERVE:
Remove the pieces of lamb from the pan and strain the cooking liquid into a bowl. Carefully spoon off any fat that surfaces. Pour the liquid

171

into a clean pan, add the meat, carrots, turnips, and onions, cover, and simmer for 10 minutes. Add the snow peas, broad beans or limas, and peas, and cook, covered, 10 minutes more.

Add salt and pepper to taste, pour the stew into a serving dish, sprinkle with the chervil or parsley leaves, and serve.

SUGGESTIONS:
Chicken or veal may be used instead of lamb.

Emincé d'agneau à la crème d'ail
SLICED LAMB WITH GARLIC CREAM SAUCE

Ingredients for 4 servings:

FOR THE STOCK:
2¼ pounds loin roast of lamb, all bones and fat removed (keep the bones for the stock) and tied with string
1 small onion, thinly sliced
1 large carrot, chopped
1 large stalk celery, chopped
Bouquet garni
2 medium tomatoes, chopped
2 cups chicken stock

FOR THE GARLIC AND SAUCE:
2 heads of garlic (about 25 large cloves, separated but unpeeled)
Milk (to cover garlic)
1 tablespoon butter
Salt, pepper
1 teaspoon sugar
⅔ cup *crème fraîche (see p. 331)* or heavy cream

FOR THE LAMB:
1 teaspoon thyme
Salt, pepper
2 teaspoons butter

172

FOR THE VEGETABLES:

¼ pound thin green beans, cut into 2-inch pieces (*cut thick green beans in half lengthwise. Ed.*)

3 teaspoons butter, in all

2 medium carrots, cut into julienne strips

4-inch piece cucumber, peeled and cut into julienne strips

2 small or 1 medium zucchini, unpeeled, cut into julienne strips

4 large mushrooms, cut into julienne strips

Salt, pepper

1 teaspoon sugar

UTENSILS:

Large cast-iron pot

2 medium saucepans

Small saucepan

Roasting pan

Large frying pan

To serve: 4 heated dinner plates and sauceboat

THE STOCK:

Preheat the oven to 425° F.

Place the lamb bones in a large cast-iron pot and cook, without adding any fat, for 15 minutes over low heat; turn the bones over a few times to brown lightly. Place the pot in the oven and cook for 15 minutes more. Leave the oven on when you remove the pot.

Add the onion, carrot, celery, and *bouquet garni.* Cook over low heat about 5 minutes, stirring frequently, to brown the vegetables lightly. Add the tomatoes and cook for 5 minutes, or until most of their moisture has evaporated. Add the chicken stock, stirring to detach the juices stuck to the bottom of the pan, bring to a boil, lower the heat, and simmer, uncovered, for 40 minutes, skimming off any foam that surfaces.

Strain the stock into a clean saucepan, pressing on the vegetables to extract any juices, and reserve.

THE GARLIC:

Place the unpeeled cloves of garlic in a saucepan, add enough milk to cover, and bring to a boil. Boil for 1 minute, then drain.

Heat the butter in a roasting pan and add the garlic. Season generously with salt and pepper, add the sugar, then cook over moderate heat for 2 minutes, stirring constantly.

Place in the oven and cook 15 minutes, turning the garlic over every 5 minutes, remove from the oven, and leave the oven on.

Wrap 8 whole cloves of garlic in aluminum foil and reserve. Peel the remaining cloves and chop to a paste.

THE SAUCE:

Place the chopped garlic in the pot with the lamb stock, add the cream, bring to a boil, stirring constantly, lower the heat, and cook, uncovered, for 25 to 35 minutes, or until the liquid has reduced to about 1⅔ cups.

Strain the reduced sauce into a clean saucepan, rubbing as much of the garlic through the sieve as possible, or simply blend the sauce in a blender. Taste the sauce for salt and pepper and keep warm over very low heat while cooking the meat and vegetables.

THE LAMB:

Place the lamb roast in a lightly buttered roasting pan, season with thyme, salt, and pepper, rubbing them into the meat. Top with 2 teaspoons of butter and roast for 16 minutes.

THE VEGETABLES:

Boil the beans in lightly salted water 4 minutes, drain, and reserve.

In a large frying pan, melt 1½ teaspoons of butter. Add the carrots and cook over moderate heat 3 minutes, shaking the pan several times. Add another 1½ teaspoons of butter. When melted, add the cucumber, zucchini, and mushrooms. Season with a little salt and pepper and the sugar. Cook over moderate heat 7 minutes longer, stirring frequently, stir in the green beans, and remove the pan from the heat.

TO SERVE:

When the meat is done, place it on a cutting board. Place the 8 reserved garlic cloves in the oven to warm. Gently reheat the vegetables if necessary.

Remove the string from the meat and cut the lamb into very thin slices; it should be rare. Season lightly with salt and pepper.

Spoon a little of the sauce onto each dinner plate, place the slices of lamb in the middle, and garnish the edges with the vegetables. Spoon a little more sauce over the lamb.

Place two cloves of garlic on each plate and serve immediately, with any remaining sauce in a sauceboat.

NOTE: *The vegetables can be cooked up to an hour ahead of time and reheated quickly just before serving. Ed.*

Epaule d'agneau en saucisson
ROAST STUFFED LAMB SHOULDER

Ingredients for 5 to 6 servings:
- 1 shoulder of lamb, weighing about 3¼ pounds
- 1 large clove garlic
- 2 teaspoons butter
- 5 shallots, finely chopped
- 3 tablespoons cognac
- 6 ounces fresh pork fatback or beef suet
- ¾ cup *crème fraîche (see p. 331)* or heavy cream
- ½ teaspoon allspice
- 1 teaspoon ground black pepper
- 5 large mint leaves, cut into thin strips
- 2 tablespoons fine chopped chives
- 2 tablespoons finely chopped chervil or parsley
- 1 teaspoon salt
- 1 tablespoon cooking oil
- 1⅓ cups warm water

UTENSILS:
Small frying pan
Large mixing bowl
Small mixing bowl
Meat grinder
Trussing needle
Kitchen string
Oval or rectangular roasting pan, 14 inches long
To serve: Large heated serving platter and sauceboat

PRELIMINARY PREPARATIONS:

Bone the shoulder or have your butcher do it; save the bones.

Lay the shoulder, skin side down, on a cutting board and use a knife to cut off about ⅓ of the lean meat, taking it as evenly as possible from the sides and center of the shoulder. Reserve this meat for the stuffing.

Cut the garlic clove lengthwise into sticks—about as thick as matchsticks. Lard the entire shoulder with the garlic by making small incisions in the meat with the tip of a pointed knife and sliding sticks of garlic into them.

THE STUFFING:

Melt the butter in a small frying pan, add the shallots, and cook for 1 minute, or until soft. Add the cognac, boil for 5 seconds, and pour into a bowl to cool.

Cut half of the reserved lamb into ½-inch cubes and place in a large mixing bowl. Grind the pork fat and remaining lamb in a meat grinder, using a coarse blade, and add to the cubes of meat. Using a wooden spoon, beat in the cream, spices, herbs, salt, and reserved shallots and cognac.

Season the lamb shoulder with salt and pepper and spread the stuffing over the surface of the meat. Fold the shoulder in half lengthwise and sew the edges together with a trussing needle and kitchen string to completely enclose the stuffing. If necessary, push the stuffing well into the part which has been sewn together as you go along, in order to use as much of the stuffing as possible (it may not all fit, depending on the shape of the shoulder).

TO COOK:

Preheat the oven to 425° F.

Heat the oil in the roasting pan over moderate heat. Place the stuffed shoulder and its bones in the pan and brown, turning frequently, for about 5 minutes. Pour off any fat, arrange the bones so that you can place the shoulder on top of them, and roast for 20 minutes.

Pour off any fat, add the warm water, and roast for 25 minutes more, basting frequently.

TO SERVE:

Place the meat on a serving platter; cover loosely with aluminum foil and keep warm in the turned-off oven for 10 minutes, to let the roast rest.

Meanwhile, strain the liquid from the roasting pan into a measuring cup. There should be about ¾ cup left; if there is more, boil the liquid to reduce it to that amount. Taste for salt and pepper.

Serve the roast on a serving platter with its gravy in a sauceboat, and a vegetable of your choice.

Sauté d'agneau aux écrevisses
LAMB WITH CRAYFISH

Ingredients for 4 servings:
  1¾ pounds boneless lamb shoulder or neck
  Salt, pepper
  2 tablespoons cooking oil
  1 tablespoon butter
  1 large carrot, diced
  1 small onion, diced
  24 live crayfish (*for substitution, see Note*)
  ¼ cup olive oil
  3 tablespoons cognac
  2 medium tomatoes, chopped
  3 cloves garlic, crushed
  Bouquet garni
  1½ cups chicken stock

  UTENSILS:
  Large *sauteuse* or high-sided frying pan, about 11 inches in
    diameter, with cover
  Skimmer or slotted spoon
  Large mixing bowl
  To serve: 4 heated dinner plates

  THE LAMB:
Cut the lamb into 2- to 3-inch cubes and season with salt and pepper.

  Heat the cooking oil in a *sauteuse* or high-sided frying pan, add the lamb, and cook over moderate heat for 5 to 6 minutes turning to brown on all sides. Add the butter, carrot, and onion, and continue cooking for 3 minutes to brown the vegetables lightly. Drain the contents of the pan in a strainer over the sink. Pour off the fat from the pan; reserve the meat and vegetables.

THE CRAYFISH:

Hold each crayfish by its head, just in front of the tail, with the head pointing downward. Grasp the central fin of the tail right at its base and bend it back toward the head, twisting gently, and pull it straight out (the stringlike intestine will come out with it). Place the crayfish in a colander, rinse under cold running water, and drain.

Heat the olive oil in the pan the lamb cooked in until very hot. Add the crayfish, cover, and cook for about 7 minutes, shaking the pan often. When all the crayfish are red, lift them out of the pan with a skimmer or slotted spoon and leave until cool enough to handle.

Separate the tails from the heads. Remove the meat from each tail and reserve. Save 20 of the heads for the sauce and 4 for decorating the plates.

TO COOK AND SERVE:

Place the lamb, carrot, and onion back in the pan, warm over low heat, add the cognac, boil for 30 seconds, and add the tomatoes, garlic, and *bouquet garni*. Boil over moderate heat for about 5 minutes, or until all the water in the tomatoes has evaporated. Add the 20 crayfish heads, chicken stock, season lightly with salt and pepper, cover the pan, and simmer gently for 45 minutes, stirring occasionally.

Remove the lamb from the pan and reserve. Strain the sauce into a mixing bowl, pressing on the crayfish heads and vegetables with a wooden spoon to extract all their juices. Discard the heads and vegetables, and place the strained sauce in a clean pan with the lamb and crayfish tails.

Heat gently to warm the meat and sauce, taste for salt and pepper, then divide the meat, tails, and sauce among the dinner plates. Decorate each plate with one of the reserved crayfish heads and serve.

SUGGESTIONS:

A 3-pound chicken can be cut into 8 pieces and used instead of lamb.

Homemade pasta (*see p. 256*) is excellent with this dish.

NOTE: *A 2¼-pound lobster may be used instead of the crayfish. Boil it for 9 minutes in salted water, timing from the moment the water comes* back to a boil. *Remove the tail and claw meat from the shell and cut it into slices. Chop the head into several pieces and use as described for the crayfish heads. Ed.*

Epaule d'agneau Papadinas
LAMB PAPADINAS

Ingredients for 4 to 5 servings:
    1 shoulder of lamb with bone, weighing 4 pounds (trim off the fat)
    Salt, pepper
    2 tablespoons cooking oil
    1 teaspoon butter
    3 large onions, thickly sliced
    1 tablespoon sugar
    1 tablespoon thyme flowers or leaves
    1 bay leaf (whole)
    2 cups water

    UTENSILS:
    Large stew pot
    To serve: Large heated serving platter

    TO COOK AND SERVE:
Preheat the over to 400° F.
    Season the lamb generously with salt and pepper, rubbing it into the meat.
    Heat the oil in a large stew pot until almost smoking, add the lamb, and brown on both sides over moderate heat for 6 to 8 minutes. Lift the lamb out of the pot and reserve.
    Pour off all the fat, add the teaspoon of butter, onions, sugar, and a little salt and pepper, and cook over low heat for about 8 minutes, or until the onions start to brown—do not allow to burn.

179

Put the meat back into the pot, add the thyme, bay leaf, water, and a little salt and pepper. Bring to a boil, cover, and place in the oven for 1 hour and 20 minutes.

To serve, remove the meat from the pot and slice. Place the slices on a serving platter, taste the cooking liquid for seasoning (discard the bay leaf), spoon everything over the meat, and serve.

Cari d'agneau
LAMB CURRY

Ingredients for 4 servings:
    2¼ pounds boneless shoulder of lamb, cut into 1½-inch cubes
    1½ teaspoons mild curry powder
    Salt, pepper
    2 tablespoons olive oil
    1⅓ cups water

    1 tablespoon olive oil
    1 large onion, coarsely chopped
    1 clove garlic, quartered
    2 medium tomatoes, chopped
    Bouquet garni
    2 tablespoons mild curry powder
    Pinch cayenne pepper
    1 cup yogurt
    ½ teaspoon salt

       FOR THE GARNISH:
    2 tablespoons butter
    ½ banana, diced
    2 medium tomatoes, peeled and diced
    ½ apple, peeled, cored, and diced
    1 small onion, finely chopped
    Salt, pepper

UTENSILS:
Large frying pan
Skimmer or slotted spoon
2 large saucepans
Small frying pan
To serve: Serving dish

THE MEAT:

Sprinkle the pieces of lamb with 1½ teaspoons curry powder, salt, and pepper, rolling the meat in the spices to coat thoroughly.

Heat 2 tablespoons of olive oil in a large frying pan, add half the lamb, and brown over high heat on all sides (allow about 5 minutes). Drain the lamb on a cloth or paper towels while browning the remaining meat (add another tablespoon of oil if necessary). Remove from the pan and drain.

Pour all the fat from the pan, place it back over moderate heat, and add the water, stirring to detach any juices stuck to the bottom of the pan. Boil for 1 minute and reserve.

THE CURRY:

Heat 1 tablespoon of olive oil in a large saucepan, add the onion, garlic, tomatoes, and *bouquet garni*. Sauté over moderate heat for 5 minutes. Stir in 2 tablespoons of curry powder, the cayenne, yogurt, and the reserved pan juices. Add the meat, the salt, and a little more water if necessary (the liquid should not quite cover the meat), and simmer, uncovered, for 1 hour and 15 minutes.

THE GARNISH:

When the curry is almost done, heat the butter in a small frying pan. When very hot, add the banana, tomatoes, apple and onions and sauté over moderate heat for 5 minutes, turning the fruit gently to brown evenly. Season with salt and pepper and reserve.

TO FINISH AND SERVE:

Lift the pieces of meat out of the curry with a skimmer or slotted spoon and reserve. Boil the sauce for about 3 minutes (there should be about 2 cups of sauce left after reducing) and strain the sauce into a clean saucepan. Press on the vegetables with a wooden spoon to extract all of their juices, then add the meat and the garnish to the sauce. Heat gently for 3 to 4 minutes, taste for seasoning, and serve with rice, pasta, or (what's best) boiled cracked wheat (bulgur).

SUGGESTIONS:

Chicken or pork may be used instead of lamb.

For a spicier curry, omit the fruit from the garnish.

For a more unusual taste, add a little cinnamon, cumin, or star anise with the curry powder.

Goujonnettes d'agneau
LAMB GOUJONNETTES WITH BÉARNAISE SAUCE

Ingredients for 4 servings:

1 pound lean boneless lamb, from the leg

Salt, pepper

FOR THE SAUCE:

¼ pound butter *(see Suggestions)*

3 shallots, finely chopped

30 mint leaves, chopped, in all

10 peppercorns, coarsely ground or crushed

3 tablespoons sherry vinegar

3 tablespoons white wine vinegar

1 large egg yolk

Salt

FOR DEEP FRYING:

Oil

1 egg

Salt, pepper

1 cup bread crumbs

UTENSILS:

Small saucepan

Medium saucepan

Wire whisk

Skimmer or slotted spoon

Large saucepan or deep fryer

Deep-frying thermometer
To serve: Heated serving platter and sauceboat

PRELIMINARY PREPARATIONS:
Cut the lamb into thin strips about 3 inches long, ½ inch wide, and ½ inch thick. Season with salt and pepper and reserve.

Melt the butter in a small saucepan over low heat; when the butter begins to bubble and a whitish foam appears, use a small spoon to remove all the impurities that float to the surface. Remove from the heat and reserve.

THE SAUCE:
Make a béarnaise as described in the recipe for **Boiled beef tenderloin with béarnaise sauce** *(see p. 159),* using the ingredients and measurements given here.

TO FRY THE LAMB AND SERVE:
Heat the oil to 375° F in a large saucepan or deep fryer.

Beat an egg in a soup plate or shallow dish with salt, pepper, and 2 tablespoons of water. Place the breadcrumbs in another soup plate.

Dip each piece of lamb first into the egg, then into the bread crumbs, patting off any excess bread crumbs; place the prepared lamb on a plate.

When the oil is hot, drop in the pieces of lamb and fry for 1 minute. Lift the meat out with a skimmer or slotted spoon and drain for a few seconds on paper towels. Place on a serving platter and serve with the sauce on the side.

SUGGESTIONS:
Softened butter can be broken into small pieces and used instead of the clarified butter. In this case, add the butter as described for the foamy butter sauce in the recipe for **Hot fish terrine** *(see p. 84).* The finished sauce can be reheated over low heat if you are careful to whisk it constantly and heat it to warm, not hot.

✿✿✿ *Jarret de porc caramelisé aux choux verts*
✿✿✿ CARAMELIZED PORK SHANK WITH CABBAGE

Ingredients for 4 to 6 servings:
  1 pork shank, weighing approximately 4½ pounds
  Salt
  ½ cup granulated sugar
  2 tablespoons olive oil, in all
  1½ tablespoons butter
  2 medium carrots, chopped
  1 large onion, chopped
  3 cloves garlic, chopped
  2 stalks celery, chopped
  2 leeks, white part only, chopped
  Bouquet garni
  3 tomatoes, chopped
  1⅔ cups water
  2 pointed or early green cabbages, weighing about 1½ pounds each,
    or 1 round 3-pound cabbage
  Pepper

  UTENSILS:
  Large rectangular roasting pan, 14 inches long
  Large saucepan
  Bowl
  To serve: Large heated serving platter

  THE PORK:
Two hours before cooking the pork, prepare it as follows: with a sharp knife, make several diagonal slits, about an inch deep, on the top and bottom of the shank. Pour table salt generously over all the surfaces of the shank and rub it into the meat. The shank should be caked in salt. Set it aside on a large platter.

After two hours, rinse off all the salt under running water and pat the meat dry with a cloth.

Preheat the oven to 450° F.

Rub the sugar all over the shank to coat it completely. Place 1 tablespoon of olive oil in a large roasting pan, add the pork, and roast for 30 minutes, basting occasionally and turning the pork 2 to 3 times to brown it evenly on all sides. Take the pork out of the pan and rinse the

184

pan to remove any burned matter stuck to the bottom. Lower the oven to 400° F.

Place the cleaned roasting pan on top of the stove, add the remaining tablespoon of olive oil and the butter, heat until very hot, then add the carrots, onion, garlic, celery, leeks, *bouquet garni,* and tomatoes. Sauté the vegetables over moderate heat for 6 to 7 minutes to soften, then place the pork on top of them, and return the pan to the oven. After 15 minutes, turn the pork over; 15 minutes later add the water, and continue roasting for 1 hour, basting 2 to 3 times with the cooking liquid.

THE CABBAGE:

Slice each cabbage in half lengthwise, cut out the central core, and cut the leaves into strips about ¼ inch wide. In a large saucepan of rapidly boiling salted water, boil the strips for 3 minutes from the time the water returns to a boil, drain, cool under running water, and drain again. Pat the cabbage dry in a cloth or towel.

TO FINISH AND SERVE:

Remove the pork from the oven, place it on a plate, and strain the cooking liquid into a bowl. Press down on the vegetables with a wooden spoon to extract all of their juices; discard the vegetables.

Rinse the roasting pan and place the strips of cabbage in it. Salt and pepper the cabbage, add the strained cooking liquid, place the pork shank on top, and roast for 30 minutes.

Place the pork on a cutting board and slice. Place the cabbage and cooking juices on a large serving platter, sprinkle with a little pepper, lay the slices of pork on top, and serve.

Sauté de porc Apicius
PORK APICIUS

Ingredients for 4 servings:

FOR THE DRIED FRUITS:
½ cup raisins
1 tablespoon honey

½ teaspoon caraway seeds
1 teaspoon dill seed
5 mint leaves, cut into thin strips
15 peppercorns, coarsely ground or crushed
6 tablespoons red wine
¼ pound dried apricots

FOR THE PORK:
1¾ pounds boneless pork shoulder, cut into 2-inch cubes
Salt, pepper
⅓ cup olive oil
⅔ cup wine vinegar
6 shallots, sliced
1 large carrot, diced
3 stalks celery, diced
2 medium tomatoes, coarsely chopped
Bouquet garni
1 cup chicken stock

UTENSILS:
2 mixing bowls
Sauteuse or high-sided frying pan, with cover, 9 to 10 inches in
    diameter
Skimmer or slotted spoon
Large saucepan
To serve: Large heated serving dish

PRELIMINARY PREPARATIONS:
The day before cooking the pork, place the raisins in a bowl with the
honey, caraway, dill, mint, peppercorns, and red wine. Stir to dissolve
the honey, cover the bowl with aluminum foil, and leave overnight.
    Place the dried apricots in another bowl, cover with warm water,
and leave to soak overnight.

THE PORK:
Generously salt and pepper the meat. Heat the olive oil in a *sauteuse*,
or high-sided frying pan brown the pork on all sides over moderate heat
for about 10 minutes, lift it out of the pan with a skimmer or slotted
spoon, and drain on paper towels.
    Pour all the fat from the pan and place the pan back over moderate
heat. Add the vinegar, stirring to detach the juices stuck to the bottom

of the pan, and boil for 2 to 3 minutes, or until almost all the vinegar has evaporated and it is the consistency of a thick glaze. Add the shallots, carrot, celery, tomatoes, and *bouquet garni*, stir over moderate heat to soften the vegetables, then add the pork and chicken stock. Bring to a boil, lower the heat, and simmer, uncovered, for 15 minutes. Then cover the pan and simmer for 1 hour 10 minutes longer.

TO FINISH AND SERVE:

Lift the pork out of the pan and reserve. Strain the cooking liquid into a large, clean saucepan, pressing on the vegetables with a wooden spoon to extract all their juices.

Drain the apricots and add them, as well as the raisins and their marinade, to the strained sauce. Place the pork back into the sauce and simmer slowly, uncovered, for 25 minutes.

Skim off any fat that surfaces, taste for salt and pepper, and place in a serving dish.

SUGGESTIONS:

Pork cooked this way is excellent with a carrot or celeriac purée.

Sauté de porc à la chinoise
PORK SAUTÉED CHINESE STYLE

Ingredients for 4 servings:

FOR THE PORK:

1¾ pounds boneless pork shoulder, cut into 1½-inch cubes
Salt, pepper
¼ cup granulated sugar
2 tablespoons cooking oil
3 tablespoons vinegar
½ tablespoon tomato paste
1⅓ cups chicken or beef stock

FOR THE VEGETABLES:
1 cup lightly packed julienne strips of carrots
1 cup lightly packed finely shredded green cabbage
3 tablespoons olive oil
1½ cups bean sprouts
Salt, pepper

UTENSILS:
Large frying pan
Large pot
Small frying pan
To serve: Large heated serving platter

THE PORK:

Season the pieces of pork generously with salt and pepper, then roll them in the sugar.

Heat the cooking oil in a large frying pan until very hot, add the pork, and brown over moderately high heat. The pork should be in a single layer and the sugar should caramelize, but not burn (lower the heat if necessary).

When the pork has browned, add the vinegar, stirring in any meat juices and sugar stuck to the bottom of the pan. Lower the heat and boil gently for 2 minutes, then add the tomato paste and stock. Bring to a boil, stirring constantly, lower the heat, and simmer for 50 minutes, uncovered, turning the pork over once or twice.

THE VEGETABLES:

Bring a large pot of salted water to a boil and add the carrots. Boil for 2 minutes, then add the cabbage; cook 1 minute longer. Drain, cool under running water, and drain again.

Heat 3 tablespoons of olive oil in a small frying pan until very hot, add the bean sprouts, salt, and pepper, and sauté for 3 minutes. Drain the sprouts on paper towels.

TO SERVE:

Taste the pork for salt and pepper.

Wipe the oil from the small frying pan and place the pan over moderate heat.

Place the pork and its sauce on a large serving platter, then rapidly sauté all the vegetables in the hot pan to reheat. Sprinkle them over the pork and serve.

SUGGESTIONS:
A greater variety of vegetables can be used. For instance, green peas, lima beans, green beans, or small pieces of cucumber could be added to the vegetables listed above, or used instead of them.

Sauté de porc aux jus de fruits
PORK WITH ORANGE AND LEMON SAUCE

Ingredients for 4 servings:

FOR THE MARINADE:
Juice of 2 oranges
Juice of 2 lemons
½ teaspoon cinnamon
¼ teaspoon powdered oregano
2 cloves garlic, crushed
Salt, pepper
1¾ pounds boneless pork shoulder, cut into 12 pieces

FOR THE SAUCE:
2 tablespoons cooking oil
2 medium tomatoes, peeled, seeded, and chopped
Bouquet garni
¾ cup chicken stock
Salt, pepper

UTENSILS:
Large mixing bowl
Wire whisk
Skimmer or slotted spoon
Sauteuse or high-sided frying pan with cover, 9½ inches in diameter
To serve: Serving dish

TO MARINATE:
The day before cooking the pork, whisk together in a large bowl the fruit juices, cinnamon, oregano, and garlic. Salt and pepper the pieces

189

of pork and add them to the bowl; the liquid should just cover the pork (if not, use a smaller bowl). Cover with aluminum foil and refrigerate overnight.

TO COOK:

An hour before cooking, remove the meat from the refrigerator. Lift the pork out of the marinade with a skimmer or slotted spoon and drain it in a sieve over the bowl containing the marinade. Dry the pork on paper towels.

Heat the oil in a *sauteuse* or high-sided frying pan. When very hot, add the pork and brown over high heat for about 2 minutes, stirring frequently, lower the heat, and brown 5 minutes longer over moderate heat.

Remove the pork with the slotted spoon and drain on paper towels. Pour off the fat in the pan and pat the pan dry with paper towels. Pour the marinade into the pan, place over moderate heat, and stir, scraping the bottom of the pan with a wooden spoon to dissolve any meat juices stuck to it. Boil for about 2 minutes, or until the liquid has reduced by half, add the tomatoes, *bouquet garni*, stock, and a little salt and pepper. Add the pork, cover, and simmer gently for 30 minutes.

TO SERVE:

Skim off any fat on the surface of the cooking liquid. Remove the *bouquet garni*, season the sauce generously with salt and pepper, and serve.

SUGGESTIONS:

Duck may be used instead of pork and grapefruit juice instead of the combined orange and lemon juices.

Either rice or spinach is an excellent garnish for this dish, and wedges of orange and lemon may be placed on each dinner plate as a garnish as well.

Ris de veau à la crème de poivrons
SWEETBREADS WITH RED PEPPER, ZUCCHINI, AND EGGPLANT

Ingredients for 4 servings:
1½ pounds veal sweetbreads

FOR THE SAUCE:
1½ tablespoons butter
10 peppercorns, coarsely crushed
¼ cup sherry vinegar
2 cups heavy cream
1 large red bell pepper, coarsely chopped
Salt, pepper

FOR THE GARNISH:
2 tablespoons butter
9 pearl onions, thinly sliced
2 medium red bell peppers, seeded and cut into julienne strips
1 medium zucchini, seeds removed, cut into julienne strips (do not
   peel)
1 small eggplant, seeds removed, cut into julienne strips (do not
   peel)
Salt, pepper
1 tablespoon cooking oil (for the sweetbreads)
1 tablespoon butter (for the sweetbreads)

UTENSILS:
Large bowl
2 medium saucepans
Blender or food processor
Small saucepan
Wire whisk
Large frying pan
Roasting pan
To serve: Heated serving platter, or 4 heated dinner plates

PRELIMINARY PREPARATIONS:
The night before cooking the sweetbreads, place them in a large bowl of

191

cold water and refrigerate until the next day. Change the water at least once.

THE SAUCE:

Drain the sweetbreads and pat them dry in a towel. With a paring knife, carefully remove the whitish membrane as well as any bits of fat or reddish spots. Save these parings for the sauce. Reserve the sweetbreads on a plate.

In a medium saucepan, heat 1½ tablespoons of butter. When very hot, add the sweetbread parings and the peppercorns and cook, stirring often, for 3 minutes, or until the bits of meat begin to color lightly. Add the vinegar and boil for 45 seconds, scraping the bottom of the pan to dissolve any meat juices.

Add the cream, stir, and bring to a boil. Lower the heat and boil very gently for 25 to 30 minutes. Skim off any foam that surfaces while the sauce is cooking. Strain the sauce into a clean saucepan (there should be 1¼ cups) and reserve.

While the sauce is cooking, purée the chopped pepper in a blender or food processor. Strain the purée into a small saucepan, pressing on the solids with a wooden spoon to extract as much liquid as possible— there should be approximately 6 tablespoons of pepper juice. Place the saucepan over moderate heat and boil for 3 to 4 minutes, or until there are 1½ tablespoons left. Whisk this into the sauce, taste for salt and pepper, and reserve.

THE VEGETABLE GARNISH:

Melt 2 tablespoons of butter in a large frying pan. When very hot, add the onions, lower the heat, and cook for 2 minutes, or until soft and transparent—they should not brown. Add the strips of pepper, cook for 2 minutes over moderate heat, stirring frequently, then add the zucchini and eggplant, sprinkle with salt and pepper, and cook for 2 minutes more, stirring frequently. Reserve.

THE SWEETBREADS:

Preheat the oven to 450° F.

Season the sweetbreads on both sides with salt and pepper.

In a roasting pan, heat the oil. When very hot, add the butter, and when it has melted, add the sweetbreads. Brown over moderate to high heat on all sides (allow about 5 to 6 minutes total), then place in the oven and roast for 5 minutes more, turning them over halfway through their cooking time.

TO SERVE:
Cut the sweetbreads into slices about ¼ inch thick and sprinkle with salt and pepper.

Reheat the vegetables if necessary and place them in the center of the serving platter or the dinner plates. Spoon the sauce over and around the vegetables, arrange the slices of sweetbread on top of the vegetables, and serve immediately.

Ris de veau pierrette
SWEETBREADS PIERRETTE

Ingredients for 4 servings:
    1½ pounds veal sweetbreads
    ½ small or ¼ large ripe avocado

    FOR THE STOCK:
1 tablespoon butter
½ pound chicken necks, wings, or backs, cut into pieces
5 shallots, sliced
1 medium tomato, seeded and diced
1½ cups water
Salt, pepper

    FOR THE SWEETBREADS:
1 tablespoon butter
1 carrot, diced
1 onion, diced
⅔ cup heavy cream

    FOR THE SAUCE:
2 teaspoons butter (for the shellfish)
8 uncooked *langoustines (or shrimp, Ed.)*, peeled
2 tomatoes, peeled, seeded, and diced
1½ tablespoons butter (for the sauce)
2 large basil leaves, finely chopped

193

UTENSILS:
Large bowl
Small bowl
Medium saucepan
High-sided frying pan or *sauteuse,* 10½ inches in diameter
Small frying pan
Wire whisk
To serve: Heated serving dish

PRELIMINARY PREPARATIONS:

The night before cooking the sweetbreads, place them in a large bowl of cold water and refrigerate until the next day. Change the water at least once.

Drain the sweetbreads and cut off the whitish membrane that surrounds them, as well as any fat or reddish spots. Reserve the sweetbreads on a plate, and keep the parings for making the stock.

THE STOCK:

In a medium saucepan, melt a tablespoon of butter and add the parings from the sweetbreads and the chicken parts. Brown lightly, add the shallots and tomato, and cook over moderate heat for about 9 minutes, or until everything has browned nicely and some of the juices have caramelized on the bottom of the pan. Add the water, scraping the bottom of the pan to dissolve the juices, season lightly with salt and pepper, and cook, uncovered, at a gentle boil for 25 minutes. Strain the stock and skim off the fat; there should be ¾ cup of degreased stock.

THE SWEETBREADS:

Pat the sweetbreads dry in a towel.

In a high-sided frying pan or *sauteuse,* melt the butter and add the carrot and onion. Cook gently for 2 minutes to soften them slightly, push the vegetables to the sides of the pan, and place the sweetbreads in the middle. Over moderate heat, brown the sweetbreads lightly on all sides (if necessary, add a little more butter to keep them from sticking), about 3 minutes. Add the cream, scraping the bottom of the pan to dissolve any meat juices stuck to it, lower the heat, and boil very gently, uncovered, for 15 minutes. Turn the sweetbreads over, add the stock, bring to a boil, and boil gently for 10 minutes more.

TO FINISH THE SAUCE AND SERVE:

Melt 2 teaspoons of butter in a small frying pan. When very hot, add the peeled *langoustines* and brown them rapidly on both sides. This should take from 3 to 5 minutes depending on their size. Reserve.

Rub the pulp of the avocado through a sieve with a wooden spoon; there should be 2 tablespoons of avocado purée.

Lift the sweetbreads out of the frying pan and place them on a serving dish. Whisk into their cooking liquid, in the following order, the diced tomatoes, the avocado purée, and the butter. Taste for salt and pepper, then add the *langoustines* and basil. The sauce should be very hot, but do not allow it to boil. Pour it over the sweetbreads and serve immediately.

SUGGESTIONS:
An equal weight of calves' or lambs' brains may be used instead of sweetbreads.

Mint may be used instead of basil.

Ris de veau aux petits oignons confits
SWEETBREADS WITH LITTLE ONIONS

Ingredients for 4 servings:
1½ pounds veal sweetbreads

FOR THE SAUCE:
1½ tablespoons butter
5 peppercorns
4 very large shallots, finely chopped
1 tomato, diced
3 tablespoons cognac
2 tablespoons vinegar
1½ cups chicken stock
1 teaspoon cornstarch
1½ tablespoons softened butter, broken into pieces

FOR THE ONIONS:
1 pound pearl onions (60 to 80), peeled
1 tablespoon butter
Salt, pepper
½ teaspoon sugar

FOR THE SWEETBREADS:
Salt, pepper
2 tablespoons butter

UTENSILS:
Large bowl
3 medium saucepans
Skimmer or slotted spoon
Wire whisk
Small frying pan
Roasting pan
To serve: 4 heated dinner plates

PRELIMINARY PREPARATIONS:
The night before cooking the sweetbreads, place them in a large bowl of cold water and refrigerate until the next day. Change the water at least once.

THE SAUCE:
Drain the sweetbreads and pat them dry with a cloth. Use a paring knife to remove the surrounding membrane, any bits of fat, and reddish spots from the sweetbreads. Keep all the parings for making the sauce.

Heat 1½ tablespoons of butter in a medium saucepan. Over moderate heat, add the parings from the sweetbreads, stir, and brown for about 5 minutes. Add the peppercorns, shallots, and tomato and cook for 3 minutes over high heat to evaporate the moisture from the tomato. Add the cognac and vinegar, boil to reduce for 2 minutes over moderate heat, then add the stock and bring to a boil. Lower the heat and simmer the sauce very slowly for 15 minutes, skimming off any foam that surfaces with a skimmer or slotted spoon.

To thicken the sauce, mix the cornstarch with a little water and pour this mixture into the sauce very slowly, whisking constantly. Bring to a boil, still whisking, lower the heat, and simmer for 10 minutes. Strain the sauce into a clean saucepan, pressing on the vegetables to extract all their juices. Add salt and pepper if needed, skim off the fat, and reserve.

THE ONIONS:
Cook the onions in boiling salted water for 10 minutes, then drain. Place them in a small frying pan with the butter and brown over moderate heat. Season with salt, pepper, and sugar, lower the heat, and cook slowly 12 minutes, shaking the pan frequently.

THE SWEETBREADS:

Preheat the oven to 450° F.

Heat 2 tablespoons of butter in a roasting pan and brown the sweetbreads until well colored on all sides (allow about 5 minutes). Place in the oven and roast for 5 minutes, turning the sweetbreads over halfway through the cooking time.

TO FINISH THE SAUCE AND SERVE:

While the sweetbreads are in the oven, heat the sauce over low heat and whisk in the softened butter. Taste for salt and pepper and remove from the heat.

Place the sweetbreads on a cutting board and cut them into ¼-inch slices. Pour any juices into the sauce and salt and pepper the slices. Place the onions on one half of each dinner plate, spoon the sauce on the other, place the slices of sweetbread in the sauce, and serve immediately.

SUGGESTION:

The whites of small leeks may be used instead of pearl onions.

NOTE: *If a more copious dish is desired,* **homemade pasta** *(see p. 256) or spinach, prepared as for* **Turbot with curry sauce and spinach** *(see p. 128) may be served as a garnish. Ed.*

Ris de veau à sec aux cinq légumes
SWEETBREADS WITH FIVE VEGETABLES

Ingredients for 4 servings:
  1½ pounds veal sweetbreads

FOR THE VEGETABLES:

3 teaspoons butter, in all
2 medium carrots, cut into julienne strips
4-inch piece cucumber, peeled and cut into julienne strips
2 small zucchini, cut into julienne strips (do not peel)
4 large mushrooms, cut into julienne strips

Salt, pepper

1 teaspoon sugar

¼ pound thin green beans, cut in half, boiled 4 minutes, and drained

FOR THE SWEETBREADS:

Salt, pepper

2 tablespoons butter

UTENSILS:

Large bowl

Large frying pan

Roasting pan

To serve: 4 heated dinner plates

PRELIMINARY PREPARATIONS:

The night before cooking the sweetbreads, put them into a large bowl of cold water and refrigerate until the next day. Change the water at least once.

The next day, drain the sweetbreads and pat them dry with a towel. Use a sharp knife to remove the surrounding membrane, any bits of fat, and any reddish spots from the sweetbreads.

Preheat the oven to 450° F.

THE VEGETABLES:

In a large frying pan, melt 1½ teaspoons of butter. Add the carrots and cook over moderate heat for 3 minutes, shaking the pan several times. Add the rest of the butter; when it has melted, add the cucumber, zucchini, and mushrooms. Season with salt, pepper, and the sugar. Stir the vegetables together, cook 4 minutes, add the green beans, cook for 2 minutes, and reserve.

THE SWEETBREADS:

Salt and pepper the sweetbreads.

Melt 2 tablespoons of butter in a roasting pan. Brown the sweetbreads until well colored on all sides (allow about 5 minutes), then place in the oven and roast 5 minutes more, turning the sweetbreads over once halfway through the cooking time.

TO SERVE:

Quickly reheat the vegetables if necessary.

Slice the sweetbreads on a cutting board and arrange them on the dinner plates. Salt and pepper lightly, place the vegetables around the sweetbreads, and serve.

SUGGESTIONS:
Wild mushrooms (chanterelles, boletus, and so on) may be used instead of ordinary mushrooms.

Both the vegetables and the sweetbreads may be seasoned with a pinch of saffron and a pinch of curry.

Rognons de veau Berkeley
VEAL KIDNEYS BERKELEY

Ingredients for 4 servings:
    2 whole veal kidneys, weighing about 12 ounces each, outer membrane and fat removed
    Salt, pepper
    2 tablespoons cooking oil
    8 shallots, chopped
    2 medium carrots, cut into thick sticks
    ½ teaspoon thyme leaves
    2 medium tomatoes, chopped
    6 tablespoons madeira
    1½ cups water
    1⅓ cups *crème fraîche (see p. 331)* or heavy cream
    2 generous tablespoons canned *mousse de foie gras (for substitution, see Note)*
    5 teaspoons Dijon mustard

    UTENSILS:
    Oval or rectangular roasting pan, 12 inches long
    Skimmer or slotted spoon
    To serve: Heated serving platter, or 4 heated dinner plates and sauceboat

THE KIDNEYS:

Preheat the oven to 425° F.

Lightly salt and pepper each kidney. Heat 2 tablespoons of oil in a roasting pan and brown the kidneys over moderate heat for 4 minutes, turning frequently. Remove the kidneys from the pan with a skimmer or slotted spoon and reserve on a plate, covered with aluminum foil.

Add the shallots and carrots to the roasting pan, sprinkle with the thyme, and cook for 3 minutes to soften. Add the tomatoes and cook over moderate heat 3 minutes longer. Place the kidneys on top of the vegetables and roast for 12 minutes. Place the kidneys on a plate, cover with aluminum foil, and keep warm in the oven with the door ajar while making the sauce.

THE SAUCE:

Place the roasting pan over moderate heat and boil the vegetables and cooking liquid for 3 minutes or until all the liquid has evaporated. Add the madeira and boil for 2 minutes, scraping the bottom of the pan to mix in any meat juices stuck to it. When the madeira has reduced by half, add the water and boil for about 7 minutes, or until the liquid has reduced to a little less than ½ cup. Add the cream, stir, and boil for about 5 minutes to thicken the sauce. Reserve.

In a small mixing bowl, beat the *mousse de foie gras* with the mustard until a smooth paste is formed. Strain the sauce onto the mixture, whisking to combine. Taste the sauce and add salt and pepper if needed. The sauce can be gently reheated, but it should not boil.

TO SERVE:

Remove the kidneys from the oven; they can be served whole on a serving platter with the sauce in a sauceboat, or sliced (salt and pepper the slices) and served on individual dinner plates with the sauce spooned over them.

SUGGESTION:

Sweetbreads can be cooked exactly as described for the kidneys.

NOTE: *Canned foie gras is used in making the sauce, but an acceptable substitution can be made with chicken livers. Heat a tablespoon of butter in a small frying pan, add 3 chicken livers, 1 finely chopped shallot, and a pinch of thyme. Cook over high heat for about 2 minutes, pour off all the fat, deglaze the pan with a teaspoon of sherry, then pour everything into a blender and blend to a purée. Allow to cool before using to make the sauce. Ed.*

Rognons de veau aux échalotes roties
VEAL KIDNEYS WITH ROAST SHALLOTS

Ingredients for 4 servings:

FOR THE SHALLOTS:
1½ pounds shallots, unpeeled
Salt, pepper
2 teaspoons sugar
3 tablespoons softened butter, broken into small pieces

FOR THE STOCK:
1½ tablespoons butter
1½ pounds chicken wings, chopped into large pieces
1 large carrot, diced
1 large onion, chopped
1 stalk celery, chopped
Bouquet garni
4 small tomatoes, chopped
4 large mushrooms, chopped
2 cups water

FOR THE KIDNEYS:
¼ pound fresh pig's caul (lace fat); *(see Note)*
2 veal kidneys, about 12 ounces each, outer membrane and fat removed
Salt, pepper
1 teaspoon butter
6 tablespoons *crème fraîche (see p. 331)* or heavy cream
Salt, pepper

UTENSILS:

Oval or rectangular roasting pan, 16 inches long (for the shallots)
Small saucepan
Large saucepan
Skimmer or slotted spoon
Blender or food mill
2 mixing bowls
Small roasting pan, 12 inches long (for the kidneys)
Wire whisk
To serve: 4 heated dinner plates and sauceboat

THE SHALLOTS:

Preheat the oven to 425° F.

Line a large roasting pan with aluminum foil, spread the shallots over the bottom of the pan in a single layer, sprinkle with salt, pepper, and sugar, and dot with the softened butter. Cover with aluminum foil and bake for 30 minutes. Turn the shallots over, lower the oven temperature to 350° F, and bake for 30 minutes more.

Set aside 20 of the largest ones for garnish. Cut the root ends off the remaining shallots and squeeze to force the cooked pulp from the skins. Chop the pulp to a paste and reserve in a small saucepan.

THE STOCK:

Melt 1½ tablespoons of butter in a large saucepan, add the chicken wings, and brown for about 10 minutes. Add the carrot, onion, celery, and *bouquet garni,* and cook over moderate heat 4 minutes. Add the tomatoes and mushrooms, season lightly with salt and pepper, and boil to evaporate all the vegetable moisture. Add the water, bring to a boil, skim off any foam with a skimmer or slotted spoon, and simmer, uncovered, for 45 minutes to 1 hour. Strain the stock, pressing on the vegetables with a wooden spoon to extract all the liquids. You will need 1 cup of stock once the surface fat has been removed. Place the degreased stock in the saucepan with the chopped shallot pulp and reserve.

THE KIDNEYS:

Soak the pig's caul in a large bowl of cold water for about 1 hour before using. Drain it, squeeze out the water, then spread it out and pat dry with a towel.

Preheat the oven to 425° F.

Season the kidneys generously with salt and pepper and wrap each one in pig's caul. Put them in a roasting pan with a teaspoon of butter and roast for 10 minutes. Turn the kidneys over and roast 8 minutes more (they should be slightly rare when done). After the kidneys have been turned over, wrap the whole shallots reserved earlier in a piece of aluminum foil and reheat in the oven while the kidneys finish cooking.

TO FINISH THE SAUCE AND SERVE:
Whisk the cream into the stock-shallot mixture and simmer for 12 minutes. Season with salt and pepper if needed, pour the sauce into a blender, and blend until smooth, or work it through a food mill.

Remove the kidneys and whole shallots from the oven. Place the kidneys on a cutting board, remove any pieces of fat remaining, cut them into thin slices, and season with salt and pepper.

Place a little of the shallot sauce on each of the hot dinner plates, arrange the slices of kidney on top, garnish each plate with 5 whole shallots, and serve.

SUGGESTIONS:
A simpler version of the sauce can be made by eliminating the stock and heating the chopped shallots with 1⅓ cups of cream before blending (this is easier to do, but not nearly as tasty).

Veal sweetbreads can be soaked overnight, then prepared exactly as described for the kidneys.

NOTE *Pig's caul (lace fat) should be used if possible, but a table-spoon of lard can be rubbed on each kidney before roasting if lace fat is unavailable. In this case, baste the kidneys 2 or 3 times while roasting. Ed.*

Courtinandise
CALF'S HEAD IN CHAMPAGNE ROBERT COURTINE

Ingredients for 5 to 6 servings:

FOR THE STOCK:
2½ pounds breast of veal
1 bottle champagne *(or other white wine. Ed.)*
2 tablespoons olive oil
1 teaspoon butter
Salt, pepper
2 carrots, diced
2 stalks celery, diced
Bouquet garni
2 onions, diced
1 pound tomatoes, diced
1 clove garlic, crushed
4 cups water

FOR THE CALF'S HEAD AND FOOT:
1½ pounds boneless calf's head
1 whole calf's foot
1 lemon, cut in half
3 medium carrots, cut into olive-like pieces, or cut into quarters
3 medium turnips, prepared like the carrots
½ pound celeriac (celery root), prepared like the carrots, or 2 stalks
    celery, cut into 1-inch pieces
Flour (for sealing the pot)

FOR THE ONIONS:
2 teaspoons butter
½ pound pearl onions, peeled
Salt, pepper
½ teaspoon sugar

UTENSILS:
Roasting pan
Skimmer or slotted spoon
2 large pots (5½-quart capacity each)
Small mixing bowl

Large frying pan
Medium saucepan
3-quart stewing and serving pot, with cover
Small frying pan, with cover

THE VEAL STOCK:
Preheat the oven to 425° F.

Bone the breast of veal; place the bones in a roasting pan and roast for 45 minutes, turning frequently to brown. Remove from the oven, lift out the bones with a skimmer or slotted spoon, place them in a large pot, and reserve. Pour off any fat in the roasting pan.

Pour ⅔ cup of the champagne into the roasting pan, scraping the bottom of the pan with a wooden spoon; pour into a bowl and reserve.

Cut the meat from the breast of veal into large cubes.

Heat the olive oil and butter in a large frying pan, add the pieces of veal, season generously with salt and pepper, and brown over moderate heat on all sides. Lower the heat and simmer for 6 minutes. Remove the veal from the pan with a skimmer or slotted spoon and place in the pot with the bones.

Add the carrots and celery to the frying pan and simmer to soften for 6 minutes, then add them to the pot with the veal. Place the pot over moderate heat, add the *bouquet garni* and the onions, and simmer for 3 minutes. Add the tomatoes and garlic and boil rapidly for about 5 minutes to evaporate most of the liquid given off by the vegetables. Add the champagne remaining in the bottle and that used to deglaze the roasting pan. Bring to a boil, add the water, and bring back to a boil.

THE CALF'S HEAD AND FOOT:
Cut the head into 10 to 12 pieces. Leave the calf's foot whole. Rub both with lemon, place them in a large pot, and add enough cold water to cover by several inches. Bring to a boil, boil over high heat for 2 minutes, drain, and cool under cold running water.

Add the head and foot to the boiling stock, lower the heat, cover the pot, and simmer for 1 hour, skimming off any foam that appears.

Preheat the oven to 425° F.

Cook the carrots, turnips, and celeriac for 3 minutes in a large pot of rapidly boiling salted water, drain, and cool under running water.

Lift the pieces of calf's head out of the stock and place them in the stewing pot with the carrots, turnips, and celeriac. Bone the foot, cut it into large pieces, and add it to the pot. Strain the stock, pressing on the vegetables and meat to extract their juices (do not discard the meat; *see Note*), and ladle enough of the strained stock into the pot to almost cover the meat. Taste and season generously with salt and pepper. Seal the pot with a mixture of flour and water (for instructions, *see Note* under **Chicken with 40 cloves of garlic,** page 207), then bake for 30 minutes.

TO FINISH AND SERVE:

Melt 2 teaspoons of butter in a small frying pan, add the pearl onions, salt, pepper, and sugar. Shake the pan and cook the onions over moderate heat for a minute or two, then add enough water to almost cover the onions (they should not float). Half cover the pan and boil rapidly to evaporate the water and glaze the onions (allow about 10 minutes).

Remove the calf's head from the oven, pry open the lid of the pot, add the onions, and serve (preferably with champagne).

NOTE: *Any remaining stock can be reheated with the pieces of veal used in making it, to make a nice stew. Bind the cooking liquid with egg yolk and cream, add a little lemon juice, and you have one of the many versions of* blanquette de veau. *(A few baby carrots, onions, and button mushrooms can be added as well.) Ed.*

Les volailles & gibiers
POULTRY & GAME

Poulet aux 40 gousses d'ail
CHICKEN WITH 40 CLOVES OF GARLIC

Ingredients for 4 servings:

FOR THE GARLIC:
2 tablespoons olive oil
Salt, pepper
½ teaspoon sugar
40 large cloves garlic (about 4 large heads), separated but unpeeled

FOR THE CHICKEN:
½ cup olive oil
1 chicken, weighing 3 pounds
Salt, pepper
2 tablespoons finely chopped parsley
2 tablespoons finely chopped chervil
2 tablespoons finely chopped chives
2 teaspoons finely chopped coriander leaf (cilantro)
2 teaspoons finely chopped basil
1 teaspoon thyme leaves
½ bay leaf
About 1½ cups flour (for sealing the pot)

UTENSILS:
Large 4- to 5-quart oval pot, with cover
Pastry brush

THE GARLIC:
Place 2 tablespoons of olive oil on a plate, season with salt, pepper, and sugar, and roll the unpeeled cloves of garlic in the mixture to coat them completely.

TO COOK:
Preheat the oven to 425° F.

Heat ½ cup of olive oil in an oval pot. Generously salt and pepper the chicken inside and out and place it in the pot. Distribute the cloves of garlic around the chicken, sprinkle the herbs over everything, seal the pot (see Note), and bake for 1 hour.

TO SERVE:
Take the pot to the table and break the seal in front of your guests. Cut the chicken into pieces, sprinkle each one with a little salt and pepper, spoon the herbs and garlic over the chicken, and serve. Each person should split the cloves of garlic open with a knife and eat the creamy inside as a vegetable.

NOTE: *Add enough water to the flour to make a soft dough. Roll the dough between the palms of your hands, or on the table, to form a sausage (or 3 to 4 smaller ones) long enough to go around the edge of the pot. With a pastry brush dipped in water, dampen the edge of the pot, place the sausage(s) around the edge, and press down to hold in place. Lightly brush the dough with water, put the cover of the pot into place, press it down, and fold any excess dough up over the edge of the cover, pressing on it as you do so. Ed.*

Poulet Maître Dufour
CHICKEN DUFOUR

Ingredients for 4 servings:
fritter batter *(see p. 266)*
1 small chicken, weighing about 2¼ pounds, with liver, heart, and
gizzard
1 cooked lamb's brain *(see Note)*, cut into ½-inch cubes (optional)

Salt, pepper
2 tablespoons butter, in all
1 onion, diced
1 carrot, diced
Bouquet garni
1 cup heavy cream
1 small or ½ large ripe avocado
Oil for deep frying

UTENSILS:
Cleaver
Small saucepan
High-sided frying pan or *sauteuse*, 9½ inches in diameter
Large saucepan or deep fryer
Deep-frying thermometer
Wire whisk
To serve: Heated serving platter or 4 heated dinner plates, small
heated serving platter and sauceboat

PRELIMINARY PREPARATIONS:
Cut the legs, neck, and wings from the chicken. Cut the drumsticks
from the thighs and reserve on a plate.

With a large knife or cleaver, separate the back from the breast and
reserve on another plate with the wings and neck.

With a cleaver, split the breast by cutting through the breastbone.
Cut each half breast in two and reserve with the legs.

Clean the gizzard and cut it into four pieces. Remove any greenish
parts from the liver and cut it into four, cut the heart in half, and place
all of them on a third plate with the pieces of lamb's brain.

THE CHICKEN AND THE AVOCADO:

Season the legs and breasts with salt and pepper. Melt a tablespoon of butter in a high-sided frying pan or *sauteuse,* add the onion, cook for 1 to 2 minutes to soften, then add the carrot, a little salt and pepper, and simmer for 3 to 4 minutes. Add the remaining butter, raise the heat, and add the chicken legs and breasts. Brown over moderate heat for 3 to 4 minutes, add the back, wings, and neck, the *bouquet garni,* and about ¾ cup of water (the liquid should about half cover the pieces of chicken—add more if needed). Bring to a boil, cover the pan, lower the heat, and simmer for 11 minutes. Turn the breasts and legs over after about 6 minutes.

Lift the legs and breasts out of the pan, skim off any foam that has surfaced, and boil the liquid with the bones and vegetables until it has almost completely evaporated. Add the cream, place the legs and breasts back in the pan, and simmer for 5 minutes. Cover and keep warm.

Peel the avocado, remove the seed, and purée the pulp by working it through a sieve with a wooden spoon. Place the purée in a small saucepan, cover, and reserve for making the sauce.

THE FRITTERS:

Heat the oil to 375° F in a large saucepan or deep fryer. Dip the pieces of lamb's brain, chicken liver, gizzard, and heart into the batter and drop them into the hot oil. Fry for 3 to 4 minutes, or until golden brown, and drain on paper towels while finishing the sauce.

TO FINISH THE SAUCE AND SERVE:

Place the chicken legs and breasts on a serving platter, or divide them up among 4 dinner plates, with a piece of breast and a piece of leg on each one. Keep warm.

Spoon off as much fat as you can from the surface of the sauce, then strain it into the pan containing the avocado purée. Press gently on the bones and vegetables to extract their juices. Whisk the avocado sauce over very low heat until very hot but not boiling, taste for salt and pepper, and pour it into a sauceboat. Spoon a little of the sauce over the chicken, place the fritters on a separate small platter, and serve, with the sauce on the side.

NOTE: *To prepare the lamb's brain, soak it for 2 hours in cold water, changing the water several times. Then, with your fingers, carefully peel off the thin membrane that surrounds it. Place 2 cups of water, 2 tablespoons of vinegar, and a pinch of salt in a small saucepan, bring to a boil, add the lamb's brain, and poach for 5 minutes. Drain on a cloth and allow to cool completely before cutting it into pieces. Ed.*

Pigeons aux poireaux confits
ROAST SQUAB WITH LEEKS

Ingredients for 2 servings:
    2¼ pounds leeks, white part only
    2 squabs, pigeons, or doves, weighing about ¾ pound each
    Salt, pepper
    1½ tablespoons plus 1 teaspoon butter, in all
    2 teaspoons sugar
    ⅔ cup water

UTENSILS:
Large saucepan
Kitchen string
Large oval or rectangular roasting pan, 12 to 13 inches long
Smaller roasting pan, 10 to 11 inches long
Bowl
To serve: 2 heated dinner plates

PRELIMINARY PREPARATIONS:
Cut the white of each leek into pieces about 2 inches long and cut each piece in half lengthwise. Separate the leaves and wash in cold water. Drain well, then boil in rapidly boiling salted water for 3 minutes. Drain, cool under running water, drain again, and reserve.

    Cut the neck and wings off of each squab. Salt and pepper each bird inside and out, then tie them with string to hold the legs close to the body.

THE LEEKS AND SQUAB:
Preheat the oven to 475° F.

Heat 1½ tablespoons of butter in a large roasting pan, add the leeks, season generously with salt and pepper, add the sugar, and sauté for 6 to 7 minutes, or until all the liquid in the pan has evaporated. Reserve.

In a smaller roasting pan, heat 1 teaspoon of butter, brown the squabs, their wings, and necks over moderately high heat, turning frequently to avoid burning, for about 6 minutes.

Place both the roasting pans in the oven and cook for 12 minutes. Turn the birds over halfway through the cooking time; the leeks should brown slightly in the oven.

TO FINISH AND SERVE:

Turn the oven off and place the squabs on top of the leeks to keep warm inside the oven while making the sauce.

Place the necks and wings on a plate and pour all the fat from the squab roasting pan.

Put the necks and wings back in the pan, place over high heat, add the water, and boil rapidly for 4 minutes to make a light sauce. Add salt and pepper as needed, then strain into a bowl.

Remove the leeks and squabs from the oven, divide the leeks between the plates, place 1 squab on top, spoon over the sauce, and serve.

NOTE: *If possible, cut birds into quarters after they are cooked and serve this way, rather than whole. Although slightly more complicated, the presentation is nicer and the birds are much easier to eat. Ed.*

Pigeons rôtis aux fèves et aux pois gourmands
ROAST SQUAB WITH BROAD BEANS AND SNOW PEAS

Ingredients for 4 servings:

FOR THE STOCK:

4 squabs, pigeons, or doves, weighing about ¾ pound each *(for substitution, see Note)*
1 teaspoon butter
1⅔ cups water

FOR THE SQUAB:

Salt, pepper
1 tablespoon cooking oil
1 tablespoon butter

FOR THE VEGETABLES:

12 pearl onions, peeled
2 tablespoons butter
2 pounds broad beans, shelled and with the skin around each bean
    removed, or fresh lima beans, shelled
½ pound snow peas, strings removed
Salt, pepper
¼ teaspoon rosemary leaves, finely chopped
½ teaspoon sugar

UTENSILS:

Small saucepan
Mixing bowl
Kitchen string
Oval or rectangular roasting pan, 13 inches long
Medium saucepan
Large frying pan
To serve: 4 heated dinner plates and sauceboat

THE STOCK:

Cut off the neck and wings of each squab (or use ½ pound of chicken wings). Heat a teaspoon of butter in a small saucepan, add the wings and necks, and brown for 3 to 4 minutes. Add the water, bring to a boil, stirring to detach the meat juices stuck to the bottom of the pan, and boil for 15 minutes, or until the liquid has reduced almost by half. Strain the stock into a measuring cup; there should be ¾ cup below the layer of fat on the surface. Spoon off the fat, season with salt and pepper, and reserve in a bowl.

THE SQUAB:

Preheat the oven to 425° F.
    Season the squabs generously inside and out with salt and pepper and tie them for roasting.
    Heat the oil and butter in a roasting pan, add the squabs, and brown over moderate heat for 6 minutes, then roast them for 12 minutes, basting them several times.

THE VEGETABLES:

Boil the onions in a saucepan of rapidly boiling water for 4 minutes, then drain.

Melt 2 tablespoons of butter in a large frying pan, add the broad beans and snow peas, and sauté over moderate heat for 2 minutes. Season with salt and pepper, lower the heat, and cook 4 minutes, covered, stirring occasionally. Add the onions, rosemary, sugar, salt, and pepper and sauté 4 minutes more, uncovered.

TO FINISH AND SERVE:

Remove the string from the squabs. Place the vegetables on dinner plates and place the squabs on top. Pour all the fat from the roasting pan, add the stock, bring quickly to a boil, stirring to detach any caramelized meat juices, then strain the sauce into a sauceboat. Serve with the sauce on the side.

NOTE: *A 3½-pound duck may be used instead of the squab. It will take a bit longer to brown before roasting, and duck should roast for 30 minutes, rather than 12. Ed.*

Pigeons pékinois
SQUAB PEKING STYLE

Ingredients for 4 servings:

 4 squabs, doves, or pigeons, weighing about ¾ pound each *(for substitution, see Note)*

FOR THE MARINADE:

2 cups white wine
¾ cup light corn syrup
¾ cup dark corn syrup
6 tablespoons soy sauce

FOR THE STOCK:
1 teaspoon butter
½ pound chicken necks, wings, or backs
2 tomatoes, chopped
4 shallots, chopped
Salt, pepper
2 cups water

FOR THE LIME AND GINGER JULIENNE:
Zest of 2 limes, cut into julienne strips
3-inch long piece fresh ginger, peeled and cut into julienne strips
2 cups water
¼ cup granulated sugar

UTENSILS:
Kitchen string
Large wide bowl
2 medium saucepans
Small saucepan
Wire whisk
Large oval roasting pan, 13 to 14 inches long
To serve: 4 heated dinner plates and sauceboat

TO MARINATE:
The day before, cut the neck and wing tips off of each bird and reserve them for making the stock.

Tie the birds for roasting.

In a bowl large enough to hold the squabs in one layer, whisk carefully the wine, the corn syrups, and soy sauce for 3 to 4 minutes to mix the ingredients well, place the squabs in the marinade, and cover the bowl. Refrigerate for 24 hours to marinate (if the birds are not completely covered by the marinade, turn them over every 6 to 8 hours).

Remove the bowl from the refrigerator an hour or two before cooking the squabs.

THE STOCK:
In a medium saucepan, melt a teaspoon of butter, add the reserved necks and wing tips and the chicken parts, and sauté quickly to brown. Add the tomatoes and shallots, salt and pepper lightly, and boil for

about 5 minutes, or until almost all of the water given out by the tomatoes has evaporated. Add the water, bring to a moderate boil, and cook, uncovered, for 25 to 30 minutes. Strain the stock into a clean saucepan, pressing on the meat and vegetables to extract all the juices; there should be ¾ cup of stock left. Skim off any fat and reserve.

THE LIME AND GINGER JULIENNE:

Place the julienne of lime zest and ginger in a small saucepan with the water and sugar, bring to a boil, lower the heat, and simmer very slowly for 25 minutes. Drain the julienne and place it in the saucepan with the strained stock.

Place the saucepan over very low heat and simmer for 20 minutes, or until there is ⅔ cup of stock, lime, and ginger left. Reserve.

THE SQUAB:

Preheat the oven to 450° F.

Lift the squab out of the marinade, then pour half of the marinade (about 2 cups) into a roasting pan. On top of the stove, bring the marinade to a boil, then place the squab in the pan on their sides. Roast for 10 minutes, turn the birds over, and roast 10 minutes on the other side. Turn the birds over on their backs and roast a final 10 minutes. Untie the birds, place them on a platter, and put them back into the turned-off oven with the door ajar.

TO FINISH THE SAUCE AND SERVE:

Place the roasting pan back over high heat and boil the cooking liquid for 3 minutes. Measure out ⅔ cup of the reduced liquid and add it to the saucepan with the stock, lime, and ginger. Reheat if necessary.

Place a squab on each dinner plate, spoon some of the sauce over each one, and serve, with the rest of the sauce in a sauceboat.

SUGGESTIONS:
Serve the squabs accompanied either with fresh green peas, or soy bean sprouts that have been sautéed in a little oil and seasoned with salt, pepper, and a touch of soy sauce.

NOTE: *Duck may be used instead of squab. Buy one weighing about 3¼ pounds, cut off the wing tips and neck, and marinate as described for the squab. Roast for 1 hour and 20 minutes, turning and basting it every 10 to 15 minutes, to brown evenly on all sides. Because of the longer cooking time, there is no need to boil and reduce the cooking liquid. Skim the fat off before measuring and adding it to the stock, lime, and ginger mixture. Carve the duck, place a piece on each dinner plate, and serve as described for the squab. Ed.*

Sauté de canard au vinaigre de xeres
DUCK WITH SHERRY VINEGAR SAUCE AND STUFFED TURNIPS

Ingredients for 2 servings:
  1 duck, weighing 2¾ pounds

    FOR THE STOCK:
  2 tablespoons cooking oil
  1 small carrot, diced
  1 small onion, diced
  ½ stalk celery, diced
  ½ medium tomato, diced
  1 clove garlic, cut in half horizontally
  ¼ teaspoon whole coriander seeds
  ¼ teaspoon coarsely crushed peppercorns
  Bouquet garni
  3 tablespoons sherry vinegar
  1½ tablespoons white wine
  3¼ cups chicken stock
  ¼ teaspoon tomato paste
  1 teaspoon coarse salt
  ½ teaspoon Dijon mustard
  1½ tablespoons softened butter

FOR THE TURNIPS:
4 small round turnips (about ¾ pound)
1 shallot, finely chopped
2 teaspoons finely chopped parsley
Salt, pepper
2 teaspoons butter

UTENSILS:
Cleaver
Large stewing pot
Bowl
Wire Whisk
Medium saucepan
Small saucepan
Melon-ball cutter
Large saucepan
Mixing bowl
Small frying pan
2 small roasting pans
To serve: 2 heated dinner plates

PREPARING THE DUCK:
Cut the legs off the duck and reserve. Cut off the back, neck, and wings, and reserve.

Cut the breast in half lengthwise with a cleaver.

THE STOCK:
Heat the oil in a large stew pot, add the duck back, wings, and neck, and brown over moderate heat, stirring frequently, for about 15 minutes. Lift the pieces of duck out of the pot, pour off all the fat, and lightly wipe the bottom of the pot with paper towels to remove any excess fat. Place the pieces of duck back in the pot with the carrot, onion, celery, tomato, garlic, coriander seeds, peppercorns, and *bouquet garni* and cook over moderate heat for about 3 minutes to soften the vegetables. Add the vinegar and wine, boil rapidly for 4 to 5 minutes, then add the stock, tomato paste, and salt. Boil for 35 minutes, or until the liquid has reduced to 1 cup. Strain the stock into a bowl, pressing on the vegetables and bones to extract all their juices. Skim off any fat. Whisk in the mustard and reserve 6 tablespoons of the finished stock in a small saucepan for making the sauce.

218

Place the rest of the stock in a small roasting pan for cooking the stuffed turnips.

THE TURNIPS:

Cut a thin slice off the bottom of each turnip so that it will stand upright. Peel the turnips and use a melon-ball cutter to hollow them out (be careful not to puncture the sides or bottom). Drop the hollowed-out turnips in a large saucepan of lightly salted boiling water, boil for 3 minutes, cool under running water, drain, and leave to dry, inverted on a towel, while making the stuffing.

Bone the duck legs and discard the skin and bones. Coarsely chop the meat and place it in a mixing bowl with the chopped shallot and parsley. Season with salt and pepper and stir well.

Heat the butter in a small frying pan. Make four little balls with the seasoned duck meat and fry them for about 4 minutes to brown on all sides, remove them from the pan, and drain on paper towels.

When the balls of stuffing are cool enough to handle, place one in each of the hollowed out turnips, and place them in the roasting pan with the stock.

TO COOK:

Preheat the oven to 425° F.

Season the duck breasts with salt and pepper. Place them in a small roasting pan, without any butter or oil, and roast for 10 minutes; turn the pieces over and place the roasting pan with the turnips in the oven. Cook for 10 minutes more, then remove everything from the oven. Drain the duck on a cloth for a few seconds.

TO FINISH THE SAUCE AND SERVE:

Heat the stock, reserved earlier, until warm, then whisk in 1½ tablespoons of softened butter, little by little, to finish the sauce (do not allow to boil).

Skin and bone each duck breast and cut the meat into thin slices. Garnish each dinner plate with the slices of duck and two stuffed turnips, spoon over the sauce, and serve.

Magrets de canard au miel et aux fleurs de thym
DUCK STEAKS WITH HONEY AND THYME SAUCE

Ingredients for 4 servings:
  2 ducks, weighing 4 to 4½ pounds each *(see Note)*

FOR THE STOCK:
1 teaspoon butter
1 tablespoon cooking oil
1 onion, finely chopped
2 carrots, finely chopped
Bouquet garni
1 stalk celery, finely chopped
2 medium tomatoes, chopped
1 small clove garlic, crushed
5 medium mushrooms, chopped
Salt, pepper
1 quart water

FOR THE SAUCE:
2 tablespoons honey
¼ teaspoon thyme leaves or flowers
2 tablespoons wine vinegar
½ teaspoon salt
Pepper

FOR THE DUCK STEAKS:
Salt, pepper
2 tablespoons butter
2 tablespoons honey, in all
1 teaspoon thyme leaves or flowers, in all

UTENSILS:
Cleaver
Large stock pot
Skimmer
Small bowl
Small saucepan
Large frying pan
To serve: 4 heated dinner plates and sauceboat

220

PRELIMINARY PREPARATIONS:

Cut the legs from each duck and reserve for use in other recipes (*see Note*). Cut each breast off, keeping your knife close to the bone to make thick steaks. Remove the skin from each duck steak and trim off all but a very thin layer of fat.

Cut off the wings and chop the duck carcasses into large pieces with a cleaver; reserve for making the stock.

THE DUCK STOCK:

Heat the butter and oil in a large pot, add the duck bones and wings, and brown for about 8 minutes (be careful not to let them burn). Add the onion, carrots, *bouquet garni*, celery, tomatoes, and garlic and cook for 4 minutes. Add the mushrooms and a little salt and pepper and cook for 4 minutes more. Pour in the water, bring to a boil, and cook, uncovered, at a gentle boil for 40 minutes, skimming off any foam that surfaces. Strain the stock into a measuring cup (do not press on the bones or vegetables); there should be 1⅓ cups of stock below the layer of fat on the surface. Use a spoon to remove all the fat, pour the stock into a small bowl, and reserve.

THE SAUCE:

Heat the honey and thyme leaves or flowers in a small saucepan; cook until the honey turns a dark brown and begins to caramelize. Add the vinegar, stirring to mix well together. Add the strained duck stock, lower the heat, and simmer very slowly for 10 minutes. Taste for salt and pepper and keep the sauce warm while cooking the steaks.

TO COOK THE DUCK AND SERVE:

Lightly salt and pepper the duck.

Heat 2 tablespoons of butter in a large frying pan, add the steaks, skinned side down, and brown over moderate heat for 2 minutes. Turn the steaks over and cook 2 minutes longer, then spread ½ tablespoon of honey over each one, sprinkle each with ¼ teaspoon thyme leaves or flowers, and cook 2 to 3 minutes (the steaks should be slightly rare).

Drain the steaks for a few seconds on a paper towel and place each one on a dinner plate. Serve immediately with a vegetable of your choice and the sauce on the side.

NOTE: *Only the breast meat and carcasses are used in this recipe. Save the legs for making* **Preserved duck** *(see p. 228) or* **Stuffed duck legs with pasta** *(see p. 225). Ed.*

221

Magrets de canard au zeste d'orange et poivre vert
DUCK STEAKS WITH ORANGE ZEST AND GREEN PEPPERCORNS

Ingredients for 4 servings:
  2 ducks, weighing 4 to 4½ pounds each

  FOR THE STOCK *(see Suggestions)*:
  2 teaspoons butter, in all
  2 teaspoons cooking oil, in all
  3 small carrots, diced
  3 small onions, diced
  1 stalk celery, diced
  4 tomatoes, diced
  5 medium mushrooms, quartered
  2 cloves garlic, crushed
  Bouquet garni (including 2 green leek leaves)
  15 peppercorns
  7⅓ cups water

  FOR THE STEAKS:
  Zest of 1 orange, cut into julienne strips
  3 tablespoons bottled green peppercorns, in all
  1 teaspoon butter
  1 teaspoon cooking oil

  UTENSILS:
  Cleaver (optional)
  Large pot or *sauteuse*
  Frying pan
  Skimmer or slotted spoon
  2 small saucepans
  2 small bowls
  Large frying pan
  Ladle
  To serve: Heated serving platter and sauceboat

  PRELIMINARY PREPARATIONS:
With a large knife, cut the wings and legs off of the ducks. They will not

222

be used in this recipe; save them for making **Preserved duck** *(see p. 228)* or, if you prefer, the legs may be used for making **Stuffed duck legs with pasta** *(see p. 225)*.

Carefully slice the breast meat off of the bones, leaving as little meat on the carcasses as possible. If the duck is very fatty, remove the skin and some of the fat so that the meat is covered by a layer of fat about ⅛ inch thick. Reserve the breasts on a plate.

Cut the tail off of each carcass and discard. Chop the carcasses into pieces with a cleaver or a large knife.

THE STOCK:

In a large pot or *sauteuse*, heat a teaspoon each of butter and oil until very hot. Add the pieces of duck carcass and brown them on all sides, stirring frequently. Be careful not to let them burn. When brown, lower the heat and cook slowly for 20 minutes, stirring occasionally.

In a frying pan, heat the remaining teaspoon each of butter and oil. When very hot, add the carrots, onions, and celery. Cook over moderate heat for 5 minutes, or until the vegetables begin to brown, stirring frequently.

When the duck bones have cooked 20 minutes, add to them the cooked vegetables, the tomatoes, mushrooms, garlic, and *bouquet garni*. Stir well together, add the peppercorns, and cook, stirring, for 4 minutes. Add the water, bring to a boil, salt lightly, and cook at a moderate boil for 1 hour and 20 minutes, skimming off any foam that appears and frequently spooning off the fat.

When the stock is cooked, strain it, pressing on the bones and vegetables with a wooden spoon to extract all the juices. There should be 2½ cups of stock once all remaining fat has been spooned off the surface.

Place the degreased stock in a small saucepan over moderate heat and boil for about 15 minutes, or until the sauce has reduced to 1¼ cups; reserve.

THE ORANGE ZEST AND GREEN PEPPERCORNS:

Place the julienne of orange zest in a small saucepan, cover with cold water, bring to a boil, and boil for 1 minute. Drain, cool under running water, and drain again. Reserve in a small bowl.

Reserve ¼ of the green peppercorns on a small plate for cooking the duck steaks. Place the remaining peppercorns in a bowl and reserve for the sauce.

THE DUCK STEAKS:

Season the duck steaks on both sides with salt. On a cutting board, spread out the green peppercorns reserved for the steaks and squash them under the blade of a large knife. Spread the crushed peppercorns over both sides of the duck steaks, pressing down into the meat with the knife blade.

Heat the butter and oil in a large frying pan until almost smoking, then add the duck steaks, skin (fat) side down. Cook over high heat for 2 minutes, turn the steaks over, and cook for 4 minutes more. Drain on paper towels and keep warm while finishing the sauce.

TO FINISH THE SAUCE AND SERVE:

Place the sauce over moderate heat and bring just to a boil, add ¾ of the orange zest, lower the heat, and simmer for 3 minutes.

Pour all the fat from the frying pan the steaks cooked in and pat the bottom of the pan dry with a paper towel. Place the pan back over the heat and add a ladleful of the sauce, scraping the bottom of the pan with a wooden spoon to dissolve all the caramelized meat juices. Add the contents of the pan to the sauce.

The duck steaks can be served either whole or sliced. If sliced, sprinkle each slice with a little salt and pepper.

Place the steaks on a platter, strain the sauce into a sauceboat, stir in the reserved orange zest and green peppercorns, and serve immediately.

SUGGESTIONS:

If you don't want to make the stock, pour 1 cup of heavy cream into the frying pan the steaks cooked in, after pouring off the fat and patting the pan dry. Bring to a boil, add salt, pepper, and ¾ of the orange zest, and boil for 3 minutes, or until the sauce has thickened slightly. Strain it, stir in the remaining zest and peppercorns, and serve as described.

Jambonnettes de canard 🔥🔥🔥
STUFFED DUCK LEGS WITH PASTA 🔥🔥🔥

Ingredients for 4 servings:
  2 ducks, weighing 4¼ pounds each

FOR THE STUFFING:
¼ pound pork fatback
2 duck (or 4 chicken) livers
6 tablespoons *crème fraîche (see p. 331)* or heavy cream
1 generous teaspoon finely chopped parsley
1 generous teaspoon finely chopped chervil
1 generous teaspoon finely chopped chives
½ teaspoon thyme leaves
1 tablespoon cognac
Pinch allspice
Salt, pepper

FOR THE STOCK:
3 medium tomatoes, chopped
1 small carrot, finely chopped
1 very small onion, finely chopped
1 stalk celery, finely chopped
2 cloves garlic, crushed
Bouquet garni
1 teaspoon tomato paste
7½ cups water
Salt
15 peppercorns

FOR COOKING THE LEGS:
2 tablespoons cooking oil
Salt, pepper
1 tablespoon butter
10 shallots, finely chopped
1 large stalk celery, finely chopped
1 generous teaspoon peppercorns, coarsely crushed
2 cups red wine
2 teaspoons thyme leaves

225

Homemade pasta *(see p. 256)*

UTENSILS:
Small boning knife
Meat grinder or food processor
Large mixing bowl
Trussing needle
Kitchen string
Cleaver
Large *sauteuse* or stewing pot, 10 to 11 inches in diameter
Small saucepan
To serve: 4 heated dinner plates and sauceboat

TO STUFF THE LEGS:

Remove the legs from the ducks; remove the breast meat as well and reserve for making either **Preserved duck** *(see p. 228)* or one of the recipes for **duck steaks** *(see p. 220 or p. 222)*. Save the wings, neck, and carcass of one of the ducks for making the stock for this recipe.

Place the duck legs, skin side down, on a board and with a small knife slit them lengthwise on the inner side. Carefully debone first the thigh, then the drumstick (do not cut them apart). Be careful not to cut or puncture the skin.

Carefully cut away half of the duck meat from each leg, horizontally and as evenly as possible. Place this meat, with the pork fatback and duck livers, in a meat grinder or food processor and grind to a paste. Transfer the mixture to a bowl and add the cream, herbs, cognac, and allspice; salt and pepper generously and beat with a spoon for several minutes.

Using a trussing needle and kitchen string, tie the small end of each drumstick. Spread the legs out on a clean surface, skin side down, and lightly salt and pepper the meat. Spread a quarter of the stuffing out over each leg, then fold the legs in half lengthwise so that the edges touch. Using the needle and string, sew the edges together, enclosing the stuffing, and making 4 approximately triangular pouches. Reserve on a plate while making the stock.

THE STOCK:

Chop the reserved duck carcass, wings, and neck into pieces with a cleaver. Place them in a large saucepan and brown over low heat for about 10 minutes (no fat need be added). Add the tomatoes and boil for

226

about 8 minutes, stirring frequently, to evaporate their water, then add the carrot, onion, celery, garlic, and *bouquet garni*. Simmer 8 minutes longer to soften the vegetables, then add the tomato paste, water, a little salt, and the peppercorns, and boil slowly, uncovered, for 90 minutes. Skim off any foam that surfaces. Strain the stock (there should be about 2 cups) and spoon off any fat from its surface. Reserve.

TO COOK THE LEGS:
Heat 2 tablespoons of oil in a pot large enough to hold all four legs in one layer with a little space around them. Season them with a little salt and pepper, prick each one once with a trussing needle, and place them in the hot oil. Brown evenly over moderate heat for about 8 minutes, turning them over with a wooden spoon. Place on paper towels to drain and reserve.

Pour off the fat from the pan and place the pan back over moderate heat. Heat the tablespoon butter, add the shallots, celery, and peppercorns, and simmer for about 5 minutes, or until the shallots are soft. Add the wine, raise the heat, and boil rapidly for 14 minutes, or until all but about a tablespoon of the wine has evaporated.

Preheat the oven to 425° F.

Place the duck legs in the pot with the reduced wine mixture and add the stock reserved earlier (the legs should be half-covered by the liquid). Add the thyme leaves, cover the pot, and bake for 32 minutes.

TO SERVE:
Place the legs on a cutting board.

Strain the cooking liquid into a measuring cup and skim off the fat. If there is more than 1⅓ cups left, pour the liquid into a clean saucepan, and boil rapidly to reduce it to that amount.

Carefully remove the string from each leg.

Spoon a little of the sauce onto each dinner plate, then pour the rest of the sauce into a sauceboat. Place a stuffed leg on each plate and serve with **homemade pasta** *(see p. 256)*, the perfect accompaniment for the taste of both the duck and the sauce.

Canard confit
PRESERVED DUCK

Ingredients for about 1½ pounds:
    1 duck, weighing about 3¼ pounds
    1 clove garlic, cut in half
    2 tablespoons coarse salt
    1 teaspoon thyme leaves
    1 teaspoon coarsely ground peppercorns
    3¼ pounds goose fat }

    UTENSILS:
Mixing bowl
Large saucepan
2 one-quart preserving jars (glass or stoneware)

    SALTING THE DUCK:
The day before cooking, cut the legs off the duck and separate the thighs from the drumsticks.

    Cut off the breast meat and wings, then cut off one half of each breast lengthwise. Rub each piece of duck with garlic.

    Mix the coarse salt, thyme, and pepper in a bowl and rub each piece of duck with this mixture. Shake off any excess salt, place the duck on a plate, covered loosely, and refrigerate for 24 hours before cooking.

    COOKING THE DUCK:
Wipe each piece of duck with a cloth and reserve.

    Melt the goose fat in a large saucepan. When hot, place the pieces of duck in it (they should be completely covered) and simmer for 1 hour over low heat. Then skim off any foam that has appeared and simmer for 30 minutes more. Test the duck to see if it has cooked through: if the meat comes easily away from the bone, it is done; if not, cook a bit longer and test again.

    STORING THE DUCK:
Lift the duck out of the fat and place the pieces in the jars (place the long piece with the wing in first, upright, then fit in the other half of the breast and a thigh and drumstick, for each jar). Pour or ladle the fat

through a sieve into the jar until the duck is covered, then store the jars in the refrigerator. The preserved duck can be kept for several months if left untouched.

TO USE THE DUCK:

Preserved duck is used in several recipes in this book, generally one jar (¾ pound) at a time.

To remove the duck from the jar, place the jar in a slow oven to melt the fat, remove the pieces, and drain on a cloth before following the cooking instructions given in any recipe.

SUGGESTIONS:

Goose or pork can be preserved in the same way; use an equal weight of fat as you have of meat to preserve (if preserving pork, use lard).

Canard sauvage rôti, salade d'épinards crus et oranges
WILD DUCK WITH SPINACH SALAD AND ORANGES

Ingredients for 4 servings:

FOR THE SALAD:
1 pound fresh young spinach, stems and ribs removed
3 medium oranges, preferably seedless
1 tablespoon finely chopped parsley
1 tablespoon finely chopped chervil
1 tablespoon finely chopped chives
3 shallots, finely chopped

FOR THE VINAIGRETTE:
1 teaspoon wine vinegar
2½ teaspoons sherry vinegar
3 tablespoons salad oil
Salt, pepper

FOR THE DUCKS:
2 wild ducks, weighing about 1½ pounds each when cleaned *(see Note)*
2 teaspoons butter
Salt, pepper

UTENSILS:
Large mixing bowl
Small mixing bowl
Wire whisk
Large roasting pan
To serve: 4 heated dinner plates

THE SALAD:
Cut the spinach into thick strips and place it in a large mixing bowl.

Cut off the orange peel and white pith with a knife, then cut out each section from between the membranes. Remove any seeds if necessary. Add the orange sections, the herbs, and shallots to the spinach and reserve.

Make a vinaigrette by whisking together the two vinegars, the oil, and a little salt and pepper. Reserve.

THE DUCKS:
Preheat the oven to 475° F.

Lightly salt and pepper each duck inside and out, then place them on their sides in a large roasting pan. Place a teaspoon of butter on each duck and roast for 13 minutes. Turn the ducks so that they rest on the other side and roast 13 minutes more, basting them with their juices 2 to 3 times.

TO FINISH AND SERVE:
Cut the legs and breasts off each duck. Cut the drumsticks from the thighs and slice the breast meat crosswise to make finger-length pieces. Lightly salt and pepper.

Add the vinaigrette to the spinach salad and toss to mix. Divide the salad among the plates, place half a duck (thigh, drumstick, and slices of breast meat) on each portion, and serve immediately.

NOTE: *One ordinary duck weighing about 4 pounds can be used instead of the two wild ducks. Cook the duck for 1 hour, resting it on* each breast, then each leg, and finally the back as it roasts. Carve as described, but each person will only get half a leg and half a breast in this case. Ed.

Pintadeau rôti en croûte
GUINEA HEN PASTRIES

Ingredients for 4 servings:
>   2 guinea hens, weighing about 1½ pounds each *(for substitutions, see Note)*
>   ½ pound barding fat *(see Note)*
>   Salt, pepper
>   ⅓ cup tightly packed diced pork fatback *(see Note)*
>   2 teaspoons butter
>   3 shallots, finely chopped
>   3 medium mushrooms
>   1 tablespoon cognac
>   2 teaspoons finely chopped parsley
>   2 teaspoons finely chopped chervil
>   2 teaspoons finely chopped chives
>   Pinch allspice
>   3 tablespoons *crème fraîche (see p. 331)* or heavy cream
>   4 teaspoons cooking oil
>   1⅔ cups water
>   9 ounces (250 g) **puff pastry** *(see p. 271)*
>   1 egg, beaten

>   UTENSILS:
>   Cleaver
>   Kitchen string
>   Oval or rectangular roasting pan, about 13 inches long
>   Meat grinder or food processor
>   Mixing bowl

Medium saucepan
Large saucepan
Small saucepan
Rolling pin
Pastry brush
Baking sheet
To serve: 4 heated dinner plates and sauceboat

PRELIMINARY PREPARATIONS:

Cut the legs and wings from each guinea hen. Break off the lower half of the backbone and reserve. Use a cleaver to separate the rest of the back from the breasts.

Lightly salt and pepper the breasts, wrap them in barding fat, and tie with string. Place in a roasting pan and reserve.

Remove the skin from the legs, debone them, cut the meat into ½-inch cubes, and reserve.

Use the cleaver to chop the bones into small pieces and reserve with the backs and wings.

THE STUFFING:

Grind half of the leg meat from the guinea hens with the fatback in the meat grinder or food processor. Mix this with the remaining cubes of meat and reserve.

Melt the butter in a saucepan, add the shallots, and cook over low heat 3 to 4 minutes to soften, then add the mushrooms, salt and pepper, and cook 4 minutes more, stirring frequently, or until all the moisture from the mushrooms has evaporated. Pour into the bowl with the meat, stir in the cognac, herbs, salt, pepper, allspice, and cream, and reserve.

THE SAUCE:

Heat the oil in a large saucepan and add the bones, wings, and backs from the birds. Lower the heat and brown slowly for 30 minutes, stirring frequently (do not allow to burn).

Remove everything from the pan and pour off all the fat; gently pat the bottom of the pan dry with a paper towel. Return the bones, wings, and backs to the pan, add the water, and bring to a boil, scraping the bottom of the pan to dissolve the meat juices stuck to it. Boil for 10 minutes, or until the liquid has reduced by about half, strain into a clean saucepan, spoon off the fat that surfaces, and reserve.

THE PASTRIES:

On a lightly floured table, roll out the dough into a rectangle about 8 ×
14 inches. Using a saucer 5 inches across as a guide, cut out two
circles with a pointed knife or pastry wheel. Pack the scraps of dough
into a ball and roll them out again into a rectangle the same size as
before. This time, cut about ¼ inch away from the edge of the saucer to
make two circles 5½ inches in diameter.

Brush off any excess flour on the pastries.

Place the two smaller circles on a lightly buttered baking sheet.
With a pastry brush, draw a narrow border of beaten egg around the
rims of the pastries, being careful not to let any egg drip over the edge.
Place half of the stuffing on each circle, spreading it out as much as
possible, but staying inside the ring of egg. Cover the stuffing with the
two larger circles, pressing them down all around the edges so that they
stick to the bottoms. Lightly brush the surface of each finished pastry
with the beaten egg and refrigerate for 25 minutes before baking.

TO COOK AND SERVE:

Preheat the oven to 425° F.

Bake the prepared breasts and pastries for 15 minutes. Remove the
pastries and turn the breasts over and bake 10 minutes more.

Remove the barding fat and skin from the breasts and cut the meat
into thin slices; lightly salt and pepper the meat.

Reheat the sauce; season with salt and pepper as needed.

Cut each pastry in half and place half on each plate. Arrange the
slices of breast meat in front of the cut side of the pastries, and serve
immediately, with the sauce on the side.

NOTE: *An equal weight of salt pork or bacon, placed in cold water,
brought to a boil and drained, may be used to replace either the
fatback, or the barding fat, or both.*

*Two rock Cornish game hens, pheasants, or 1 chicken (3 pounds)
may be used instead of guinea hens. Ed.*

Pintadeau au thé noir
GUINEA HEN POACHED IN TEA

Ingredients for 2 servings:
> 2¼-pound guinea hen *(for substitutions, see Suggestions)*
> 2½ quarts water
> 2 generous tablespoons Ceylon tea
> 1½ teaspoons coarse salt
> 1 large carrot, diced
> 1 large turnip, diced
> 1 cup diced green beans
> ¼ pound peas, shelled
> ⅓ cup *crème fraîche (see p. 331)* or heavy cream
> 1½ teaspoons tea leaves (for the sauce)
> Salt, pepper

UTENSILS:
Large (4-quart) oval pot, with cover
Large mixing bowl
Large pot
Large saucepan
Large frying pan or *sauteuse*
Skimmer or slotted spoon
To serve: Large heated serving platter, or 4 heated dinner plates

THE GUINEA HEN:
Cut the neck and wings off the bird and reserve.

Bring the water to a boil in a large pot. Place the tea in a large mixing bowl, pour the boiling water over it, cover with aluminum foil, and leave to infuse for 10 minutes.

Strain the tea back into the pot used to boil the water, add the coarse salt, and bring to a boil. Add the guinea hen, its neck and wings, cover the pot, and simmer for 25 minutes (11 minutes per pound). Turn the bird over halfway through the cooking time if not completely covered by the tea.

THE VEGETABLES:
Bring a large pot of lightly salted water to a boil, add the carrot, turnip, beans, and peas, and boil for 6 minutes, cool under running water, and drain. Reserve.

THE SAUCE:

Cut off the breasts and legs of the guinea hen, remove the skin, and reserve.

Cut the carcass into 3 to 4 pieces and place it in a saucepan with the skin from the legs and breasts, the neck, and the wings. Add 1½ cups of the cooking liquid and boil rapidly for 4 to 5 minutes, or until the liquid has reduced by half, add the cream, and boil slowly 7 minutes longer.

TO FINISH AND SERVE:

Remove the sauce from the heat. Add 1½ teaspoons of tea leaves, stir, cover the pan, and allow to infuse for 1 minute. Strain the sauce into a large frying pan or *sauteuse*, pressing on the bones and tea to extract as much flavor as possible. Skim off any fat that surfaces, place the vegetables and pieces of guinea hen in the sauce, and heat gently 3 to 4 minutes to warm through.

With a skimmer or slotted spoon, lift the pieces of guinea hen and vegetables out of the pan and place them on a large serving platter or individual dinner plates; taste the sauce, add salt and pepper if needed, spoon over the guinea hen, and serve.

SUGGESTIONS:

A small chicken or an equal weight of veal or pieces of turkey can be cooked and served in the same way.

Tourte de faisan
PHEASANT WITH PEARS AND SPINACH IN A PASTRY SHELL

Ingredients for 2 servings:

  7 ounces (200 g) **puff pastry** (*see p. 271*)
  1 small egg
  1 pheasant, weighing about 1¼ pounds, cleaned (*see Note*)
  Salt, pepper
  ¼ pound chicken necks
  1 teaspoon butter
  2 tablespoons madeira
  ⅔ cup warm water

FOR THE PEARS:

1 teaspoon butter
1 large pear (½ pound), peeled, cored, and cut into 8 wedges
Salt, pepper
½ teaspoon granulated sugar
2 tablespoons cognac
⅓ cup *crème fraîche (see p. 331)* or heavy cream

FOR THE SPINACH:

1 teaspoon butter
½ pound fresh spinach, stems and ribs removed
Salt, pepper

UTENSILS:

Rolling pin
Pastry brush
Baking sheet
Small roasting pan
2 wooden spoons
Cake rack
Cleaver or large knife
Small saucepan, with cover
2 small frying pans, with covers
To serve: 2 heated dinner plates and sauceboat

PRELIMINARY PREPARATIONS:

On a lightly floured table, roll out the dough into a large rectangle about 7 x 14 inches. Using a plate as a guide, cut out two circles 6½ inches wide. With a pastry brush, brush off any excess flour and place the circles of dough on a baking sheet, leaving quite a bit of space between them.

Beat a small egg with a pinch of salt and brush each circle with a little of it—do not allow the egg to drip over the edge of the dough, as this would keep it from rising properly. With the tip of a pointed knife, draw a shallow circle about ½ inch inside the edge of each circle; this will form the pastry's top.

Allow the dough to rest for 15 minutes before baking.

THE MEAT, THE PASTRY AND THE SAUCE:

Preheat the oven to 425° F.

Cut off the neck and end section of each wing of the pheasant. Lightly salt and pepper the bird inside and out.

Heat a teaspoon of butter in a roasting pan; add the chicken wings, the wing tips, and neck of the pheasant, and the pheasant itself. Lay the pheasant on its side and brown for 2 minutes, then, using two wooden spoons, turn the bird over and brown for 2 minutes on the other side.

Place the pheasant, still on its side, in the oven and roast for 6 minutes. Turn the bird to its other side, place the pastry in the oven and bake for 7 minutes. Place the pheasant upright and finish baking the pastry and pheasant for 9 minutes more.

When done, remove the pheasant and pastry from the oven and reduce the oven heat to 350° F. Place the pastries on a cake rack and the pheasant on a cutting board.

Pour any fat from the roasting pan, but keep the wings and necks in it. Cut the leg and breast meat into thin slices, place it on a plate, and cover with aluminum foil.

Use a cleaver or large knife to chop the pheasant bones into large pieces and put them back in the roasting pan. Cook the bones for about 2 minutes over low heat, add the madeira, and boil rapidly until it has completely evaporated. Add the warm water, scraping the bottom of the pan with a wooden spoon, and simmer for 11 minutes. Strain the liquid into a saucepan, taste for salt and pepper, cover, and reserve.

THE PEAR AND SPINACH GARNISH:

Heat a teaspoon of butter in a small frying pan, add the pear wedges in one layer, salt and pepper lightly, sprinkle with the sugar, and lightly brown over moderate heat for about 2 minutes. Add the cognac and boil to evaporate it completely, add the cream, and boil for 2 minutes longer. Cover and keep the pears warm while cooking the spinach.

Melt a teaspoon of butter in another frying pan, add the spinach, salt, and pepper. When the spinach has melted down, cook for 2 minutes, stirring frequently, cover and reserve.

TO SERVE:

Run the tip of a knife around the top of each pastry and lift the tops off carefully. Place the pastries back into a 350° F oven for about 3 minutes to reheat (the pheasant can also be reheated if kept covered with foil—count about 5 minutes).

Reheat the sauce prepared with the pheasant bones and pour it into a sauceboat.

Remove the pastry shells from the oven and place one on each dinner plate. Divide first the spinach, then the pears, between them, placing the pears and their sauce on a bed of spinach inside the pastries. Finish filling the shells with the pheasant—it should form a mound. Place the pastry tops in place and serve with the sauceboat on the side.

NOTE: *Any game bird or rock Cornish game hen may be used instead of pheasant. Roast as described, counting about 16 minutes per pound.*

If preferred, the rectangle of dough can be cut in half to form two squares, rather than circles. Trim all the edges to insure even rising. Ed.

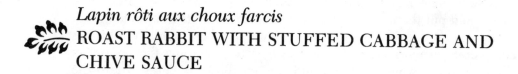

Lapin rôti aux choux farcis
ROAST RABBIT WITH STUFFED CABBAGE AND CHIVE SAUCE

Ingredients for 4 servings:
  4 generous tablespoons finely chopped chives
  3 tablespoons softened butter
  4½-pound rabbit
  12 ounces pig's caul (lace fat—*see Note*)

  FOR THE SAUCE:
  2 teaspoons butter
  1 small carrot, chopped
  1 small onion, chopped
  1 small *bouquet garni*
  8 teaspoons madeira
  2 cups heavy cream

  FOR THE CABBAGE:
  2 teaspoons butter
  2 shallots, finely chopped
  1 medium tomato, peeled and chopped
  2 medium mushrooms, chopped

Salt, pepper
12 whole outer cabbage leaves, unbroken, spines trimmed

4 teaspoons cooking oil (for the rabbit)
2 teaspoons butter (for the cabbages)

UTENSILS:
2 small bowls
Cleaver
Medium high-sided frying pan or *sauteuse*
Small saucepan
Small frying pan
Large saucepan
Oval or rectangular roasting pan, 13 to 14 inches long (for the rabbit)
Oval or rectangular roasting pan 12 inches long (for the cabbages)
Wire Whisk
To serve: Heated serving platter, or 4 heated dinner plates and
   sauceboat

PRELIMINARY PREPARATIONS:
Place the chives and butter in a bowl and beat together with a wooden
spoon, then place in a sieve over a mixing bowl. Rub the chives and
butter through the sieve with the wooden spoon and reserve for
finishing the sauce.
   Cut the rabbit in half just below the rib cage. Cut the bottom half
into three pieces (two legs and the back) and reserve.
   Debone the upper half of the rabbit using a small knife. Save the
bones for making the sauce. Dice the meat and reserve.
   Soak the pig's caul in cold water for 1 hour, drain, and pat dry with a
clean cloth.

THE SAUCE:
Chop the reserved rabbit bones into pieces with a cleaver. Melt 2
teaspoons of butter in a high-sided frying pan or *sauteuse,* add the
bones, and brown over moderate heat for 8 minutes. Add the carrot,
onion, and *bouquet garni*, simmer 5 minutes, add the madeira, and boil
for 5 seconds; stir in the cream. Lower the heat and simmer for 15
minutes. Remove 4 tablespoons of the sauce and reserve for the stuffing,
then cook the remaining sauce for 5 to 10 minutes more, or until there is
about 1 cup of liquid left. Spoon off any fat that surfaces, strain the sauce
into a small saucepan, and reserve.

THE STUFFING:

Melt 2 teaspoons of butter in a small frying pan, add the shallots, and cook for 2 minutes to soften, then add the diced rabbit meat, tomato, mushrooms, and a little salt and pepper. Cook over moderate heat for about 5 minutes, or until all of the liquid given out by the meat and vegetables has evaporated. Add the 4 tablespoons of sauce reserved earlier, bring to a boil, and pour into a bowl to cool before stuffing the cabbage leaves.

THE CABBAGE:

Boil the cabbage leaves in a large saucepan of rapidly boiling salted water for 6 minutes, drain, cool under running water, drain again, and spread the leaves out on a cloth to dry.

Place a quarter of the stuffing in the center of a cabbage leaf and fold in the edges of the leaf to cover it. Place a second leaf over the opening at the top and wrap it around. Finish by enclosing the package in a third leaf, making the cabbage roll as round as possible.

Take between ½ and ⅔ of the pig's caul and cut it into 4 squares. Wrap each stuffed cabbage roll in a square of pig's caul so it will hold its shape and reserve.

TO COOK:

Preheat the oven to 425° F.

Wrap the back and each of the two rabbit legs in a piece of the remaining pig's caul. Heat the cooking oil in the larger roasting pan, add the back and legs, and brown, turning frequently, for about 4 minutes. Roast for 5 minutes.

While the rabbit is roasting, heat 2 teaspoons of butter in the smaller roasting pan and brown the stuffed cabbages over moderate heat for 2 to 3 minutes, turning often. Place in the oven and cook the cabbage and the rabbit for 12 minutes, turning both over after 6 minutes. At the end of the 12 minutes, remove the back from the oven but continue cooking the legs and cabbage 6 minutes more.

TO FINISH THE SAUCE AND SERVE:

Remove the pig's caul from the rabbit and slice all the meat. Place it on a plate with the cabbage, cover with aluminum foil, and keep warm in the oven with the door ajar while finishing the sauce.

Heat the sauce, but do not allow to boil. Taste, add salt and pepper if needed, and whisk the chive butter, little by little, into the sauce.

Either serve the rabbit and cabbages on a serving platter, with the sauce on the side, or place a cabbage on each of 4 dinner plates, arrange the rabbit meat around or next to it, spoon the sauce over the rabbit, and serve.

SUGGESTIONS:
Parsley or tarragon can be mixed with the butter and sieved as described for the chives to make a different sauce. Since tarragon is quite strong, use only half as much.

NOTE: *If pig's caul is unavailable, tie the stuffed cabbages with kitchen string and add 2 tablespoons of lard to the butter in the roasting pan used to cook them. Also add 2 tablespoons of lard to the pan used for the rabbit; baste both the meat and the cabbages as they roast, if lard is used instead of lace fat. Ed.*

Fricassée de lapin à l'estragon et à l'ail
RABBIT WITH TARRAGON AND GARLIC

Ingredients for 4 servings:

FOR THE RABBIT:
4¼-pound rabbit
8 large sprigs fresh tarragon
Salt, pepper
1 tablespoon cooking oil
2 teaspoons butter
¼ cup tarragon-flavored vinegar
4 medium tomatoes, peeled, seeded, and chopped
1½ cups *crème fraîche (see p. 331)* or heavy cream

FOR THE GARLIC:
16 large cloves garlic, unpeeled
1 cup milk
1 tablespoon butter
Salt, pepper
1 teaspoon sugar

UTENSILS:

2 large frying pans, one with cover
Slotted spoon
Small saucepan
Small frying pan
Wire whisk
To serve: Large heated serving platter

PRELIMINARY PREPARATIONS:

Only the back and back legs of the rabbit are used in this recipe. Cut the rabbit in half just below the rib cage (use the top half of the rabbit for stock). Cut the legs from the back. Cut each leg in half at the knee, and cut the back crosswise into 4 pieces.

Remove the leaves from the tarragon stems and reserve.

Tie the stems of the tarragon in a bunch.

THE RABBIT:

Salt and pepper the rabbit generously. Heat the oil in a large frying pan and add the rabbit. When it starts to brown, add the butter, lower the heat, and brown on all sides for about 10 minutes, shaking the pan often to avoid sticking. With a slotted spoon, remove the rabbit from the pan and reserve.

Pour all the fat from the pan and pat it dry with a paper towel. Add the tarragon vinegar, stirring to detach any meat juices stuck to the bottom of the pan, and place over high heat. Boil the vinegar for about 30 seconds, or until it has almost completely evaporated, add the tomatoes and the bunch of tarragon stems, and cooked slowly for 4 minutes. Add the cream, salt, and pepper, then add the rabbit, cover the pan, and simmer for 15 minutes.

THE GARLIC:

Place the cloves of garlic in a saucepan, add the milk, and bring to a boil. Boil gently 4 minutes and drain.

Heat the butter in a small frying pan, add the garlic, salt, pepper, and sugar. Cook over very low heat for 15 minutes, stirring often, to color and caramelize the garlic on all sides without burning.

TO SERVE:

Lift the pieces of rabbit out of the sauce with the slotted spoon and place them on a plate. Measure the sauce; if there is more than 1⅔ cups, boil it to reduce to that amount, then strain it into a clean frying pan. Taste for salt and pepper, then heat the rabbit in the sauce.

Place the rabbit on a serving platter, spoon the sauce over it, and sprinkle with the freshly chopped tarragon. Placed the caramelized cloves of garlic around the rabbit, and serve.

Homemade pasta *(see p. 256)* makes an excellent accompaniment to this dish.

SUGGESTIONS:
Instead of rabbit 2¾ pounds chicken legs and breasts or 1¾ pounds boneless veal (cut into 8 pieces) may be used.

Fresh basil or fennel may be used instead of tarragon; in this case, use ordinary wine vinegar, preferably made from white wine.

Cuissot de marcassin du mendiant
HAUNCH OF VENISON BAKED IN CLAY

(color picture VI)

Ingredients for 6 to 8 servings:
   1 haunch of venison or wild boar, weighing about 3½ pounds
   About ¼ pound pork fatback, for larding (use about 10% of the
      weight of the meat)
   1 large carrot, diced
   2 small onions, diced
   5 shallots, diced
   1 stalk celery, diced
   ½ head of garlic (cut horizontally)
   10 peppercorns
   2 cloves
   8 coriander seeds, coarsely crushed
   6 juniper berries, coarsely crushed
   Bouquet garni (thyme, rosemary, and parsley)
   5 cups red wine
   6 tablespoons wine vinegar
   Salt, pepper
   1 tablespoon cooking oil

FOR THE SAUCE:

6 tablespoons cognac
2 tablespoons madeira
3 medium tomatoes, seeded and chopped

FOR THE HERB BUTTER:

2 tablespoons finely chopped parsley
2 tablespoons finely chopped chives
2 tablespoons finely chopped chervil
½ teaspoon chopped sage
½ teaspoon chopped savory
½ teaspoon chopped rosemary
½ teaspoon chopped thyme
1 bay leaf, broken
6½ tablespoons softened butter

UTENSILS:

Larding needle
Oval enameled cast-iron pot, with cover (about 4-quart capacity)
Small square of muslin
Large bowl
Skimmer or slotted spoon
Wooden mortar and pestle
Parchment paper
Kitchen string
4½ pounds potter's clay
Roasting pan or baking dish
Hammer
To serve: Sauceboat

TO MARINATE:

Three days before cooking, bone the venison and remove the large tendon at the base of the leg. Keep the bones and any scraps of meat.

Cut the fatback into long thin strips and use a larding needle to lard the venison with it.

Place the bones, scraps of meat, and the venison in an enameled cast-iron pot with the carrot, onions, shallots, celery, and garlic. Tie the peppercorns, cloves, coriander seeds, and juniper berries in a square of muslin and place next to the meat. Add the *bouquet garni,* wine, and vinegar, cover the pot, and refrigerate for a total of 72 hours, turning the meat after the first 36 hours.

PRELIMINARY COOKING AND SAUCE:

Several hours before cooking, lift the meat out of the marinade and place it in a colander over a large bowl or platter to drain completely. Strain the marinade; discard the spices in the muslin and the *bouquet garni*, but reserve the liquid and the vegetables for later use.

Preheat the oven to 550° F.

Generously season the venison with salt and pepper.

Heat 1 tablespoon of cooking oil in the pot the meat marinated in. Place the bones in the pot, put the meat on top of them, and spread the vegetables from the marinade around the meat. Roast for 30 minutes to brown the meat, turning it once while roasting. Put the meat on a cutting board to cool.

Place the pot with the vegetables and bones still in it on top of the stove, add the cognac and madeira, and boil for 1 minute, scraping the bottom of the pot to detach the meat juices stuck to it. Add the tomatoes and the strained liquid from the marinade and boil slowly for about 1½ hours, skimming off any foam that surfaces. Strain the sauce into a saucepan and spoon off all the fat that surfaces; there should be 1⅔ cups of sauce remaining. Taste for salt and pepper, and reserve.

THE HERB BUTTER:

Place all the herbs in a mortar and pound to a paste, add the softened butter, and mix it into the herbs with a fork; reserve.

TO BAKE AND SERVE:

Preheat the oven to 425° F.

Spread the herb butter all over the cold venison. Wrap the meat in a large sheet of parchment paper to enclose it completely. Fold up the ends of the paper and tie the package with kitchen string, at the ends and around the middle.

Spread a damp dish towel out on the table. Place the clay in the center of it and press it out with your hands into a circle about ¼ inch thick and large enough to completely cover the venison. Place the venison in the center of the clay and lift the corners of the towel to encase the venison, pressing and smoothing the edges of the clay together to seal them. Use your fingers or a knife blade to smooth out the clay and eliminate any cracks. (*Keep the moist towel wrapped around it until ready to bake. Ed.*) Place the venison in a roasting pan or baking dish. With a skewer or trussing needle, make two holes in the top of the clay (one at each end) to allow steam to escape and bake for 1 hour.

245

When the meat has finished cooking, reheat the sauce and pour it into a sauceboat. Use a hammer to break open the hardened shell of clay and remove the larger pieces. Then cut open the paper and carve the meat, spooning as much of the herb butter as possible over each portion, and pass the sauce.

SUGGESTIONS:
The ideal accompaniments for this dish are **sweet potato purée** *(see p. 254)* and **Turnip darphin** *(see p. 254)*. Prepare the vegetables while the meat is baking in the clay and serve in vegetable dishes.

NOTE: *The sauce may be made and the venison may be roasted and wrapped in clay several hours in advance. Ed.*

Les légumes & accompagnements
VEGETABLES & GARNISHES

Haricots verts Eventhia
STRING BEANS EVENTHIA

Ingredients for 4 servings:
  1¼ pounds thin string beans
  4½ tablespoons olive oil
  3 medium onions, thinly sliced
  3 large tomatoes, peeled, halved, and seeded
  Salt, pepper
  A small sprig thyme

  UTENSILS:
  Large mixing bowl
  Large frying pan, with cover
  To serve: Vegetable dish

  PRELIMINARY PREPARATIONS:
String the beans, wash them in cold water and leave to soak in a large
bowl of cold water for about 5 minutes.

TO COOK AND SERVE:

Heat the olive oil in a large frying pan, add the onions, stir, and cook over low heat for 5 minutes, or until transparent.

Lift the beans out of the cold water with your hand, shake them once over the sink, then add them to the pan (the water remaining on the beans will be enough to cook them). Cook the beans over low heat 5 minutes, then take the tomato halves and squeeze them in your hand over the pan; the water from the tomatoes and their pulp will fall into the pan. Season with salt and pepper, add the thyme, stir, cover, and cook over very low heat for 1 hour (*see Note*).

Remove the thyme and serve in a vegetable dish.

SUGGESTIONS:

Fresh white beans, limas, or any other fresh bean can be cooked this way.

NOTE: *Cooking times will vary depending on the thickness of the beans, so taste from time to time; when done, they should be tender, but still slightly crisp. Ed.*

Gratin d'épinards
SPINACH AU GRATIN

Ingredients for 3 to 4 servings:

FOR THE SPINACH:
2¼ pounds fresh young spinach, stems and ribs removed (*see Note*)
1 tablespoon butter
Salt, pepper

FOR THE MUSHROOMS:
2 teaspoons butter
½ pound mushrooms, sliced
Salt, pepper
3 tablespoons madeira
1 cup *crème fraîche* (*see p. 331*) or heavy cream

½ clove garlic (for the dish)
Melted butter (for the dish)
1 egg yolk

UTENSILS:
2 large frying pans or *sauteuses*
Oval gratin dish, 10 inches long, or round dish 8½ inches in
    diameter
Pastry brush

THE SPINACH:
Heat a tablespoon of butter in a large frying pan or *sauteuse*, add as
much spinach as the pan will hold, stir constantly, and as the spinach
melts down, add more to the pan. When all the spinach has been added
and has melted down, season with salt and pepper and cook over
moderate heat for 4 minutes, stirring frequently. Remove from the heat
and reserve.

THE MUSHROOMS:
Melt 2 teaspoons of butter in a large frying pan and add the
mushrooms, stirring constantly in the beginning to avoid burning.
When the mushrooms begin to give out water, season them lightly with
salt and pepper, and cook for about 2 minutes, or until their water has
evaporated and they have begun to brown. Add the madeira, boil until
it has evaporated, then add the cream, and boil rapidly for 1 minute;
remove the pan from the heat and reserve.

TO SERVE:
Preheat the broiler.
    Rub a gratin dish with the half clove of garlic, then brush it lightly
with melted butter. Reheat the spinach if necessary and cover the
bottom of the dish with it.
    Stir the egg yolk into the mushroom-cream mixture, taste for salt
and pepper, and pour over the spinach, spreading it out so that the
spinach is entirely covered. Place under the broiler for 1 to 2 minutes,
or until the surface has browned, and serve immediately.

SUGGESTIONS:
An equal weight of lettuce or Swiss chard leaves may be prepared as
described for the spinach.
    This dish is excellent with any grilled meat or fish.

NOTE: *If the spinach you buy has thick dark green leaves, rather than small, tender, light green ones, parboil it for 2 minutes in rapidly boiling salted water, drain, cool under cold running water, and press dry in the palms of your hands before preparing it as described. Ed.*

Gratin arlequin
MIXED VEGETABLES AU GRATIN

Ingredients for 4 servings:
> 2 medium potatoes
> 2 medium carrots
> 2 medium turnips
> ½ clove garlic
> Salt, pepper
> 1⅔ cups heavy cream
> 2 cups grated Swiss cheese
> 2 tablespoons butter, broken into pieces

UTENSILS:
Round deep gratin dish, 8½ inches in diameter

TO MAKE AND SERVE:
Preheat the oven to 350° F.

Peel the vegetables and cut them into thin slices. Wash the slices thoroughly and dry them in a towel.

Rub the gratin dish all over with the garlic, then cover the bottom of the dish with about a quarter of the mixed vegetable slices. Season with salt and pepper, add a quarter of the cream, and sprinkle with a quarter of the grated cheese. Make four layers in this manner and top the last layer of cheese with the dabs of butter.

Bake for 25 minutes, lower the temperature to 325° F, and continue baking 30 minutes more, or until the surface of the dish is golden brown. Serve immediately.

Gratin de pommes de terre
POTATOES AU GRATIN

Ingredients for 4 to 5 servings:

2¼ pounds potatoes
1 clove garlic, cut in half
Salt, pepper
1⅔ cups heavy cream
2 cups grated Swiss cheese
2 tablespoons butter, broken into pieces

UTENSILS:
Oval gratin dish, 13 to 14 inches long

TO BAKE AND SERVE:
Preheat the oven to 400° F.

Peel the potatoes and cut them into slices about 1⁄16 inch thick. Wash in cold water, drain, and pat dry in a towel.

Rub the gratin dish with the halves of garlic, then cover the bottom of the dish with about a quarter of the potato slices. Sprinkle with salt and pepper, pour a quarter of the cream over them, and sprinkle with a quarter of the cheese. Make four layers in this manner, dotting the last layer of cheese with the butter.

Bake the potatoes for 20 minutes, then lower the oven to 325° F, and bake 25 minutes more, or until golden brown. Serve immediately.

SUGGESTION:
Try using sliced turnips or celeriac (celery root) instead of potatoes.

Pommes de terre Archestrate
ARCHESTRATE POTATOES

Ingredients for 2 servings:

¾ pound large, starchy potatoes
2 tablespoons butter
Salt, pepper

UTENSILS:

Small frying pan, 9½ inches in diameter (preferably nonstick) or an enameled cast-iron gratin dish

To serve: Heated serving platter

PRELIMINARY PREPARATIONS:

Peel, wash, and dry the potatoes. Slice very thinly, as if making potato chips, and reserve.

Melt the butter in a frying pan or gratin dish, remove the pan from the heat, and tip and turn to coat the bottom evenly with the butter.

TO COOK AND SERVE:

Away from the heat, lay the potato slices in the pan one by one, making a circle around the edge. Place the potatoes so that each slice covers half of the preceding one. Continue making concentric, overlapping circles, until the bottom of the pan is covered, then make a second layer in the same way.

Salt and pepper the top of the potatoes, place the pan over moderate heat, and cook for 2 minutes, then lower the heat and cook 4 minutes longer. Shake the pan gently to avoid sticking. When the bottom potatoes have browned, use a spatula to turn over the "pancake," season again with salt and pepper, and cook 5 minutes, or until the second side has browned. Slide onto a platter and serve (if using a gratin dish, the potatoes may be served in it, if preferred).

Galettes de pommes de terre rapées
POTATO PANCAKES

Ingredients for 2 servings:

    1 pound potatoes
    Salt, pepper
    Nutmeg
    3 tablespoons butter

UTENSILS:
Small saucepan
Vegetable grater
2 blini pans *(see Note)*
Basting brush
To serve: Serving platter

PRELIMINARY PREPARATIONS:
Peel, wash, and dry the potatoes. Grate them coarsely, salt and pepper generously, add a little nutmeg, and cover. Reserve.

Clarify the butter by melting it in a small saucepan and spooning off any foam that surfaces. Reserve.

TO COOK:
Generously butter the blini pans, using a basting brush, and heat over moderate heat until the butter is almost smoking. Add a handful of grated potatoes to each pan, shake the pan for a few seconds to make sure they don't stick, then flatten the pile of potatoes with the back of a spoon to make a pancake a little less than ½ inch thick. With the basting brush, dab a little of the butter over each pancake and cook over moderate heat, shaking the pan often, for 3 minutes, or until the bottom of each pancake has browned. Flip each pancake out onto a plate, browned side up. Lightly brush each pan with a little more butter, then slide the pancakes into them, uncooked side down, and lower the heat. Brown on the second side for 4 to 5 minutes, then slide the pancakes out onto a paper towel to drain for a few seconds. Place them on a platter and keep warm while making the remaining pancakes (there will be 2 to 3 pancakes per person, depending on the thickness).

SUGGESTIONS:
Freshly chopped herbs such as parsley, chives, tarragon, etc., and a few chopped mushrooms may be added to the grated potatoes before cooking.

If desired, one large pancake may be made in a frying pan, preferably nonstick.

NOTE: *Blini pans are small individual frying pans, generally made of iron and about 4 inches in diameter. Ed.*

Darphin de navets
TURNIP DARPHIN

Ingredients for 4 servings:

1¼ pounds turnips
½ pound potatoes
Salt, pepper
6 tablespoons butter

UTENSILS:
Vegetable grater
Mixing bowl
Small saucepan
2 to 4 blini pans (*see Note* to **Potato pancakes,** p. 252)
Basting brush
To serve: Large serving platter

PRELIMINARY PREPARATIONS:
Peel, wash, and dry the turnips and potatoes, then grate them coarsely.
Place them in a mixing bowl, season generously with salt and pepper,
mix well together, and reserve.
Clarify the butter as described for **Potato pancakes** (*see p. 252*).

TO COOK:
Make individual pancakes exactly as described for **Potato pancakes,** but
when cooking the second side, do not lower the heat and cook for only 3
minutes.

SUGGESTION:
Celery root (celeriac) may be used instead of turnips.

Purée de patates douces
SWEET POTATOES PURÉED WITH APPLES
AND BANANAS

Ingredients for 6 to 8 servings:

2 tablespoons butter, in all
1 large apple, peeled, cored, and cut into 8 wedges

2 pinches paprika, in all
1 small banana, sliced

Juice of 1 small orange
Juice of 1 small lemon
1 cup sugar
2 cups water
3¼ pounds sweet potatoes, peeled and diced
3 tablespoons *crème fraîche (see p. 331)* or heavy cream
Salt, pepper

UTENSILS:
Small frying pan
Mixing bowl
Large saucepan, with cover
Food mill or potato masher
Medium saucepan
To serve: Serving dish

THE APPLE AND BANANA:
Melt 1 tablespoon of butter in a small frying pan, add the apple wedges and brown, turning once, for about 4 minutes. Season with paprika, pour into a bowl, and reserve.

Add 1 tablespoon of butter to the pan, brown the slices of banana on both sides for about 4 minutes, season with paprika, and pour into the bowl with the apple. Reserve.

THE SWEET POTATOES:
Place the orange and lemon juices in a large saucepan with the sugar, bring to a boil, and cook for about 13 minutes, or until the sugar has caramelized. Add the water and sweet potatoes, bring to a boil, pressing the sweet potatoes down into the liquid, lower the heat, and cook, covered, stirring occasionally, for 30 to 35 minutes, or until soft.

TO PURÉE AND SERVE:
Using a food mill or potato masher, purée the potatoes and their liquid with the apple and banana. Pour the purée into a saucepan; over very low heat, stir in the cream. Taste for salt and pepper, spoon into a serving dish, and serve.

SUGGESTIONS:
The banana may be omitted.

255

This purée is especially good with game—*see* **Haunch of venison baked in clay** *(see p. 243).*

Pâtes fraîches aux épinards
HOMEMADE SPINACH PASTA

Ingredients for 8 servings as a garnish:

1 pound fresh spinach, ribs and stems removed
3 cups water
2½ cups all-purpose flour
1½ teaspoons salt
2 whole eggs
4 egg yolks
1 tablespoon cooking oil

1 generous tablespoon butter
Salt, pepper

UTENSILS:
Heavy-duty blender or food processor
Saucepan
Small bowl
Large mixing bowl
Mixer with dough hook (optional)
Large, very sharp knife or pasta machine
Broom handle or clean cloth
Large pot
To serve: Serving dish

THE GREEN COLORING:
Place 1 cup of water in a blender or food processor with a third of the spinach and blend to a purée; strain into a saucepan, stirring and pressing on the residue left in the sieve to extract all the liquid. Do the same with the remaining water and spinach.

Bring the spinach liquid to a boil: a thick foam will rise to the surface. Boil for 45 seconds, then strain. There should be about 2 tablespoons of green coloring matter left in the sieve. Place this in a bowl and refrigerate. Discard the liquid.

THE DOUGH:

In a large mixing bowl place the flour, salt, eggs, egg yolks, cooking oil, and green coloring. Mix all the ingredients together, then knead the dough until a smooth, rather stiff dough of a uniform green color is formed. If preferred, the dough can be made using a mixer equipped with a dough hook (run the machine in short bursts).

Form the dough into a ball, cover, and allow to rest for 15 minutes.

CUTTING THE PASTA:

The pasta dough may be cut either by hand or using a pasta machine.

By hand: On a lightly floured surface, roll the dough out into a thin, regular sheet, turning it to insure even rolling. Allow the dough to dry until it feels leathery but the edges are not yet brittle (about 20 to 30 minutes), then roll it up into a sausage and make noodles by cutting the sausage into slices about ¼ inch wide, using a large, very sharp knife.

With a manually operated pasta machine: Divide the ball of dough into 4 pieces. Flatten each piece between the palms of your hands, flour it lightly, and run it through the machine on the widest setting. Run it through the successive settings to number 4 or 5 (do not make the dough *too* thin) and allow the dough to dry for 20 to 30 minutes or until leathery. Insert the crank handle at the proper cutter width and run the dough through to form noodles.

Whether cutting the noodles by hand or with a machine, allow them to dry, either by draping them over a broom handle set between two chairs, or by placing them in loose bunches on a cloth. If the sheets of dough have dried correctly, the noodles will not stick together.

TO COOK AND SERVE:

Bring a large pot of salted water to a boil. Add the noodles and boil for 2 to 3 minutes (they should be cooked "al dente": tender, but firm to the bite). Drain them in a colander, rinse very rapidly under cold water, and drain again.

Place the butter in the pot over very low heat, add the noodles, salt and pepper, and toss to heat the noodles and melt the butter. Serve immediately.

SUGGESTIONS:

A spoonful of truffle juice may be added to the pot with the butter and tossed with the noodles just before serving.

The green coloring may be made with watercress or lettuce instead of spinach. Use 3 bunches of watercress (6 cups leaves) or a pound of lettuce.

Or, if preferred, 2½ tablespoons of carrot juice or mushroom purée may be added instead of the coloring to the ingredients used in making the dough.

Les pâtes à pain & à pâtisserie
BREADS, PASTRY DOUGHS
& BATTERS

Pain
DINNER ROLLS

Ingredients for 8 rolls:

FOR THE STARTER:
⅓ cake (⅕ ounce) compressed baker's yeast or a generous ¼
   teaspoon active dry yeast
6 tablespoons warm water
1 generous tablespoon honey
1 scant cup all-purpose flour
4 teaspoons rye flour
Generous ¼ teaspoon salt

FOR THE DOUGH:
⅔ cake (⅖ ounce) compressed baker's yeast or ¾ teaspoon active dry
   yeast

¾ cup warm water
2½ cups all-purpose flour
2 tablespoons rye flour
¾ teaspoon salt

UTENSILS:
Medium mixing bowl
Large mixing bowl
Electric mixer with dough hook (optional)
Large bowl
Baking sheet
Roasting pan
Very sharp knife or razor blade
Pastry brush
Cake rack

THE STARTER:

The night before making the bread, place the yeast in a medium mixing bowl (if using compressed yeast, break it into small pieces), and add the warm water. Set aside for about 5 minutes, whisking occasionally. When the yeast is completely dissolved, stir in the honey, the two flours, and the salt. Beat vigorously with a wooden spoon to form a smooth sticky dough, then cover the bowl with aluminum foil and leave overnight at room temperature.

THE DOUGH:

The next day, the starter should have doubled in size, and bubbles should have formed on the surface. With a spoon, stir down the starter and form it more or less into a ball in the bottom of the bowl.

In a large mixing bowl, make the dough: dissolve the yeast in the water as described above, then stir in the two flours and the salt. Beat just long enough to mix all the ingredients well together and form a dough. Place the starter in the bowl with the dough.

If using a mixer with a dough hook, beat the dough and starter together about 3 minutes, making sure the two are perfectly mixed.

If kneading by hand, knead for 5 to 7 minutes on a lightly floured table, stretching and folding the dough over on itself to mix and make it perfectly smooth and elastic.

The finished dough should be soft but not sticky. Form it into a ball, flour it lightly, place it in a clean, large bowl, and cover with aluminum foil. Leave in a warm place (about 75° F to 80° F) for about 1½ hours, or until the dough has doubled in size.

TO MAKE AND BAKE THE ROLLS:

Preheat the oven to 425° F.

Lightly grease a baking sheet.

Lightly flour the table, then dump the dough onto it. Punch the dough down, shape it into a ball, and divide it into two equal parts with a sharp knife. Roll each half of the dough into a sausage shape about 2 inches thick and 6 inches long and cut each sausage into 4 pieces. Form each piece into a little oblong roll about 4 inches long, and place them on the baking sheet, leaving at least 2 inches between them. Cover with a towel and leave to rise in a warm place for 15 to 20 minutes, or until the rolls have nearly doubled in size.

Fill a roasting pan half full of water and bring to a boil over high heat; place it in the bottom of the oven (the steam will keep the rolls from drying out and make them brown better).

With a very sharp knife or a razor blade, make 5 shallow slits in the top of each roll, cutting at an angle, and holding the blade at a slight tilt.

Bake the rolls for 6 minutes at 425° F, lower the oven to 400° F, and bake for 25 minutes. With a pastry brush, brush the top of each roll with a little of the water in the roasting pan, then bake for 15 minutes more. Test to see whether the rolls are done: pick one up and with your knuckle tap the bottom of it; if a hollow sound is produced, the rolls are done. If a dull thump is the result, bake them longer. Cool on a cake rack.

SUGGESTIONS:

Caraway rolls: These are made exactly as described, but after slitting the top of the rolls, brush them with a little warm water, and sprinkle each one generously with caraway seeds. Bake as described. Caraway rolls are especially good with Munster cheese.

Pains aux noix et aux raisins
WALNUT AND RAISIN DINNER ROLLS

Ingredients for 5 rolls:

⅓ package (⅕ ounce) compressed baker's yeast or a generous ¼
    teaspoon active dry yeast
½ cup lukewarm milk
1½ tablespoons granulated sugar
½ egg, beaten
1¾ cups all-purpose flour
¾ teaspoon salt
2 tablespoons melted butter
⅓ cup golden raisins
¼ cup dried currants
Scant ½ cup walnut meats

UTENSILS:
2 mixing bowls
Wire whisk
Wooden spoon or electric mixer with dough hook
Baking sheet
Very sharp knife
To serve: Bread basket

THE DOUGH:
Place the yeast in a mixing bowl (if using compressed yeast, break it
into small pieces). Whisk in the warm milk, leave for about 15 minutes,
then whisk again. When the yeast has completely dissolved, whisk in
the sugar. Add the beaten egg, stirring it in with a wooden spoon, then
stir in the flour and salt.

Knead the dough, either by hand or using a mixer equipped with a
dough hook, for 4 to 5 minutes, or until it forms a ball, then knead in
the melted butter. When the butter has been mixed in, knead in the
raisins, currants, and nuts.

Place the finished dough in a mixing bowl and cover with aluminum
foil. Put it in a warm place (in an oven with the pilot light on, for
example) to rise for 1½ to 2½ hours, or until doubled in size. With
lightly floured hands, punch the dough down, form it once again into a
ball, cover with foil, and refrigerate for 35 minutes.

TO MAKE AND BAKE THE ROLLS:

Preheat the oven to 400° F.

Lightly grease a baking sheet.

On a lightly floured table, roll the dough out into a sausage about 2 inches thick. Cut the dough into 5 equal pieces, then roll each piece into a ball between the palms of your hands.

Place the rolls on the baking sheet with plenty of space between them. Leave them in a warm place for 30 to 45 minutes, or until doubled in size.

With a very sharp knife, slit the top of each roll, then immediately place the baking sheet in the oven. Bake for 10 minutes at 400° F, lower the oven to 350° F, and bake for 25 minutes more.

When done, place the rolls in a basket until ready to serve.

Walnut and raisin dinner rolls are delicious with cheese, especially goat cheeses.

Brioche fine
BRIOCHE

Ingredients for 1 brioche, serving 4 to 6:

FOR THE YEAST STARTER:

½ package compressed baker's yeast or ½ teaspoon active dry yeast
2 tablespoons warm milk
4½ tablespoons all-purpose flour

FOR THE DOUGH:

1 generous cup all-purpose flour
2 tablespoons granulated sugar
½ teaspoon salt
2 eggs
¼ pound softened butter, broken into pieces
1 egg beaten with a pinch of salt (to brush on brioche)

UTENSILS:

1 bowl
2 large mixing bowls
Mixer with dough hook
Mold (1-quart capacity, *see Note* for types of molds)
Pastry brush
Trussing needle or metal cake tester
Cake rack

THE YEAST STARTER:

Place the yeast in a small bowl (if using compressed yeast, break it into small pieces) and stir in the warm milk. Allow to sit for 5 to 10 minutes, then whisk. When the yeast has completely dissolved, stir in the flour, mix until perfectly smooth. Form the dough into a mound in the bottom of the bowl, cover with aluminum foil, and set in a warm place (75° to 80° F) to rise for about 20 minutes; the dough should double in size.

THE DOUGH:

In a large mixing bowl, place the flour, sugar, salt, and eggs. Mix together with a wooden spoon, then beat the dough vigorously for 1 to 2 minutes, or until it forms a ball around the spoon. Replace the spoon with a mixer equipped with a dough hook and continue beating the dough for 3 to 5 minutes, or until smooth. Add the yeast starter and beat for 2 minutes, or until it has been completely incorporated. Beat in the butter piece by piece; it should take about 3 to 4 minutes to add all the butter and mix it completely with the dough, which will have become very creamy.

Place the dough in a clean large bowl and cover with a thick folded towel or aluminum foil. Place in a warm place for 2½ to 4 hours, or until the dough has doubled in volume (the rising time varies greatly depending on the yeast; fresh yeast tends to act more quickly than dry activated yeast).

When the dough has finished rising, beat it down with a wooden spoon, cover once again, and refrigerate it for 2 to 2½ hours. At the end of this time, it should be rounded on top. Punch it down with your hands and either proceed to mold and bake it, or cover and refrigerate overnight.

TO MOLD, BAKE, AND SERVE:
Press the dough into a lightly buttered brioche mold (if you have left the dough overnight, work it with your hands to warm it up a bit before placing it in the mold). The mold should be about half filled.

Leave the dough to rise in a warm place for about 2½ hours, or until it has risen about ¾ inch above the top of the mold.

Preheat the oven to 400° F.

When the dough has finished rising, paint the top with the beaten egg, using a pastry brush.

Bake for 8 minutes, lower the oven to 375° F, and bake for 35 to 40 minutes more, or until the brioche is a rich golden brown and a trussing needle or metal cake tester plunged into the center comes out clean and hot. (If the top darkens too much while the brioche is baking, cover it with aluminum foil.)

Turn the brioche out onto a cake rack as soon as it comes from the oven. Serve it either warm or cool, or cut it into slices, toast them, and serve with stewed fruit or a fruit salad.

SUGGESTIONS:
A few chopped candied fruits may be added to the dough before adding the butter.

NOTE: *A brioche may be molded to almost any shape. A cylindrical brioche* (brioche mousseline) *is made in a cylindrical mold—a 1-quart can is a good substitute for a* mousseline *mold. This shape is used when making a brioche for the* **Hot guava** *or* **apple charlottes** *(see p. 306 or p. 309).*

A bread pan may also be used. The brioche will be prettier if the dough is divided into four or six pieces, each piece rolled into a ball, and the balls laid in the mold next to each other.

A Parisian brioche is made in a round, ribbed brioche mold. Divide the dough into two pieces, one about 3 times the size of the other. Roll each one into a ball. Place the large one in the mold and make an indentation in the center. Set the small ball into the depression. This is the brioche most often seen in French pastry shops. Ed.

Pâte à beignets (principe et suggestions)
FRITTER BATTER AND BASIC DEEP-FRYING TECHNIQUE

Ingredients for 4 servings of fritters *(see Suggestions)*:

¼ package compressed baker's yeast or ¼ teaspoon active dry yeast
1 cup beer
¾ teaspoon salt
1½ cups all-purpose flour, measured and then sifted

Cooking oil

UTENSILS:
Mixing bowl
Wire whisk
Large pot or deep fryer
Deep-frying thermometer
Fork
Skimmer or slotted spoon
Salt shaker or sugar dredger
To serve: Serving platter

THE BATTER:

In a mixing bowl, dissolve the yeast in 2 tablespoons of beer, (if using compressed yeast, crumble it into small pieces) then whisk in the rest of the beer and add the salt. Add the sifted flour all at once, whisking rapidly to dissolve it and to make a smooth batter. Cover the bowl and set aside at room temperature for at least 3 hours.

PRELIMINARY PREPARATIONS:

Half fill a large pot or deep fryer with cooking oil. Heat it to 375° F (this should take about 15 minutes).

Line a large flat platter with several thicknesses of paper towel for draining the fried food.

Have ready a fork for dipping the food into the batter, a skimmer or slotted spoon, a serving platter, and a salt shaker or sugar dredger.

Pat the food to be fried with a towel to remove any excess moisture.

COOKING:

When the oil is hot, drop the pieces of food into the fritter batter; make sure they are completely coated. One by one, lift the pieces out of the batter with the fork and drop them into the hot oil. (Fritters must be dropped into the oil one at a time, or they will stick together in a huge mass.) Depending on the size of the pot, and the size of the fritters, anywhere from about 8 to 20 fritters may be fried at a time. Do not crowd them; if the fritters must be cooked in several batches, preheat the oven to 250° F and keep the finished ones hot while cooking the rest.

When the fritters are golden brown on one side, turn them over using the fork, the skimmer or slotted spoon; it generally takes about 2 to 3 minutes to brown each side. If they brown much faster than this, lower the heat—the oil is getting too hot. If it takes much longer, raise the heat—the oil is not hot enough and the fritters may be greasy.

When the fritters are nicely browned on each side, lift them out of the oil with the skimmer or slotted spoon and drain them on the paper towels. Place them on a serving platter and sprinkle with salt (meat or fish fritters) or sugar (fruit fritters).

SUGGESTIONS:
The following suggestions for meat, fish, or fruit fritters are for 4 servings:

MEAT OR FISH:
1 to 1½ pounds of calf's or lamb's brains, or fish fillets, cut into 1-inch cubes
20 to 24 sea scallops, or 1½ pounds bay scallops, left whole

FRUIT:
About 1 pound pears or apples, peeled, cored, and cut into wedges or slices, or bananas, sliced
About 2 pounds melon or pineapple, peeled, seeded or cored, and cut into wedges or slices
About 1 pint strawberries, hulled and left whole

NOTE: *Oil used for deep frying may be used several times if strained and stored, covered, in a glass jar. It should be discarded when it begins to turn dark (slightly brownish).*

The same oil may be used for frying meat or fruit, but oil used for fish should be used for fish only. Ed.

♠♠♠ *Biscuit à la cuillère*
LADYFINGER PASTRY FOR CHARLOTTES

Ingredients for lining a 6¼-inch charlotte mold:

    3 egg yolks
    4½ tablespoons granulated sugar, in all
    3 egg whites
    6 tablespoons all-purpose flour, sifted (measure before sifting)

    UTENSILS:
Mixing bowl
Wire whisk
Wooden spatula
Baking sheet
Flexible rubber scraper
Flexible-blade metal spatula
Large cake rack
6¼-inch charlotte mold

    THE BATTER:
In a mixing bowl, whisk the egg yolks and 1½ tablespoons of sugar together until the mixture is smooth and has lightened in color.

    In another bowl, beat the egg whites until firm but not stiff, add 3 tablespoons of sugar, and continue beating until very stiff. Using a wooden spatula, fold ¼ of the egg whites into the egg yolk mixture, then fold in the remaining egg whites. When smooth, fold in the sifted flour; the finished batter should be perfectly smooth and creamy.

    TO BAKE:
Preheat the oven to 400° F. Lightly butter and flour a baking sheet.

    With the handle of the wooden spatula, draw a rectangle 7½ inches × 13½ inches in the center of the baking sheet.

    Scrape the batter from the bowl into the center of the rectangle using a flexible rubber scraper. With a flexible-blade metal spatula, spread the batter out so that it fills the rectangle and smooth the surface.

    Bake for 15 to 20 minutes, or until the top is golden brown and it begins to resist when pressed lightly.

    Remove the pastry and detach it from the baking sheet by sliding the flexible-blade metal spatula under it. Slide it onto a cake rack and allow to cool completely.

TO CUT:

When cool, place the pastry on a table. Set a 6¼-inch charlotte mold on it at one corner, as close to the edge as possible. With a sharp knife, cut out a circle, using the bottom of the mold as a guide.

Cut the rest of the pastry into straight bands about 1 inch wide, then cut each band in half crosswise; you should have 14 bands measuring about 1 × 3½ inches each (plus a few left-over ends).

When making a charlotte, the circle and bands are used to line the mold, with the top-crust sides touching the mold.

NOTE: *This method of baking and cutting the pastry is much easier than the traditional method of making individual ladyfingers with a pastry bag; it also makes lining the bottom of the mold very simple. Ed.*

Pâte sablée amandine
SWEET SHORT PASTRY WITH ALMONDS

Ingredients for 10½ ounces dough (for an 8-inch tart):
  1 scant cup all-purpose flour
  ⅓ cup ground blanched almonds
  5 tablespoons butter, softened and broken into pieces
  ½ a beaten egg
  ⅓ cup granulated sugar, or ½ cup confectioner's sugar
  ¼ teaspoon vanilla extract

UTENSILS:
Food processor (optional)
2 bowls
Wire whisk

TO MAKE THE DOUGH WITH A FOOD PROCESSOR:

In the bowl of the processor, place the flour, almonds, and butter. Using the chopping blade, run the machine for 3 minutes.

In a bowl, beat the egg with the sugar and vanilla until the mixture becomes very pale. Add this to the contents of the processor and run the machine for 2 minutes more.

Remove the dough from the processor, pack it into a ball, place in a bowl, cover with a folded dish towel, and refrigerate for at least 2 hours before using as described in specific recipes.

TO MAKE THE DOUGH BY HAND:

In a bowl, beat the egg with the sugar and vanilla until the mixture becomes very pale.

Place the flour and almonds in a bowl or on the table, mix together, and make a well in the center. Place the bits of butter on the flour and place the egg mixture in the well. Rapidly mix everything together with a pinching motion.

When all the ingredients have been more or less mixed together, fraiser *the dough: with the heel of your hand, push bits of the dough against the table and away from you. When all the dough has been crushed in this way, scrape it off the table with a rigid plastic scraper, pack all the pieces loosely together, and* fraiser *once more, bit by bit.*

Pack the finished dough into a smooth ball, place in a bowl, cover with a folded dish towel, and place in the refrigerator for at least 2 hours before using. Ed.

COMMENT:

This dough is very fragile. Rather then rolling it out, the ball of dough may be flattened with your hand, placed in the mold or pie pan, and pressed in with your fingers.

The dough becomes very hard in the refrigerator, so it is best to leave it at room temperature for about 15 minutes before using it.

Pâte feuilletée
PUFF PASTRY

Ingredients for 21 ounces (600 g) puff pastry:

1¾ cups flour *(see Comment)*
¾ teaspoon salt
2½ tablespoons softened butter, broken into small pieces
½ cup cold water
½ pound minus 2 tablespoons chilled butter

Ingredients for 42 ounces (1200 g) puff pastry:

3⅝ cups flour *(see Comment)*
1½ teaspoons salt
5 tablespoons softened butter, broken into small pieces
1 cup cold water
¾ pound plus 4 tablespoons chilled butter

COMMENT: *Although any flour may be used in making puff pastry, a mixture of 3 parts all-purpose flour to 1 part cake flour gives the best results. Ed.*

UTENSILS:
Bowl
Sharp knife
Food processor (optional)
Plastic wrap
Rolling pin
Pastry brush

MAKING THE DOUGH:
By hand:
Place the flour in a bowl or on a table and sprinkle with the salt. Dot the pieces of softened butter over the flour, make a well in the center of the flour, and pour in the water. With a finger, stir the water around in the well, adding the flour little by little, knocking it into the well with the other hand, until a mixture the consistency of a thin paste has been formed. Incorporate the rest of the flour and the butter all at once with a pinching motion, using both hands. Although the dough should not be worked too long, it should be the same consistency throughout. If

271

working on a table top, the dough may be worked and chopped with a plastic scraper.

Form the dough into a ball, flatten it slightly with your hand, slit the top in a large crisscross pattern with the tip of a sharp knife, place the dough in a plastic bag, and leave in the refrigerator for at least 2 hours.

In a food processor:

Place the flour in the processor bowl, add the salt, and sprinkle in the pieces of softened butter. Run the processor for 45 seconds, then add the water through the opening in the top; continue running the machine for 1 minute more, or until the dough has formed itself into a ball. Do not run the machine too long, or the dough will become elastic and hard to work.

Form the dough into a ball, slit it, and chill it as described above.

ROLLING OUT THE PASTRY:

Place the chilled butter between two sheets of plastic wrap and hit it a few times with a rolling pin. Then continue flattening it with the palm of your hand until it forms a square or rectangle ½ to ¾ inch thick.

Lightly flour the table. Roll out the chilled dough into a square roughly twice the size of the square of butter. The center of the square of dough should be considerably thicker than the edges.

With a pastry brush, brush any excess flour off the surface of the dough. Place the butter in the center of the dough and fold 2 sides of the dough over it; the dough should overlap in the center. Brush off any flour, then fold the other 2 sides of the dough over the butter, pressing them down; they should overlap as well.

Lift the package of dough off the table. Lightly flour the table, as well as the bottom and top of the dough, then place it back on the table with the fold perpendicular to you and the open end of the envelope to your right. Puff pastry should always be rolled in the direction of the fold, never across it, while giving it its "turns."

Place the rolling pin in the center of the block of dough and roll away from you. Lift the rolling pin up, place it back in the center, and roll away from you again. Replace the rolling pin in the center. This time roll toward you. Repeat this motion and continue in this way, always placing the rolling pin in the center of the dough and rolling either away from or toward you until you have a long band of dough a little less than ½ inch thick. It should be slightly thicker in the center than at the ends. Periodically lift it up to make sure it is not sticking to the table, flour the table and dough lightly, and continue.

When the dough is the right thickness, brush off any excess flour. Fold the top end of the rectangle toward you, leaving the bottom third of the dough exposed. Brush it off, then fold the bottom end over, covering the first flap. Brush it off again. You have just given the dough its first "turn."

Give the dough a quarter of a turn so that the fold is again perpendicular to you, and give it a second turn, exactly as you did the first.

Place the folded dough on a plate, cover with aluminum foil or plastic wrap, and refrigerate for at least 30 minutes.

Give the dough 2 more turns as described above, chill for 30 minutes, then give it 2 final turns, for a total of 6 turns. After a final rest of 30 minutes, it is ready to be rolled out and cut into the desired shapes.

Once the dough has been cut, allow it to rest for at least 15 minutes before baking it.

NOTE: *The recipes in this book call for either 7, 9, or 10½ ounces (200, 250, or 300 grams) of the dough, to be cut into various shapes. The metric measurements are helpful here because the mathematical relationship between the various weights is more obvious. So if you have made 21 ounces (600 g) of dough, and need 10½ ounces (300 g) for a recipe, you should use half of the dough you have made; if you made 42 ounces (1200 g) you need a quarter of it. The other proportions are: 7 ounces (200 g) is ⅓ (or ⅙) of the total; 9 ounces (250 g) is halfway between ⅓ and ½ (or ⅙ and ¼), respectively.*

Puff pastry freezes very well, which is why the recipe given here is for making larger amounts than are ever called for at one time. Cut the dough into sections of the desired weights, depending on the recipes you intend to try eventually. Then either roll out and cut each section into the desired shapes, place flat in freezer bags (or in one bag in several layers separated by sheets of plastic) and freeze; or simply put each section in a plastic bag and freeze. In the second case, remove the dough from the freezer and place in the refrigerator for 24 hours before cutting. If using puff pastry that was cut before being frozen, it may be placed directly in the oven or thawed for 15 to 20 minutes before baking. If placing directly in the oven, count 1 to 2 minutes extra cooking time.

When rolling out the dough prior to cutting it, do not hesitate to roll in any direction, or to fold the dough if necessary; each recipe gives directions on how to roll out and cut the pastry.

When actually cutting the shapes, two things must be remembered: (1) puff pastry will not rise properly unless the edges are cut, and (2) use a large, very sharp knife; never drag it through the dough to cut it, but press down straight or use a slight rocking motion. If cutting around a saucer to obtain a circle, cut with the tip of the knife, using an up and down sawing motion.

Once the shapes are cut, turn them upside down so that the fold in the dough will be on the bottom; this is to insure even rising.

Puff pastry should always be kept in the refrigerator unless actually being rolled out, because if it becomes too warm the butter softens and breaks through the dough. For this reason, it is always best to work in a cool kitchen; do not even attempt to make puff pastry if the room temperature is above 80° F, and if it is above 70°, don't be surprised if it is a little difficult to work with.

If, for one reason or another, the butter does break through the dough, don't panic. Simply flour the broken place copiously and place the dough in the refrigerator to chill for about 15 minutes before continuing. Scrape the table (or rolling pin) clean, flour lightly, and continue rolling the dough out. The best way to avoid accidents is to check the bottom of the dough often, and flour the table any time it seems necessary. As long as the dough slides slightly on the table as it is being rolled out, there is no problem. Check it immediately if it stops moving.

Puff pastry will keep for about 4 days in the refrigerator, tightly wrapped in aluminum foil. Any scraps should be saved and packed into a ball; when rolled out, the dough will still rise, and is excellent for making **Palmiers** (see p. 326) or tart bottoms. Ed.

Les desserts

DESSERTS

Salade de fruits éxotiques
TROPICAL FRUIT SALAD

Ingredients for 6 to 8 servings:

FOR THE SYRUP:

1 clove
½ teaspoon Chinese five-spice mixture
Zest of 2 limes
Zest of 2 oranges
Zest of ½ lemon
1½ vanilla beans, split in half lengthwise
1½ bulbs fresh lemongrass (citronella), diced (*see Note*)
1 teaspoon chopped fresh ginger
3 coriander seeds
¾ cup granulated sugar
4 cups water

FOR THE SALAD:

1 ripe mango
12 ripe (wrinkled) passion fruits
3 large or 6 small kiwi fruits, peeled and sliced
½ ripe fresh pineapple, cut into chunks
Leaves from a large sprig of mint, cut into thin strips

UTENSILS:
Large saucepan
To serve: Large serving bowl

THE SYRUP:
Place all the ingredients for the syrup in a large saucepan. Bring to a rolling boil, immediately remove from the heat, and allow to cool completely.

THE FRUIT SALAD:
With a knife, peel the mango, cut the pulp off of the seed, dice it, and place in a serving bowl. Cut the passion fruits in half and scoop the seeds and pulp into the bowl with the mango. Add the sliced kiwis and pineapple chunks, strain the cold syrup over the fruit, and chill for at least 2 hours.

At the last minute, sprinkle with the strips of mint and serve.

NOTE: *In general, the ingredients used in this salad can be found in specialty shops dealing in products from Southeast Asia.*

Lemongrass (citronella) is a pale green aromatic grass with reedy leaves about a foot long growing from a bulbous base. It is often sold dried, but for this recipe it is preferable to buy it fresh. The term "bulb" used in the ingredient list refers to the whole plant (bulb and leaves). Ed.

Poires fraîches pochées au cassis
PEARS POACHED WITH BLACK CURRANTS

Ingredients for 4 servings:
   4 large or 8 small pears (2 pounds)
   ½ lemon
   10½ ounces (1½ cups) black currants in light syrup, drained
   3¼ cups water
   1¾ cups granulated sugar
   ½ vanilla bean, split in half
   3 tablespoons crème de cassis (*see Note*)

UTENSILS:
Spoon, melon-ball cutter, or apple corer
Blender
Fine sieve
Large saucepan
To serve: Large serving bowl

THE PEARS:
Peel the pears. If large, cut them in half and scoop out the core with a spoon or melon-ball cutter. If small, core them with an apple corer and leave whole. Rub the pears with ½ lemon to prevent discoloration.

THE BLACK CURRANTS:
Set aside half of the black currants for later use.

Place those remaining in a blender with 6 tablespoons of their syrup and blend to a purée. Strain the purée into a large saucepan, rubbing on the seeds and skins with a wooden spoon to extract all the juice.

TO COOK AND SERVE:
Add the water, sugar, vanilla bean, and crème de cassis to the black currant purée and bring to a boil, stirring until the sugar is dissolved. Add the pears, bring back almost to a boil, lower the heat, and simmer for 12 minutes. Add the reserved black currants and cook for 5 minutes more, pour into a large serving bowl, and allow to cool.

Chill in the refrigerator for at least 2 hours before serving.

SUGGESTION:
If desired, vanilla ice cream can be served at the same time as the pears.

NOTE: *Crème de cassis is a sweet black currant liqueur (not the syrup). A specialty of Dijon, it can be found in most liquor stores. Ed.*

Ananas Eventhia
PINEAPPLE EVENTHIA

Ingredients for 4 servings:

    1 ripe pineapple, weighing about 2 pounds
    ¾ cup raspberries
    ½ cup *crème fraîche (see p. 331)*, chilled
    2 tablespoons confectioner's sugar
    8 small or 4 regular scoops of rum-flavored ice cream (about 1 pint)
    1 pint strawberries

UTENSILS:
Blender or food processor
Fine sieve
Large mixing bowl, chilled
Wire whisk
Pastry bag with a star-shaped nozzle
To serve: 4 dessert plates

THE PINEAPPLE:

Cut the pineapple into quarters lengthwise. Remove the core on each piece and cut the pulp off the skin; be careful not to damage the skins, as they will be used to serve the dessert.

Dice the pineapple pulp, place it on a plate, and chill it in the freezer while making the raspberry cream *(see Note)*.

THE RASPBERRY CREAM:

Purée the raspberries in a blender or food processor, then work the purée through a sieve to eliminate all the seeds.

Place the cold *crème fraîche* in a chilled mixing bowl, add the confectioner's sugar and the strained raspberry purée, and whisk until the cream stands in peaks.

TO SERVE:

Place each pineapple skin on a plate. Spoon some of the diced pineapple onto each one, top each with 2 small or 1 large scoop of ice cream, and place the remaining pieces of pineapple and the strawberries over and around the ice cream. Using a pastry bag, decorate with a ribbon of the raspberry cream. Serve immediately.

NOTE: *The pineapple can be prepared up to several hours in advance. In this case, place the diced pulp in the refrigerator, not in the freezer.*

If you do not have a pastry bag, the raspberry cream can simply be served in a sauceboat on the side. Ed.

Mousse au citron et aux cerises flambées
LEMON MOUSSE WITH FLAMING CHERRIES

Ingredients for 6 individual mousses:
   Zest of 3 lemons, finely chopped
   2 tablespoons granulated sugar
   ⅔ cup dry white wine
   1½ tablespoons lemon juice

   1 tablespoon unflavored gelatin
   3 tablespoons cold water
   3 generous tablespoons lemon jelly
   7 eggs, separated
   1 tablespoon granulated sugar (for the egg whites)

   48 canned or stewed cherries
   3 tablespoons cherry syrup
   2 tablespoons granulated sugar (for the cherries)
   6 tablespoons kirsch

   UTENSILS:
   Saucepan
   2 mixing bowls
   Wire whisk or electric mixer
   Frying pan
   To serve: 6 dessert dishes, or individual soufflé molds (about 1-cup capacity)

   THE MOUSSES:
Place the chopped lemon zest in a saucepan with the sugar, wine, and lemon juice. Bring to a boil, lower the heat, and simmer slowly for 10 minutes.

Moisten the gelatin with the water.

Remove the lemon mixture from the heat and beat in the gelatin and lemon jelly.

Lightly beat the egg yolks in a mixing bowl, then pour the contents of the saucepan onto them, beating constantly. Continue beating for about 5 minutes; the mixture should cool and thicken.

Beat the egg whites until very stiff; halfway through, add the sugar. With a wooden spatula, fold a quarter of the egg whites into the cooled lemon mixture, then fold in the remaining whites; the final mixture should be perfectly smooth.

Divide the mousse among the dessert dishes or soufflé molds and refrigerate for at least 2 hours before serving.

TO SERVE:

The mousses may either be turned out (dip each mold in boiling water for a few seconds) or served in the dishes or molds.

In a frying pan, place the cherries and their syrup. Bring the liquid to a boil, add the sugar, and continue cooking until the cherries caramelize slightly. Add the kirsch and light with a match, pour the cherries over the mousses, and serve immediately.

SUGGESTION:

Orange mousses may be made in the same way, using oranges, orange juice, and orange jelly.

NOTE: *If making orange mousses, use the zest of 1½ oranges; the other measurements remain the same. Ed.*

Mousse au caramel
CARAMEL MOUSSE

Ingredients for 4 servings:
    ⅔ cup granulated sugar
    1 teaspoon lemon juice
    1½ tablespoons water
    2 eggs, separated

Scant ½ teaspoon unflavored gelatin
1½ teaspoons cold water
1⅓ cups heavy cream, whipped until stiff
Few drops lemon juice (for the egg whites)

UTENSILS:
Small saucepan
2 mixing bowls
Wire whisk or electric mixer
To serve: Serving dish, or 4 individual dessert dishes

THE CARAMEL:
In a saucepan, place the sugar, lemon juice and 1½ tablespoons of water. Bring to a boil and cook over low heat for 10 to 15 minutes, or until the syrup is a pale golden color. Swirl the pan to obtain even coloring and watch very carefully that it doesn't darken too much.

Place the egg yolks in a mixing bowl and beat them lightly.

Moisten the gelatin with 1½ teaspoons of cold water.

When the caramel is ready, remove the pan from the heat and wait a few seconds for it to stop bubbling. Then, beating the egg yolks vigorously with a whisk or electric mixer, pour the hot caramel onto them in a very thin, steady stream; a thick, creamy mixture should form. As soon as all the caramel has been added, add the gelatin. Continue beating for another 5 minutes, or until the mixture has cooled completely.

TO FINISH AND SERVE:
Using a wooden spatula, fold the whipped cream into the caramel mixture. When perfectly mixed, add a few drops of lemon juice to the egg whites, beat until very stiff, and fold them into the mixture; the final mixture should be perfectly smooth.

Pour the mousse into a large serving dish or 4 individual dishes and refrigerate for several hours before serving.

SUGGESTIONS:
One-third cup chopped almonds, walnuts, or hazelnuts may be beaten into the caramel after the gelatin has been added.

🔥 *Mousse au chocolat*
CHOCOLATE MOUSSE

Ingredients for 4 servings:
 6 ounces semisweet chocolate
 2 teaspoons softened butter, broken into small pieces
 6 tablespoons *crème fraîche (see p. 331)* or heavy cream
 1 teaspoon curaçao *(see Suggestions)*
 3 egg yolks
 4 tablespoons granulated sugar, in all
 4 egg whites
 Few drops lemon juice (for the egg whites)

UTENSILS:
Large double boiler
Mixing bowl
Wire whisk or electric mixer
To serve: Serving dish

THE CHOCOLATE:
Melt the chocolate in a large double boiler. Check from time to time to make sure that the water in the bottom of the double boiler never boils (remove from the heat if necessary).

When the chocolate has melted, stir it with a wooden spoon to make it perfectly smooth. Stir in the butter, a piece at a time. Stir in the cream little by little, then add the curaçao. The mixture should be smooth and creamy. Remove the chocolate from the heat, stir in the egg yolks and 2 tablespoons of sugar, and allow to cool until no longer warm to the touch.

TO MAKE THE MOUSSE AND SERVE:
In a mixing bowl, place the egg whites and lemon juice. Beat until very stiff, then fold in 2 tablespoons of sugar. Fold a quarter of the egg whites into the chocolate, then fold in the rest; the finished mixture should be perfectly smooth and of an even color.

Pour the mousse into a serving dish and chill for 1 to 2 hours before serving *(see Comment)*.

SUGGESTIONS:

Scotch, bourbon or other liquors may be used instead of curaçao to flavor the mousse.

One half cup chopped walnuts may be folded into the mousse with the egg whites, if desired.

COMMENT:

This mousse should be eaten the day it is made. If keeping it for more than 12 hours, cook all of the sugar to the soft-ball stage (239° F). Pour it onto the stiffly beaten egg whites, beating vigorously as you do so. Then fold the egg whites into the chocolate as described (in this case, no sugar is added to the chocolate).

Poires Colette Dufour
STUFFED PEARS COLETTE DUFOUR

Ingredients for 4 servings:

FOR THE PEARS:
4 small pears
½ lemon
2 quarts water
½ vanilla bean, cut in half lengthwise
¾ cup granulated sugar

FOR THE STUFFING:
¾ cup walnut meats
3 tablespoons light brown sugar

FOR THE SAUCE:
⅔ cup milk
⅓ cup granulated sugar
¼ cup unsweetened cocoa powder
1½ tablespoons softened butter, broken into pieces

4 scoops pistachio ice cream

UTENSILS:

Apple corer
Large saucepan
Blender or food processor
Small saucepan
Wire whisk
Ice cream scoop
To serve: 4 chilled dessert plates and sauceboat

PRELIMINARY PREPARATIONS:

The pears must be poached and allowed to cool completely before stuffing. It is best to poach the pears a day ahead of time; otherwise allow at least 3 hours for them to cool.

Peel the pears and rub each one with the half lemon to avoid discoloration. Use an apple corer to remove the central cores. Place the water, vanilla bean, and sugar in a large saucepan and bring to a boil, stirring to dissolve the sugar. Add the pears, lower the heat, and simmer 15 minutes. Remove from the heat and leave the pears to cool completely in their cooking liquid.

STUFFING THE PEARS:

Place the walnut meats and sugar in a blender or food processor and blend to a paste.

Remove the pears from their liquid and drain completely on a cloth or towel. Place them upright on a large plate and carefully fill each one with walnut paste, pushing in as much of the paste as possible without breaking the pear. Place the stuffed pears in the freezer while making the chocolate sauce (*see Note*).

THE CHOCOLATE SAUCE:

Heat the milk, sugar, and cocoa powder in a saucepan until boiling, whisking constantly, then whisk in the butter. Remove the pan from the heat and stir with a spoon for a minute or two, then pour the sauce into a sauceboat.

TO SERVE:

Place a scoop of pistachio ice cream on each chilled dessert plate. Make a depression in the center of each one, stand the pears upright in the ice cream, and serve with the chocolate sauce on the side.

NOTE: *The pears can be stuffed up to several hours in advance. If prepared more than ½ hour in advance, reserve them in the refrigerator, not in the freezer. Ed.*

Poires pochées, crème au gingembre
PEARS WITH GINGER CREAM AND CHOCOLATE MOUSSE

Ingredients for 4 servings:

FOR THE PEARS:
4 small or 2 large pears (about 1 pound)
Zest of 1 lime, finely grated
2 cups water
1¼ cups granulated sugar

FOR THE GINGER CREAM:
3 egg yolks
3 tablespoons granulated sugar
1 cup milk
½ teaspoon powdered ginger

FOR THE MOUSSE:
3½ ounces semisweet chocolate
2 teaspoons softened butter
4 teaspoons Scotch whiskey
3 egg whites
2 drops lime juice
2 teaspoons granulated sugar

UTENSILS:
Large saucepan
Large mixing bowl
Wire whisk

Double boiler
To serve: 3 serving bowls

THE PEARS:

If using small pears, leave them whole; core them with an apple corer, then peel them. Large pears should be peeled, cut into quarters, and their seeds cut out with a knife.

Place the grated lime zest in a saucepan with the water and sugar. Bring to a boil, lower the heat, and simmer for 20 minutes. Add the pears and simmer 20 minutes more. Remove from the heat and leave the pears to cool completely in the liquid.

THE GINGER CREAM:

Beat the egg yolks with the sugar until smooth and pale in color. Heat the milk and ginger in a saucepan, then whisk into the egg yolks. Continue to cook and cool the cream exactly as described for the vanilla custard in **Floating island** *(see p. 293)*. It is not necessary to strain the ginger cream.

THE MOUSSE:

Melt the chocolate in a double boiler. When melted, stir in the butter and Scotch, remove from the heat, and allow to cool until no longer warm to the touch.

In a mixing bowl, beat the egg whites and the lime juice until foamy, add the sugar, and beat until very stiff. Carefully fold the egg whites into the chocolate, then pour into a serving dish and chill for 1 to 2 hours at least before serving.

TO SERVE:

Drain the pears and place them in a serving dish.

Place the ginger cream in another bowl, then bring the three dishes (pears, cream, and mousse) to the table. Everyone should serve himself, taking a little of each.

NOTE: *Everything must be made at least 3 to 4 hours in advance in order to have time to cool. Those who prefer may prepare everything up to 24 hours in advance. Ed.*

Poires savoyardes, brioche toastée
SAVOY PEARS WITH TOASTED BRIOCHE

Ingredients for 4 servings:
    4 large pears (2 pounds)
    ½ lemon
    2 tablespoons butter
    ½ cup granulated sugar
    ⅓ cup pear brandy (*eau de vie de poire*)
    ¾ cup *crème fraîche* (*see p. 331*) or heavy cream
    20 peppercorns, coarsely crushed in a mortar
    8 slices **brioche** (*see p. 263*), ½ inch thick

UTENSILS:
Large frying pan
2 wooden spoons
To serve: Serving platter and 4 dessert plates

THE PEARS:
Peel the pears, core them, and cut each one into 6 wedges, rubbing each wedge with half a lemon to keep it from turning brown.

Melt the butter in a large frying pan, add the pears, and roll in the butter to coat each wedge. Add the sugar, raise the heat, and cook 5 minutes, turning the pears over with 2 wooden spoons to lightly caramelize them on all sides. Add the brandy and light; when the flame has died out, add the cream and peppercorns, stir, and simmer very slowly over low heat for 12 minutes.

TO FINISH AND SERVE:
Toast the slices of brioche under the broiler. They brown very quickly—30 seconds to 1 minute on each side should be enough—so watch very carefully.

Place the toasted brioche on a platter.

Place the pears and their sauce on individual dessert plates and serve with the brioche on the side.

SUGGESTION:
Apples can be prepared exactly like the pears, in which case apple brandy (calvados) should be used.

NOTE: *Although the brioche adds a nice touch, it is not absolutely essential to the taste of the dessert. Do not be afraid to eat the pieces of peppercorn—they are delicious with the pears and the sauce. Ed.*

Pêches farcies
STUFFED PEACHES

Ingredients for 4 servings *(see Note)*:

FOR THE PASTRY CREAM:
½ cup milk
¼ vanilla bean, cut in half lengthwise
2 egg yolks
2 tablespoons granulated sugar
1½ tablespoons all-purpose flour
½ teaspoon butter

¼ cup slivered almonds
4 whole canned peaches in syrup *(see Note)*
2 tablespoons raspberry liqueur *(eau de vie de framboise)*

UTENSILS:
Saucepan, with cover
2 mixing bowls
Wire whisk
Baking sheet
Round roasting pan, 8 inches in diameter
Trussing needle or large knitting needle
Pastry bag with ⅜-inch nozzle
To serve: Serving platter, or 4 dessert plates

THE PASTRY CREAM:
Place the milk and vanilla bean in a saucepan and bring to a boil, remove from the heat, cover, and leave to infuse for 9 minutes.

Beat the egg yolks and sugar until pale and creamy, then whisk in

288

the flour. Bring the vanilla infusion back to a boil and add it to the egg yolks and sugar, whisking constantly. Pour back into the saucepan and bring to a boil, whisking constantly. Boil for 30 seconds, whisk again, pour the cream into a clean mixing bowl, and remove the vanilla bean. Rub the surface of the cream with the butter to keep a skin from forming and leave to cool. When cool, whisk the cream and cover the bowl.

THE ALMONDS:
Preheat the oven to 400° F.

Spread the almonds out on a baking sheet; place in the oven for about 10 minutes, stirring about every 3 minutes, to brown them evenly. When golden brown, place in a bowl, and allow to cool.

THE PEACHES:
Raise the oven temperature to 425° F.

Drain the peaches. Place their syrup in a roasting pan and reserve.

Seed each peach by holding it in one hand and sticking a trussing needle or knitting needle into the bottom (pointed end) of the peach directly under the seed. Push gently; the seed will come out the top of the peach without damaging it.

Stir the almonds into the pastry cream. Fill a pastry bag with the cream and fill each peach with it.

Bring the syrup from the peaches to a boil, then place the peaches in it. Bake for 12 minutes, basting once or twice.

TO SERVE:
Lift the peaches out of the syrup and place them on a serving platter or dessert plates.

Place 2 tablespoons of the syrup in a small saucepan; discard the remaining syrup. Bring the syrup in the saucepan to a rapid boil, add the brandy, and light with a match. Pour flaming over the peaches and serve immediately.

SUGGESTIONS:
Pear brandy or kirsch may be used instead of raspberry liqueur. Coarsely chopped walnuts or hazelnuts may be used instead of slivered almonds.

NOTE: *In his restaurant, Alain Senderens would serve 2 peaches per person, rather than one (therefore, the proportions given here would* be for 2 servings rather than for 4). We felt that this made for a very filling dessert, but you can double all measurements for 4, if you like.

If you buy and poach fresh peaches, use 1⅓ cups of their syrup for the proportions given in the ingredient list when baking them in the oven. Ed.

Beignets de melon au coulis de fraises
MELON FRITTERS WITH STRAWBERRY SAUCE

Ingredients for 4 servings:
   fritter batter (*see p. 266*)
   1 pint strawberries
   2 tablespoons granulated sugar
   2 small cantaloupes or musk melons, about 1 pound each
   1 to 2 quarts cooking oil
   ⅔ cup confectioner's sugar
   Flour (for the baking sheet)

   UTENSILS:
   Mixing bowl
   Wire whisk
   Food processor or blender
   Fine sieve
   Deep fryer or large saucepan
   Deep-frying thermometer
   Skimmer or slotted spoon
   Baking sheet
   To serve: Serving platter, or 4 dessert plates and sauceboat

   PRELIMINARY PREPARATIONS:
Prepare the fritter batter at least 3 hours in advance.

   THE SAUCE:
Wash and hull the strawberries and purée them in a food processor or blender. Strain the purée into a bowl to remove the seeds, rubbing them with a wooden spoon to extract all the juice. Whisk in the sugar

(more or less sugar may be added, according to taste). Pour the finished sauce into a sauceboat and chill until ready to serve.

THE MELON:
Cut each melon in half and scoop out the seeds; cut each half into 6 to 8 wedges about ¾ inch wide at the base and cut off the rind. Reserve on a plate.

THE FRITTERS:
Fill a deep fryer or large saucepan halfway with cooking oil and heat to 375° F.

When the oil is hot, drop 2 to 3 wedges of melon into the batter. Make sure they are completely coated, lift them out one by one with a fork, and drop them into the hot oil. Depending on the size of the fryer or saucepan, 8 to 12 fritters may be cooked at once. After 1 to 2 minutes, they should have browned on one side. Turn them over with a wooden spoon and brown on the other side, then lift them out of the oil with a skimmer or slotted spoon and place on paper towels to drain. Cook the remaining melon wedges in the same way; 2 to 3 batches should be enough to cook them all.

TO GLAZE AND SERVE:
Preheat the broiler.

Place the confectioner's sugar in a soup plate.

Lightly flour a baking sheet.

When the fritters have drained, roll them one by one in the confectioner's sugar, place them on the baking sheet, and slide them under the broiler for about 1 minute to glaze. Watch carefully to see that they brown but don't burn.

Place the fritters on a serving platter or dessert plates and serve immediately, with the strawberry sauce on the side.

SUGGESTION:
Any fruit may be prepared in this way.

Fraises caramélisées, crème anglaise au citron
CARAMELIZED STRAWBERRIES WITH
LEMON CREAM

Ingredients for 4 servings:

FOR THE LEMON CREAM:
Zest of 1 lemon
1 cup milk or heavy cream
3 egg yolks
⅓ cup granulated sugar

FOR THE STRAWBERRIES:
1 quart strawberries
1¼ cups granulated sugar (for the caramel)
6 tablespoons water

UTENSILS:
Saucepan
Wire whisk or electric mixer
Wooden spatula
Bowl
Baking sheet or aluminum foil
Small saucepan
Trussing needle or skewer
To serve: 4 dessert plates

THE LEMON CREAM:
Chop the lemon zest, then place it in a sieve, and rinse it under cold running water. Drain thoroughly.

Make the lemon cream exactly as described for the vanilla custard for the **Floating island** *(see p. 293)*, but using the chopped lemon zest instead of vanilla and the measurements for the other ingredients listed here.

Strain the cream into a bowl and allow to cool to lukewarm, stirring occasionally.

THE STRAWBERRIES:
Wash and hull the strawberries, then set them on a cloth to dry.

Lightly oil a baking sheet or a sheet of aluminum foil.

Place the sugar and water in a small saucepan. Heat, stirring until the sugar has dissolved, then boil rapidly until the syrup begins to turn a golden yellow. Swirl the saucepan to insure even coloring, then remove it from the heat.

Stick a strawberry onto a trussing needle or skewer, dip it into the caramel, swirl it if necessary to coat it all over, then set it down on the baking sheet. (Remove the needle or skewer by pushing lightly on the strawberry with the tip of a knife.) Continue in this manner until all the strawberries are coated—if the caramel thickens too much as it cools off, place it back over the heat for a few seconds, swirling the pan to distribute the heat evenly.

TO SERVE:
If necessary, reheat the lemon cream to lukewarm, then divide it among the dessert plates. Detach the strawberries from the baking sheet, arrange them on the plates, and serve.

SUGGESTIONS:
The lemon zest may be replaced by the zest of an orange, or the two may be mixed together (use half as much of each in this case).

Raspberries may be used instead of strawberries.

Ile flottante aux pralines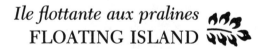
FLOATING ISLAND

Ingredients for 4 to 5 servings:

FOR THE ALMOND BRITTLE:
⅔ cup shelled almonds (3½ ounces)
6 tablespoons water
⅔ cup granulated sugar

FOR THE CUSTARD:
2 cups milk
½ vanilla bean, cut in half lengthwise
5 egg yolks
½ cup granulated sugar

FOR THE "ISLAND":
6 tablespoons water
½ cup granulated sugar
Few drops lemon juice
6 egg whites
1 tablespoon granulated sugar

UTENSILS:
Marble slab or baking sheet
3 saucepans
Baking sheet or roasting pan
Flexible-blade metal spatula
Mortar, food processor, or heavy-duty blender
Wire whisk or electric mixer
Wooden spatula
Roasting pan
Cake pan, 8 inches in diameter, 2 inches deep
To serve: Deep serving platter

THE ALMOND BRITTLE *(see Note)*:
Preheat the oven to 350° F.

Bring a saucepan of water to a boil, add the almonds, and boil for 1 minute, drain, cool under running water, and peel by squeezing them out of their skins. Dry the almonds on a cloth, then spread them out on a clean baking sheet or roasting pan, and dry them in the oven for 8 minutes.

Place 6 tablespoons of water and ⅔ cup of sugar in a saucepan and boil for 10 to 15 minutes, or until a rich, dark caramel is formed. Swirl to obtain even coloring, then stir in the almonds with a wooden spoon; they should all be coated with the caramel. Pour them onto a lightly oiled marble slab or baking sheet and spread them out with the wooden spoon into an even layer. Allow to cool and harden.

Slide a flexible-blade metal spatula under the almond brittle to detach it from the marble or baking sheet, break it into pieces, and grind it in a mortar, food processor, or blender to make a coarse powder. Reserve in a bowl.

THE CUSTARD:
Place the milk and vanilla bean in a saucepan and heat over low heat for 6 minutes; the milk should be almost boiling.

In a bowl, beat the egg yolks and sugar until very pale, then pour the hot milk onto them, whisking vigorously. Pour back into the saucepan and cook over low heat for 5 to 6 minutes, stirring constantly with a wooden spatula. The foam on the surface should disappear, and the custard should thicken enough to coat the spatula lightly. To test, lift the spatula straight out of the custard and let any excess drip off, then draw a horizontal line on the spatula with your finger. If the top edge of the line of custard holds its shape, the custard is done. Do not allow the custard to boil.

Strain the custard into a bowl and allow to cool, whisking occasionally.

THE "ISLAND":

Preheat the oven to 350° F.

Pour water about ½ inch deep into a roasting pan and place it in the oven.

Boil 6 tablespoons of water and ½ cup of sugar in a saucepan for 5 to 6 minutes, or until a dark blond caramel is formed. Do not allow it to color too much.

While the caramel is cooking, place the cake pan in the oven. When the caramel is ready, pour it into the pan and turn the pan in all directions to coat the bottom and sides completely (be very careful not to burn yourself when coating the sides).

Add a few drops of lemon juice to the egg whites and beat them until foamy, add a tablespoon of sugar, and continue beating until the egg whites are very stiff and smooth.

Sprinkle the crushed almond brittle over the egg whites and fold it in. When the mixture is uniform, pour it into the caramelized mold and smooth the surface with a wooden spoon.

Place the mold in the roasting pan and bake for 45 minutes.

TO SERVE:

Remove the "island" from the oven. Pour the custard into a deep serving platter. Run a knife around the edge of the "island," then very carefully turn it out onto the custard; the island will float. Allow to cool for 15 minutes, then serve.

NOTE: *Seven ounces ready-made nut brittle (almond or hazlenut) may be used. Grind as described—there should be 1⅓ cups ground nut brittle for this recipe.*

The floating island may be made and turned out well in advance. It is equally good served cold or lukewarm. Ed.

Blancs neige sur crème anglaise
SNOW EGGS

Ingredients for 4 servings:

FOR THE CUSTARD:
2 cups milk
½ vanilla bean, cut in half lengthwise
6 egg yolks
⅔ cup granulated sugar

FOR THE SNOW EGGS:
2 teaspoons lemon juice
6 egg whites
⅓ cup granulated sugar

FOR THE CARAMEL:
6 tablespoons water
½ cup sugar

UTENSILS:
Saucepan
Bowl
Wire whisk
Large high-sided frying pan or *sauteuse*
Cake rack
Large mixing bowl
Electric mixer (optional)
Skimmer or slotted spoon
Small saucepan
To serve: Deep serving platter

THE CUSTARD:
Make the custard as described for the **Floating island** *(see p. 293)*, using the measurements given here. Allow to cool completely.

THE SNOW EGGS:
Place a high-sided frying pan or *sauteuse* over moderate heat and fill ¾ full with water. Place a clean cloth on a cake rack (preferably one with "feet").

In a mixing bowl, add the lemon juice to the egg whites and begin beating. When foamy, add a third of the sugar. Continue beating until the whites begin to stiffen, then add a second third of the sugar. When the egg whites form soft peaks, add the remaining sugar, and beat until very stiff and smooth.

Dip an ordinary kitchen tablespoon into a bowl of water. When the water in the pan simmers, take a large spoonful of the egg white and place it in the water (hold the spoon down in the water—the egg white will float off). Place 3 or 4 of these "eggs" in the pan and poach for 3 minutes, turn them over, and poach for 3 minutes on the second side. Lift them out of the water with a skimmer or slotted spoon and drain on the cloth. Continue in this way until all the egg white has been used up.

TO SERVE:

Pour the cold custard into a deep serving platter and delicately place the snow eggs on top in a mound.

Place the water and sugar for the caramel in a small saucepan and boil for 6 to 8 minutes, or until a golden caramel is formed. Swirl the saucepan to obtain even coloring, pour over the snow eggs in a thin stream, and serve immediately.

SUGGESTION:

A fruit sauce may be used instead of the vanilla custard.

NOTE: *Any fruit may be used in making a fruit sauce. Use a pint of prepared fruit (i.e., peeled, seeded, and cut into pieces if necessary) and follow the directions and measurements given for the raspberry sauce for the* **Pear charlotte** *(see p. 300). Ed.*

Charlotte aux fraises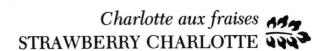
STRAWBERRY CHARLOTTE

Ingredients for 4 to 6 servings:

    2 quarts ripe strawberries
    2 tablespoons confectioner's sugar
    1 tablespoon unflavored gelatin

3 tablespoons cold water
3 egg yolks
⅓ cup granulated sugar
1 recipe **ladyfinger pastry** *(see p. 268)*
4½ tablespoons strawberry *eau de vie* (or kirsch)
½ cup heavy cream, whipped until stiff

UTENSILS:
Food processor or blender
Fine sieve
Wire whisk
Mixing bowl
Saucepan
Bowl
Electric mixer (optional)
Wooden spatula
Large bowl (optional)
Charlotte mold, 6¼ inches in diameter
Pastry brush
Ladle or large spoon
To serve: Serving platter and sauceboat

PRELIMINARY PREPARATIONS:
Wash and hull the strawberries. Measure out 1½ cups and pat them dry in a clean cloth or paper towel, cut them into quarters, and reserve in a bowl.

Purée the rest of the strawberries in a food processor or blender, then strain through a fine sieve to remove all the seeds, stirring and rubbing the pulp to extract all the liquid. Measure the juice; there should be approximately 2¾ cups.

THE STRAWBERRY SAUCE:
Set aside 2 cups of the strawberry purée for making the strawberry cream. Pour the remaining purée into a sauceboat and add the confectioner's sugar, whisking until the sugar is completely dissolved. Refrigerate until ready to serve.

THE STRAWBERRY CREAM:
Place the reserved strawberry purée in a saucepan and heat for 6 minutes over low heat, stirring occasionally. Do not allow to boil.

Moisten the gelatin with the water.

In a bowl, beat the egg yolks and sugar together until the mixture is creamy and light in color. Add the hot strawberry purée, whisking constantly. Pour back into the saucepan, place over low heat, and cook, stirring constantly with a wooden spatula, for about 4 minutes or until the thick foam on the surface has disappeared (only a few bubbles will be left) and the mixture has thickened enough to lightly coat the spatula. Test by lifting the spatula straight out of the cream and letting the excess cream drip off; draw a horizontal line in the cream on the spatula with your finger. If the top of the line holds its shape, the cream is done. Do not let the cream boil.

Pour the strawberry cream into a mixing bowl and whisk in the moistened gelatin. Allow to cool completely in the refrigerator (about 2 hours), whisking occasionally, or place the mixing bowl in a larger bowl filled with ice water and whisk frequently until cold (about 15 minutes), changing the ice and water when necessary. The cream is ready when it is cold to the touch and as thick as a pastry cream or a homemade mayonnaise.

THE CHARLOTTE:

Lightly butter the sides of the charlotte mold. Cut a circle of waxed paper to fit the bottom of the mold and put it in place. Lay the ladyfinger circle in the mold with the flat (bottom) side facing up.

With a pastry brush, paint the circle with some of the strawberry *eau de vie* or kirsch. Brush the top side of the remaining ladyfingers as well and prop them up around the sides of the mold, with the rounded (top) side touching the mold.

When the strawberry cream is cold, whisk it vigorously until perfectly smooth. Fold in the whipped cream with a wooden spatula; make sure the two creams are perfectly mixed together.

Ladle a quarter of the cream into the mold and cover it with ⅓ of the reserved quartered strawberries. Ladle in a second quarter of the cream, cover again with strawberries, and so on, finishing with a layer of cream (the completed charlotte will have 4 layers of cream and 3 layers of strawberries). Smooth the surface of the cream and refrigerate the charlotte for at least 7 to 8 hours.

TO SERVE:

Slice off the ends of the ladyfingers even with the cream.

Place a serving platter upside down over the charlotte mold, then invert everything so that the mold is sitting on the platter *(see Note)*. Lift off the mold, peel off the paper, and serve the charlotte with the strawberry sauce on the side.

SUGGESTION:
An equal amount of raspberries may be used instead of strawberries (leave the raspberries reserved for garnishing the charlotte whole).

NOTE: *If the charlotte does not come out of the mold, dip it into a bowl of hot water, carefully run a knife around the edge, and try again. Ed.*

Charlotte aux poires
PEAR CHARLOTTE

Ingredients for 4 to 6 servings:
  8 pear halves, stewed or canned in light syrup
  2 fresh pears
  Juice of 1 lemon
  ¼ vanilla bean, cut in half lengthwise
  1 tablespoon unflavored gelatin
  3 tablespoons cold water
  6 egg yolks
  ½ cup granulated sugar

  1 recipe **ladyfinger pastry** *(see p. 268)*
  1 teaspoon pear brandy *(eau de vie de poire)* (optional)
  1 egg white
  1 tablespoon granulated sugar
  1 pint raspberries
  ⅓ cup confectioner's sugar

  UTENSILS:
  2 large bowls
  Small bowl
  Blender or food processor

Saucepan
2 medium bowls
Wire whisk
Wooden spatula
Fine sieve
Charlotte mold, 6¼ inches in diameter
Pastry brush
To serve: Serving platter and sauceboat

PRELIMINARY PREPARATIONS:

Drain the pears over a large bowl to catch the syrup. Place 4½ tablespoons of the syrup in a small bowl and reserve for painting the ladyfinger pastry.

Cut 3 of the pear halves into thin slices and reserve.

Cut the remaining 5 pear halves into large pieces and place in a blender or food processor. Peel, quarter, and core the fresh pears. Add them to the blender with the lemon juice and blend to a purée. Measure the purée and add enough of the syrup in the large bowl to make 2 cups.

THE PEAR CREAM:

Place the pear purée in a saucepan with the vanilla bean. Heat the purée, make the pear cream, and cool it, as described for the strawberry cream in the **Strawberry charlotte** *(see p. 297)*, using the measurements given here.

TO LINE AND ASSEMBLE THE CHARLOTTE:

Line the charlotte mold with the ladyfinger pastry as described for the **Strawberry charlotte.** Paint the pastry with the reserved pear syrup (the pear taste may be intensified by adding the pear brandy, if desired).

When the pear cream is cold, whisk it perfectly smooth. Beat the egg white with 1 tablespoon of sugar until very stiff, then fold it into the pear cream.

Using the pear cream and slices of pear, assemble the charlotte as described for the **Strawberry charlotte.** Chill for at least 7 to 8 hours.

THE RASPBERRY SAUCE:

Purée the raspberries in a blender or food processor and strain into a sauceboat, rubbing and stirring the seeds in the sieve with a wooden spoon to extract all the juice. Whisk in the confectioner's sugar and reserve in the refrigerator until ready to serve.

TO SERVE:

Turn out and serve the pear charlotte as described for the **Strawberry charlotte.**

SUGGESTIONS:

The raspberry sauce may be replaced by a black currant or strawberry sauce, made as described above for raspberries, using the same quantities of fruit and sugar.

Or the charlotte may be served with a chocolate sauce *(see* **Stuffed pears Colette Dufour,** *p. 283).*

NOTE: *Because the taste of the charlotte is very subtle and delicate, tell your guests to take only 2 to 3 spoonfuls of the sauce and to place it around, not over, the charlotte, or serve it yourself in the kitchen. If served in this way, the sauce will bring out the taste of the pears; otherwise, the pear taste will be lost completely. Ed.*

Charlotte au coco avec coulis d'ananas
COCONUT CHARLOTTE WITH PINEAPPLE SAUCE

Ingredients for 4 to 6 servings:

FOR THE COCONUT CREAM:
1 whole coconut with milk inside *(see Note)*
2 cups milk
½ teaspoon powdered ginger
⅔ cup granulated sugar
5 egg yolks
1 tablespoon unflavored gelatin
3 tablespoons water

OTHER INGREDIENTS:
1 recipe **ladyfinger pastry** *(see p. 268)*
¾ cup heavy cream, whipped until stiff
½ small ripe pineapple (2 pound)
⅓ cup confectioner's sugar

UTENSILS:
Ice pick
Hammer
Mixing bowl
Food processor or heavy-duty blender
Wire whisk
Food mill
Saucepan
Wooden spatula
Charlotte mold, 6¼ inches in diameter
To serve: Serving platter and sauceboat

THE COCONUT:
The night before making the charlotte, remove the "milk" from the coconut: with an ice pick, pierce holes in two of the dents in the top of the coconut and pour the liquid into a mixing bowl; this is coconut milk.

With a hammer, break the coconut open and pry off the hard outer shell with a sturdy knife. Cut the coconut meat into pieces about an inch square, place ⅓ of them in a food processor or a heavy-duty blender with ⅓ of the regular milk, and purée. Add the purée to the coconut milk in the mixing bowl. Continue until all of the coconut has been puréed and added to the bowl, stir in the ginger, mix well, cover the bowl, and refrigerate overnight.

THE COCONUT CREAM:
The next day, place the coconut purée in a food mill and grind all of the liquid through, as well as some of the pulp; you will need 2 cups total for making the charlotte.

Place the coconut-flavored milk in a saucepan with ⅓ cup of sugar and bring to a boil. In a mixing bowl, beat the egg yolks with the remaining sugar until creamy and pale in color. Continue to make the coconut cream as described for the strawberry cream in the recipe for **Strawberry charlotte** *(see p. 297)*, using the measurements given here.

303

LINING THE CHARLOTTE MOLD:

Line the mold with the ladyfinger pastry as described for the **Strawberry charlotte** (the ladyfingers are used dry in this recipe).

ASSEMBLING THE CHARLOTTE:

When the coconut cream is cold, whisk it vigorously to make it smooth and fold in the whipped cream, mixing the two creams together perfectly. Pour the finished cream into the mold, smooth the surface, and chill for at least 7 hours.

THE PINEAPPLE SAUCE:

Cut the pineapple in half. Only half will be used in this recipe; the rest can be used to make a **Tropical fruit salad** *(see p. 275)*, **Five tropical fruit tartlets** *(see p. 314)*, or eaten as it is.

Remove the skin and core from the half pineapple and cut the pulp into chunks. Purée the pulp in a blender or food processor, then strain it into a sauceboat, rubbing on the fibers with a wooden spoon to extract all the juice. Whisk in the confectioner's sugar and chill until ready to serve (more or less sugar may be added according to taste).

TO SERVE:

Cut off the ends of the ladyfingers and turn the charlotte out as described for the **Strawberry charlotte**. Serve with the pineapple sauce on the side.

SUGGESTIONS:

The whipped cream may be replaced by 2 stiffly beaten egg whites, and the ginger may be replaced by ¼ teaspoon of rum or vanilla extract.

A handful of finely chopped, *unsalted* cashews can be added to the ladyfinger batter at the same time as the egg whites.

NOTE: *If fresh coconut is unavailable, 1⅔ cups of dessicated (grated) coconut, plus ¾ cup water, may be used instead. Mix this with the milk and ginger, and proceed as described for fresh coconut. Ed.*

Gâteau au café
COFFEE CHARLOTTE

Ingredients for 4 to 6 servings:

3 generous tablespoons coffee beans
2 cups milk
6 egg yolks
⅔ cup granulated sugar
1 tablespoon unflavored gelatin
3 tablespoons cold water
1 recipe **ladyfinger pastry** *(see p. 268)*
½ cup cold strong coffee (or 2 teaspoons instant coffee, dissolved in ½
    cup boiling water and allowed to cool)
1 cup heavy cream, whipped until stiff

UTENSILS:
Mortar and pestle, or bowl and smaller bowl or glass
Saucepan
Mixing bowl
Wire whisk or electric mixer
Ribbed brioche mold, 8½ inches in diameter, or charlotte mold, 6¼
    inches in diameter
To serve: Serving platter

THE COFFEE CREAM:
Coarsely crush the coffee beans in a mortar, or place them in a bowl and
crush them with the bottom of a smaller bowl or a glass.

Place the crushed coffee beans in a saucepan, add the milk, and heat
gently for 8 minutes; at the end of this time, the milk should be almost
boiling. Allow to simmer for 3 minutes more.

Beat the egg yolks and sugar in a mixing bowl until the mixture is
pale yellow, then strain the hot milk onto it, whisking constantly.

Pour the mixture back into the saucepan, finish cooking, add the
gelatin, and cool as described for the strawberry cream in the
Strawberry charlotte *(see p. 297)*.

THE CHARLOTTE:
Line the mold with the ladyfinger pastry (brush the pastry with the cold
coffee) exactly as described for the **Strawberry charlotte.**

When the coffee cream is cold, whisk it until perfectly smooth, then

305

fold in the whipped cream. Pour the finished cream into the mold, smooth the surface, and chill for 7 to 8 hours.

TO SERVE:

Cut the ends of the ladyfingers off even with the cream, turn out the charlotte as described for the **Strawberry charlotte,** and serve.

SUGGESTIONS:

The ladyfingers may be brushed with rum instead of coffee.

If desired, a few bits of leftover ladyfinger pastry may be soaked in a mixture of coffee and rum. Pour half of the coffee cream into the mold, arrange the pieces of ladyfinger on top, then pour in the rest of the cream, and finish as described.

Charlottes chaudes aux goyaves, coulis de kiwis
HOT GUAVA CHARLOTTES WITH KIWI SAUCE

Ingredients for 4 individual charlottes:

FOR THE LEMON ZEST:

Zest of 1 lemon, cut into very fine julienne strips
Juice of 1 lemon
¾ cup water
2 tablespoons granulated sugar

FOR THE SAUCE:

4 kiwi fruits *(for substitution, see Suggestions)*
Juice of 2 oranges
3½ tablespoons granulated sugar

FOR THE CHARLOTTES:

6 guavas, about 2½ pounds *(for substitutions, see Suggestions)*
1 tablespoon butter
3½ tablespoons granulated sugar
1 cylindrical **brioche** *(see p. 263)*, preferably at least a day old
5 tablespoons melted butter (for the baking sheet, molds, and
    brioche)
¼ cup apricot jam

Desserts

UTENSILS:
Small saucepan
Food processor or blender
Bowl
Frying pan
4 individual charlotte molds, 3 inches in diameter, or 4 soufflé
    molds, 4 inches in diameter (about 1-cup capacity)
Baking sheet
Pastry brush
Roasting pan or baking dish
To serve: 4 dessert plates and sauceboat

THE CANDIED LEMON ZEST:

Place the julienne of lemon zest in a strainer, rinse under cold running water, drain, and place in a small saucepan. Add the lemon juice, water, and sugar, bring to a boil, lower the heat, and simmer, uncovered, for 40 minutes (there should be about a tablespoon of the liquid left). Reserve.

THE KIWI SAUCE:

Peel the kiwis, cut into pieces, and purée in a food processor or blender.

Place the purée in a bowl, stir in the orange juice and sugar, and whisk until the sugar is dissolved. Strain the sauce into a sauceboat and chill until ready to serve.

THE GUAVAS:

With a vegetable peeler, peel the guavas and cut them into quarters; scoop out the center and seeds using a spoon.

In a frying pan, melt the butter, add the guavas, and sprinkle them with the sugar. Cook over moderate heat for 7 minutes, stirring frequently. The guavas will soften and color lightly. Reserve.

PREPARING THE BRIOCHE:

Preheat the oven to 425° F.

Cut the brioche into slices about ⅛ inch thick. Trim four slices, if necessary, to line the bottoms of the molds. Cut the edges off of the remaining slices to make squares, then cut them into bands about ¾ inch wide and the height of the molds. Make sure the bands line the sides of the mold perfectly, with no spaces between; the brioche will shrink slightly as it is toasted.

307

Remove the pieces of brioche from the molds. Lightly brush the baking sheet with melted butter, and place the brioche on it. Brush the molds with a little butter and set them aside. Brush the pieces of brioche with the remaining butter and bake them for 5 to 7 minutes, or until just beginning to turn golden brown.

Line the molds with the warm brioche, starting with the circles that line the bottoms. It is important to line the molds when the brioche comes from the oven, because it becomes very brittle when cool.

TO MAKE AND SERVE THE CHARLOTTES:

Place 3 pieces of guava in each lined mold, pressing on them as you do so. Add a tablespoon of apricot jam to each mold, then divide the candied lemon zest among the molds and finish each charlotte with a second layer of guavas. Press on the contents of the molds so that the charlottes will hold together; the molds should be filled to the brim, or very close to it.

Place the charlottes in a large roasting pan or baking dish. Butter a sheet of aluminum foil large enough to cover all of the charlottes at once, and place it on top of them, buttered side down. Bake for 20 minutes, lower the oven to 350° F, and bake for 15 minutes more.

Turn the charlottes out onto dessert plates, pour a little of the kiwi sauce around them, and serve immediately, with the rest of the sauce on the side.

SUGGESTIONS:

The kiwi sauce may be replaced by a pineapple sauce made as for the **Coconut charlotte** (see p. 302). The guavas may also be replaced by a pulp of a large, ripe pineapple, cut into chunks and prepared as described above.

If desired, a ¼ teaspoon cinnamon or Chinese five-spices mixture may be added to the guavas at the same time as the sugar.

NOTE: *If the guavas sink when baking so that the ends of the brioche stick up above them, trim the brioche so that it will be even with the filling before turning the charlottes out. Ed.*

Charlottes aux pommes chaudes
HOT APPLE CHARLOTTES

Ingredients for 4 individual charlottes:

FOR THE LEMON ZEST:

Zest of 1 lemon, cut into very fine julienne strips
Juice of 1 lemon
¾ cup water
2 tablespoons granulated sugar

FOR THE CHARLOTTES:

1 cylindrical **brioche** *(see p. 263)*, preferably at least a day old
5 tablespoons melted butter (for the baking sheet, molds, and brioche)
8 medium apples (about 2¾ pounds)
¼ cup butter
6 tablespoons granulated sugar
¼ cup apricot jam
Crème fraîche (see p. 331)

UTENSILS:

Small saucepan
4 individual charlotte molds, 3 inches in diameter, or 4 soufflé molds 4 inches in diameter (about 1-cup capacity)
Baking sheet
Pastry brush
Large frying pan
Fork
Large roasting pan or baking dish
To serve: 4 dessert plates and sauceboat

THE LEMON ZEST AND BRIOCHE:

Make the candied lemon zest, cut and toast the brioche, and line the molds exactly as described for the **Hot guava charlottes** *(see p. 306)*.

THE APPLES:

Peel and core the apples, then cut each one into 6 wedges.

Melt ¼ cup of butter in a large frying pan, then add the apples in a single layer (if necessary, use two frying pans, or cook the apples in two batches, dividing the butter and sugar between them). Sprinkle with the sugar and cook for 5 minutes, or until the first side has browned, turn the wedges over with a fork, and lightly brown the second side. Lower the heat and cook about 5 minutes more to caramelize the sugar (do not allow it to burn).

TO MAKE THE CHARLOTTES AND SERVE:
Preheat the oven to 350° F.

Place 4 pieces of apple in each lined mold, wedging them tightly together. Spoon a tablespoon of apricot jam into each mold, cover with another layer of apples, divide the candied lemon zest among the molds, and finish filling them with a third layer of apples. The apples should form a slight dome on top.

Place the charlottes in a large roasting pan or baking dish. Butter a sheet of aluminum foil large enough to cover all the molds at once and place it on top of them buttered side down. Bake for 40 minutes.

When the charlottes are done, cut the ends of the brioche off even with the apples if necessary, then turn out the charlottes onto dessert plates and serve immediately, with *crème fraîche* on the side.

SUGGESTIONS:
Pears or bananas may be used instead of apples.

A cold vanilla custard, made as described for the **Floating island** (*see p. 293*), or a strawberry or raspberry sauce made as described for the **Pear charlotte** (*see p. 300*), may be served instead of *crème fraîche*.

NOTE: *If using pears or bananas, use 8 pears or 4 large bananas. Cut the pears like the apples; cut bananas into slices about ¼ inch thick. Prepare either as described for the apples.*

Heavy cream, lightly whipped, may also be served instead of crème fraîche, *but the incomparable taste of the* crème fraîche *is worth the effort of making it. Ed.*

Tarte d'hiver
WINTER TART

Ingredients for 6 to 8 servings:
  10½ ounces **sweet short pastry with almonds** *(see p. 269)*
  ⅔ cup granulated sugar
  5 tablespoons softened butter, broken into small pieces
  ½ vanilla bean, cut in half lengthwise
  ¾ teaspoon cinnamon
  ½ cup chopped almonds
  4 apples, peeled, cored, and diced
  Crème fraîche (see p. 331) (for serving)

  UTENSILS:
  Rolling pin
  Pie pan, 8 inches in diameter
  Mixing bowl

  TO BAKE AND SERVE:
Preheat the oven to 400° F.

Roll out the dough into a circle about ⅛ inch. Line the pie pan and cut off any excess dough with a knife. Lightly press down on the dough with your fingers to eliminate air pockets.

Place the sugar and butter in a mixing bowl and beat with a wooden spoon until creamy. Split open the vanilla bean and scrape its contents into the bowl using a knife. Beat in the cinnamon and chopped almonds to make a paste of uniform appearance.

Fill the pie pan almost completely with the diced apple, then cover the surface with pieces of the almond paste. With your fingers, push the bits of paste together to form a solid layer on top of the apples, then bake for 40 minutes (the surface of the tart should be golden brown when done). Cool for 10 minutes before serving warm with a sauceboat of *crème fraîche*.

SUGGESTIONS:
Chopped walnuts may be used instead of the almonds and diced pears instead of the apples.

Tarte aux citrons
LEMON PIE

Ingredients for 6 to 8 servings:

10½ ounces **sweet short pastry with almonds** *(see p. 269)*
Zest of 2 lemons, finely chopped
1 cup cold water
Juice of 2 lemons
Juice of 2 oranges
2 eggs
⅓ cup granulated sugar
½ cup ground almonds
¼ cup melted butter

UTENSILS:

Pastry brush
Rolling pin
Pie pan, 8 inches in diameter
Bowl
Wire whisk
Mixing bowl

PRELIMINARY PREPARATIONS:

Preheat the oven to 425° F.

Lightly butter the pie pan.

On a lightly floured table, roll out the dough into a circle about ⅛ inch thick. Line the pie pan (if the dough breaks, simply push the broken edges together with your fingers). Cut off any excess dough and refrigerate while making the filling.

THE FILLING:

Place the lemon zest in a saucepan, add the water, bring to a boil, and boil for 5 seconds. Drain, cool under running water, and drain again. Reserve in a bowl. Strain the lemon and orange juices into the bowl with the lemon zest.

In a mixing bowl, whisk the eggs lightly, then add the sugar, ground almonds, fruit juices and zest, and the melted butter. Mix well and pour into the pie pan.

TO BAKE AND SERVE:

Bake the pie for 15 minutes, lower the oven to 400° F, and bake 15 to 17 minutes longer, or until the blade of a knife plunged into the center of the filling comes out clean, and the pie crust has begun to brown.

Allow to cool for about 10 minutes. Serve warm.

Tarte aux cassis
BLACK CURRANT TART

Ingredients for 6 servings:

9 ounces (250 g) **puff pastry** (*see p. 271*) or **short pastry** (*see* **Tarte tatin,** *p. 317*)

2 eggs

⅓ cup granulated sugar

3 tablespoons ground almonds

Pinch cinnamon

1½ cups heavy cream

1½ cups (10½ ounces) black currants in syrup, drained

UTENSILS:

Rolling pin

Pie pan, 8 inches in diameter, or flan ring, about 1½ inches deep

Large mixing bowl

Wire whisk

Ladle

TO MAKE THE TART AND SERVE:

Preheat the oven to 425° F.

Lightly butter the pie pan or flan ring.

On a lightly floured table, roll out the dough into a circle about 10½ inches wide. Brush off any excess flour and line the pan with the dough. Press the bottom and sides of the pan lightly with your fingertips to eliminate any air pockets, then cut off any excess dough.

Beat the eggs with the sugar, whisk in the ground almonds and cinnamon, then add the cream, whisking until perfectly smooth.

Pour the drained currants into the lined pie pan, spread them out evenly, then ladle in enough cream filling to fill the pan completely. Bake 30 to 35 minutes, or until golden brown on top.

Allow to cool for about 15 minutes. Serve warm, but not hot.

Cinq tartelettes exotiques
FIVE TROPICAL FRUIT TARTLETS

Ingredients for 4 servings:

7 ounces (200 g) **puff pastry** *(see p. 271)* or other pastry dough of your choice

¼ medium apple, cut into thin slices
Confectioner's sugar (to sprinkle over tartlets)
Softened butter to dot over apple tartlets

½ small mango, peeled, seeded, and cut into thin slices
1 small kiwi fruit, peeled and cut into thin slices
¼ medium pear, peeled, cored, and cut into thin slices
Half of a 1-inch-thick slice of fresh pineapple, cut into thin slices
Crème fraîche (see p. 331) to serve with tartlets

UTENSILS:
Rolling pin
2¾-inch round cookie cutter
2 baking sheets
Pie pan, 8 inches in diameter
Sugar dredger
To serve: 4 large dessert plates and sauceboat

THE PASTRY ROUNDS:
Preheat the oven to 425° F.

On a lightly floured table, roll out the dough to a thickness of about ¹⁄₁₆ of an inch, then cut out 20 circles with the cookie cutter. It may be necessary to cut out about half of the circles, then pack the scraps of dough into a ball, roll it out, and cut the rest.

Place 16 of the circles on a lightly buttered baking sheet. Butter a second baking sheet and place it, buttered side down, over the rounds; this will keep the rounds from rising too much.

Place the 4 remaining rounds in a lightly buttered pie pan. Cover the surface of each one with apple slices, overlapping them so that none of the dough is showing. Sprinkle with confectioner's sugar, then dot each one with a few dabs of butter.

Bake the baking sheets and the pie pan for 15 minutes. At this time, remove the baking sheets from the oven and lift off the top sheet. Allow the apple tartlets to cook for 5 minutes more.

When the ungarnished rounds have cooled, cover 4 of them with slices of mango, 4 with kiwi, 4 with pear, and 4 with pineapple. In each case the slices should overlap, and there should be no dough showing when finished.

TO GLAZE AND SERVE:

Preheat the broiler.

Sprinkle the 16 raw fruit tartlets with confectioner's sugar and place them under a moderate broiler for about 2 to 3 minutes. The tops should color slightly, but watch them carefully so they don't burn. Remove the tartlets from the broiler and place the apple tartlets under the broiler for about 45 seconds to warm them.

Place one of each kind of tartlet on each of 4 dessert plates and serve immediately, with *crème fraîche* on the side.

NOTE: *The leftover fruit may be used to make* **Tropical fruit salad** *(see* *p. 275).* *Ed.*

Tarte bonne femme
APPLE TART
(color picture VII)

Ingredients for 4 servings:
  10½ ounces (300 g) **Puff pastry** *(see p. 271)*
  3 medium apples (1 pound)
  2 tablespoons butter, broken into pieces

3 generous tablespoons granulated sugar
1 cup *crème fraîche, (see p. 331)* for serving (optional)

UTENSILS:
Baking sheet
Rolling pin
To serve: Large rectangular platter and sauceboat (optional)

TO MAKE:
Preheat the oven to 450° F.

Lightly butter and flour a baking sheet.

Roll out the puff pastry into a rectangle about 15 × 9 inches. Trim the edges with a sharp knife, then place the dough on the baking sheet, leaving a border about 1 inch wide, and prick the pastry all over with a fork to keep it from rising too much.

Peel and core the apples, cut them in half, then cut them crosswise into thin semicircular slices. Place the slices on the dough one at a time, laying them so that each one overlaps the preceding one almost completely. Cover the tart in this manner, leaving a border of about an inch all around the edge. Dot the apples with butter, sprinkle with the sugar, and bake for 16 minutes. Lower the oven to 425° F and bake for 10 minutes more.

TO SERVE:
Serve the tart as it comes from the oven, with *crème fraîche* on the side, if desired.

SUGGESTIONS:
Pears may be used instead of apples, and short pastry (see the recipe for **Tarte tatin,** *p. 317)* can be used instead of puff pastry. If short pastry is used, fold the edges up to make a border.

TARTE TATIN

Ingredients for 6 to 8 servings:

FOR THE SHORT PASTRY DOUGH:
¼ teaspoon salt
3 tablespoons cold water
1½ cups all-purpose flour
¼ pound plus 2½ tablespoons softened butter, broken into pieces

FOR THE APPLES:
6 apples (about 2¾ pounds)
¼ cup butter
1 cup granulated sugar
¼ teaspoon cinnamon
Crème fraîche (see p. 331) for serving (optional)

UTENSILS:
Small bowl or glass
Mixing bowl (optional)
Heavy metal pie pan or cake pan, or round enameled cast-iron
    baking dish, 10 to 11 inches in diameter and about 2 inches deep
Rolling pin
Pastry brush
To serve: Large round serving platter

THE DOUGH:
In a small bowl or glass, dissolve the salt in the water.

Place the flour on a clean table top, or in a mixing bowl, and distribute the pieces of butter over it. With your fingers, pinch the flour and butter together rapidly until all the butter has been incorporated and a crumbly mixture has been formed—1 minute of energetic pinching should do it. Add the salt water, mixing it in with the same pinching motion for about a minute more, then pack the dough into a ball, cover with a floured cloth or aluminum foil, and refrigerate for at least 30 minutes.

THE APPLES:
Peel and core the apples, then cut each one into 8 wedges.

Place the pie pan over moderate heat and melt the butter in it, add the pieces of apple, sprinkle with the sugar and cinnamon, and cook for 10 to 12 minutes, or until the sugar begins to caramelize, turning the apples over with a wooden spoon. Remove the pan from the heat and arrange the apple wedges in circles or rows that cover the bottom of the pan in one layer.

TO BAKE:

Preheat the oven to 425° F.

On a lightly floured table, roll the dough out a little larger than the diameter of the baking pan.

With a dry pastry brush, brush any excess flour off of the dough. Roll the dough onto the rolling pin (see Note), brushing off the flour from the bottom as you do so, then unroll it on top of the apples. Tuck the dough in around the apples and fold the edges in to form a border; if there is excess dough, cut it off with a knife.

Bake the tart at 425° F for 30 minutes, lower the oven to 350° F, and bake for 15 minutes more, or until the dough is a rich golden brown.

Remove the tart from the oven and place it over moderate heat on top of the stove for 1 minute.

TO TURN OUT AND SERVE:

Remove the tart from the heat and place a deep serving platter upside down over it. With both hands (protect your fingers with potholders), lift the pie pan up with the platter on it, press the two together, and flip everything over. Lift the pie pan off of the tart.

Allow to cool for 5 to 10 minutes, then serve the tart warm, accompanied by a dish of *crème fraîche,* if desired.

NOTE: *If using a ball-bearing rolling pin, hold it by the rolling surface when rolling the dough onto it and placing it on the tart (if held by the handles, the weight of the dough will make it unroll when picked up). Ed.*

Clafoutis aux fruits frais
GRAPE OR CHERRY CLAFOUTIS

Ingredients for 4 servings:
- 5 large or 6 medium eggs
- ½ cup granulated sugar
- ¼ teaspoon cinnamon
- ⅛ teaspoon salt
- ½ cup all-purpose flour
- 1 cup milk
- ¼ cup melted butter
- 1½ pounds cherries or grapes
- 2 generous tablespoons honey

UTENSILS:
Mixing bowl
Wire whisk
Cake pan, 10 inches in diameter
Large frying pan

THE BATTER:
Beat the eggs, sugar, cinnamon, and salt together. Sift the flour into the bowl, whisk to combine, then whisk in the milk, little by little, and add the melted butter. Whisk until smooth.

THE FRUIT:
Pit the cherries or seed the grapes if desired (this is optional). Wash and dry the fruit completely before cooking.

In a large frying pan, heat the honey, add the fruit, and cook over high heat for 10 to 15 minutes to caramelize; the fruit will give out liquid, which will have to evaporate before it begins to caramelize. Stir the fruit as little as possible. Shake the pan from time to time to roll the fruit in the caramel once it begins to form. Be careful not to let it burn.

TO BAKE AND SERVE:
Preheat the oven to 400° F.

Lightly butter the cake pan.

Whisk the batter and pour it into the cake pan, add the fruit, spreading it out evenly, and bake for 30 to 35 minutes, or until the surface is golden brown.

Remove from the oven, allow to cool 15 minutes, and serve warm.

319

Gâteau au miel et aux noisettes
HONEY AND HAZELNUT CAKE

Ingredients for 6 to 8 servings:

    4 eggs, separated
    ½ cup honey
    ⅓ cup granulated sugar
    4 tablespoons softened butter, broken into pieces
    1 scant cup all-purpose flour, measured then sifted
    1¼ cups ground hazelnuts

    2 drops lemon juice
    2 tablespoons granulated sugar (for the egg whites)

UTENSILS:

2 large mixing bowls
Wire whisk or electric mixer
Cake pan 8 inches in diameter and 1½ to 2 inches high
To serve: Cake plate

TO MAKE AND SERVE:

Preheat the oven to 400° F.

Beat the egg yolks, honey, and sugar in a large bowl until pale and creamy. Beat in the butter, then stir in the flour and ground hazelnuts to make a stiff batter.

Beat the egg whites and lemon juice in a large bowl until they stiffen, then add 2 tablespoons of sugar, and continue beating until very stiff. Fold a quarter of the egg whites onto the batter, then fold in the remaining egg whites.

Lightly butter the cake pan, pour in the batter, and bake 40 minutes, or until the cake is firm to the touch and a straw plunged into the center comes out clean and dry.

Turn the cake out on a cake plate when it comes from the oven, allow to cool for about 15 minutes, then serve.

NOTE: *Walnuts or pecans may be used instead of hazelnuts. Ed.*

Gâteau chocolaté aux noix et aux amandes fraîches
WALNUT-ALMOND CHOCOLATE CAKE

Ingredients for 6 to 8 servings:
  7 tablespoons softened butter
  ¾ cup granulated sugar
  1 large egg, separated
  ¼ teaspoon salt
  ⅔ cup milk
  2 tablespoons unsweetened cocoa powder
  1 cup all-purpose flour
  2 drops lemon juice
  ¾ teaspoons vanilla sugar
  ¼ pound blanched almonds
  ¼ pound walnut meats

  UTENSILS:
  3 mixing bowls
  Wire whisk or electric mixer
  Wooden spatula
  Pound-cake mold or loaf pan, 10 inches long
  To serve: Oval or rectangular serving platter

  THE BATTER:
In a mixing bowl, beat the butter and sugar, until very pale and creamy, add the egg yolk and salt, and whisk in the milk little by little.

In another mixing bowl, mix the cocoa powder and the flour. Whisk this mixture little by little into the butter-sugar-milk mixture. Beat the batter vigorously until very creamy and smooth.

Add two drops of lemon juice to the egg white and beat it until very stiff. Begin folding it carefully into the batter; about halfway through, add the vanilla sugar, almonds, and walnut meats, and continue folding until there are no more bits of unmixed egg white in the batter.

  TO BAKE AND SERVE:
Preheat the oven to 400° F.

Lightly butter a pound-cake mold or loaf pan.

Pour the batter into the mold and bake for 30 minutes, then lower the oven to 350° F and continue baking for 40 minutes to 1 hour. The

321

cake is done when the blade of a knife inserted into the center comes out clean and dry, and the cake begins to pull away from the sides of the mold.

Turn the cake out as soon as it comes from the oven and serve either barely warm, or cold.

Cigarettes
CIGARETTES

Ingredients for 24 to 30 cookies:
   2 egg whites
   ⅓ cup granulated sugar
   ¼ cup melted butter
   ½ cup all-purpose flour

UTENSILS:
Small saucepan
Wooden spoon
Large mixing bowl
Sifter
Baking sheet
Flexible-blade spatula
Cake rack

PRELIMINARY PREPARATIONS:
At least 24 hours before baking, make the batter: using a wooden spoon, beat the egg whites and sugar together for about 2 to 3 minutes, then beat in the melted butter little by little. When it has been perfectly mixed in, sift the flour into the batter, stirring as it is being added, then beat the batter until smooth. Cover the bowl with aluminum foil and refrigerate for at least 24 hours.

TO BAKE AND SHAPE:
Preheat the oven to 450° F.

Lightly butter a baking sheet with melted butter.

Place a teaspoon of batter on the baking sheet and spread it out with the back of the spoon to make a cookie about 3 inches wide and as thin as possible (you should be able to see the baking sheet through the batter). About 8 to 9 cookies can be placed on one baking sheet. Bake for 4 to 5 minutes, or until browned to a cinnamon color.

Using a wide, flexible-blade spatula, remove a cookie from the baking sheet; do not hesitate to push the spatula hard to remove the cookie and don't be surprised if the cookie forms pleats. Straighten the cookie out, place it on a table, and set the handle of a wooden spoon down on one edge of the cookie (the spoon end of the spoon should stick out over the edge of the table). Roll the cookie around the handle to form a tube, then slide it off, and place on a cake rack to cool. Keep the remaining cookies warm by leaving them in the oven with the door open. Since they become brittle very rapidly, the cookies must be removed from the baking sheet and shaped one by one.

Serve with coffee or dessert.

NOTE: *Since this batter will keep for several days in the refrigerator, it is best to bake the cookies as you need them. If not serving them immediately, place them in a tightly sealed cookie box as soon as they have cooled because they go stale very quickly. Ed.*

Tuiles aux amandes 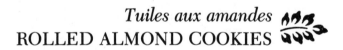 ROLLED ALMOND COOKIES

Ingredients for 24 to 30 cookies:
   2 egg whites
   ¼ cup granulated sugar
   ¼ cup melted butter
   ¼ cup all-purpose flour
   Generous ½ cup slivered almonds

   UTENSILS:
   Small saucepan
   Wooden spoon
   Large mixing bowl
   Baking sheet

Spatula
Rolling pin
Cake rack

PRELIMINARY PREPARATIONS:

At least 24 hours before baking, make the batter: Using a wooden spoon, beat the egg whites and sugar together for about 2 to 3 minutes, then beat in the melted butter little by little. When all the butter has been completely mixed in, sift the flour into the batter, stirring as it is being added. When smooth, stir in the almonds, cover the bowl with aluminum foil, and refrigerate for at least 24 hours.

TO BAKE AND SHAPE:

Preheat the oven to 450° F.

Lightly butter a baking sheet with melted butter. Drop a generous teaspoon of the batter onto the baking sheet and spread the almonds evenly throughout to make a very thin cookie about 2½ to 3 inches wide. Approximately 9 to 12 cookies can be made at once on a baking sheet. Bake for 4 to 5 minutes, or until the edges have browned to a cinnamon color—the centers will be paler.

Use a spatula to remove the cookies from the baking sheet. Lay each cookie on a rolling pin and, protecting your hand with a potholder, press the cookie around the rolling pin to shape it (keep the remaining cookies warm by leaving them in the oven with the door open). The cookies harden quickly and will become too brittle to bend if you take too many from the oven at once, so only remove as many as you can shape at a time.

Place the finished cookies on a cake rack to cool. Serve with coffee or dessert.

SUGGESTIONS:

A little finely chopped lemon or orange zest may be added to the batter, or the amount of almonds can be increased, if desired.

NOTE: *Since this batter will keep in the refrigerator for several days, it is best to bake only as many cookies as will be needed at one time. If not being served immediately, place them in a tightly sealed cookie box as soon as they are cool as they become stale very quickly. Ed.*

Financiers
FINANCIERS

Ingredients for 24 to 30 pastries:
  ¼ pound plus 2½ tablespoons butter
  4 egg whites
  ⅔ cup granulated sugar
  ⅓ cup ground almonds
  ⅓ cup all-purpose flour

UTENSILS:
Small saucepan
Wooden spoon
Mixing bowl
24 to 30 oval molds, about 3 × 1¾ × ½ deep (2-tablespoon capacity)
  (*see Note*)
Cake rack

PRELIMINARY PREPARATIONS:
At least a day before baking, make the batter: Heat the butter in a small
saucepan until it just begins to change color and stops sizzling (do not
allow to burn). With a spoon, skim off the foam on the surface, and
allow to cool.

With a wooden spoon, beat the egg whites and sugar together, then
sift in the ground almonds and flour. Stir to make a smooth batter.
Carefully pour the nut-brown butter into the batter little by little, lifting
the batter with the spoon to incorporate air as the butter is being added.
Be careful not to pour the milk solids in the bottom of the saucepan into
the batter as you add the butter.

When all the ingredients are well combined, cover the bowl with
aluminum foil and refrigerate for at least 24 hours (the batter will keep
for several days in the refrigerator).

TO BAKE:
Preheat the oven to 450° F.

Lightly butter each mold.

Beat the batter with a spoon to soften it. With an ordinary teaspoon,
take a walnut-sized lump of batter and scrape it into a mold with
another spoon. When all the molds have been filled, bake them for 10

minutes, or until golden brown; the pastries should split down the middle as they bake.

Turn the pastries out immediately as they come from the oven. Leave to cool upside down on a cake rack for about 10 minutes. Serve warm with dessert or coffee.

SUGGESTIONS:
One-third cup ground hazelnuts, walnuts, or pecans, ground in a blender or food processor, may be used instead of almonds. Or ⅔ cup dessicated (grated) coconut can be used instead of any of these.

NOTE: *The shape of the molds is not important, but the capacity is: the molds should hold 2 tablespoons (1 fluid ounce). Barquette molds, madeleine molds, or miniature cupcake molds all give equally good results. Ed.*

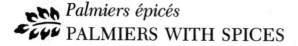

Palmiers épicés
PALMIERS WITH SPICES

Ingredients for 10 to 12 *palmiers:*
    2 tablespoons granulated sugar
    ½ teaspoon cinnamon
    ⅛ teaspoon allspice
    ⅛ teaspoon Chinese five-spice powder
    4½ ounces (125 g) **puff pastry** *(see p. 271)*
    Granulated sugar (for dipping the *palmiers*)

    UTENSILS:
Bowl
Rolling pin
Baking sheet
Flexible-blade metal spatula
Cake rack or clean baking sheet
To serve: Serving plate

TO ROLL OUT THE DOUGH:

In a bowl, mix the sugar, cinnamon, allspice, and Chinese spice powder.

Sprinkle the top and bottom of the puff pastry with some of the mixed spices and sprinkle a little on the table. Roll out the dough into a rectangle approximately 5 × 11 inches, sprinkling it and the table with the spice mixture as it is absorbed into the pastry. Use all of the spice mixture.

Starting at one of the short ends, roll the pastry until it almost reaches the center of the rectangle; roll up the other short end until it touches the first. Place the pastry on a plate, cover with aluminum foil, and refrigerate for 20 minutes.

TO CUT, BAKE, AND SERVE:

Preheat the oven to 425° F.

Cover the bottom of a plate with granulated sugar.

With a large, very sharp knife, cut the dough into 10 to 12 slices, about ⅜ to ½ inch thick. Place each slice in the granulated sugar, turn it over to coat both sides, then set it down on a lightly buttered baking sheet. Leave plenty of space between the *palmiers;* they spread a great deal while baking.

Bake the *palmiers* for 5 minutes, then turn them over with a flexible-blade metal spatula, and bake for 5 minutes more, or until golden brown and caramelized.

Slide the *palmiers* onto a cake rack or a clean baking sheet to cool for a few minutes. Serve warm, piled on a plate.

Orangettes chocolatées
CHOCOLATE-COATED ORANGE PEEL

Ingredients for 4 to 5 servings:
    2 oranges, preferably untreated
    1 cup water
    1 cup granulated sugar
    6 tablespoons Grand Marnier (or other orange-flavored liqueur)
    5 ounces semisweet chocolate, broken into pieces

UTENSILS:
Saucepan
Cake rack or drum sieve
Double boiler
Baking sheet
To serve: Serving plate

THE ORANGES:

Wash the oranges off in warm water and dry them. With the tip of a pointed knife, slit the skin into quarters. Peel the skin off, being very careful not to break it; the fruit will not be used in this recipe, so keep it for something else, such as a fruit *macédoine*.

Cut each piece of peel in half crosswise and trim the edges so that each half piece forms a rectangle. Discard the trimmings. With the knife, remove as much of the white part of the skin as possible, then cut each rectangle into 4 strips.

Place the strips of orange zest in a sieve, rinse under cold running water, and drain.

TO COOK:

Place the water, sugar, and Grand Marnier in a saucepan. Bring to a boil, add the orange zest, lower the heat, and simmer for 2 hours. (After 1 hour 15 minutes, check the syrup; if it has become very thick, add 6 tablespoons of water, stir, and continue cooking.)

Lift the strips out of the syrup with a fork and spread them out on a cake rack or drum sieve, making them as flat and straight as possible. They should not touch each other. Allow to cool completely and dry for at least 3 hours (or leave them overnight).

TO COAT WITH CHOCOLATE:

In the bottom of a double boiler, heat a little water until it simmers.

Place the chocolate in the top of the double boiler and set it in place over but not touching the water. Melt the chocolate; this should take about 5 to 6 minutes, and the water should never boil.

Stir the melted chocolate until smooth; remove the double boiler from the heat.

Place a large sheet of aluminum foil (or 2 smaller ones) on the table.

One by one, drop the strips of candied zest into the chocolate, turn them over with a fork, and lift them out, allowing the excess chocolate to drip off. Place them on the aluminum foil, as flat and straight as possible, and without allowing them to touch.

When all of the zest has been coated, allow to cool for 10 minutes. Refrigerate them for 25 to 30 minutes, lift them off the foil, and arrange on a plate. Keep refrigerated until ready to serve.

SUGGESTION:
The zest of one grapefruit may be used instead of the orange zests.

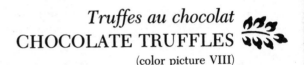

Truffes au chocolat
CHOCOLATE TRUFFLES
(color picture VIII)

Ingredients for about 20 to 25 truffles:
    1 tablespoon milk
    2 tablespoons heavy cream
    1½ tablespoons granulated sugar
    4½ ounces semisweet chocolate, broken into pieces
    1 tablespoon Scotch whiskey
    Approximately ¼ cup unsweetened cocoa powder

UTENSILS:
Small saucepan
Bowl
Pastry bag with ½-inch nozzle *(see Note)*
Large flat platter or baking sheet
To serve: Serving plate

THE TRUFFLE CREAM:
Place the milk, cream, and sugar in a small saucepan and bring slowly to a boil. Remove from the heat, add the chocolate, and stir until it has melted completely. Add the whiskey and stir until perfectly smooth. Pour it into a bowl and place it in the refrigerator, stirring occasionally with a wooden spoon for about 35 minutes, or until the chocolate cream has stiffened to the consistency of a thick chocolate icing.

MAKING THE TRUFFLES:

Beat the truffle cream with a wooden spoon to make it smooth. Spoon it into the pastry bag and squeeze it out onto a large flat platter or a baking sheet, making mounds the size of a small walnut. Place in the refrigerator to harden for 30 to 45 minutes.

Place the cocoa in a soup plate.

When the truffles are stiff, detach them from the platter with the tip of a knife and roll them in the cocoa, one at a time. Roll them rapidly between the palms of your hands to make them perfectly round, then roll them in the cocoa once more. Put the finished truffles on a clean plate and refrigerate for at least an hour before serving.

SUGGESTION:

Instead of whiskey, cognac or any fruit brandy (raspberry, strawberry, plum, and so on) may be used.

NOTE: *Instead of using a pastry bag, the mounds may be made by taking a teaspoon of truffle cream and pushing it onto the platter or baking sheet with a second spoon. Ed.*

Pruneaux Rénaudie
BRANDIED PRUNES "RÉNAUDIE"

Ingredients for a 1-quart jar:
    4 teaspoons tea leaves
    2 cups boiling water
    1 pound large prunes
    ¼ cup granulated sugar
    1 cup cognac or vodka

    UTENSILS:
    Teapot
    1-quart preserving jar

TO MAKE AND SERVE:

Place the tea leaves in a teapot and add the boiling water. Cover and allow to steep for 3 to 4 minutes.

Place the prunes in a sterilized preserving jar with the sugar and alcohol. Strain the tea into the jar, wait 15 minutes, then close the jar tightly. Place in a cupboard for 2 weeks before serving.

Serve the prunes after dinner, about 3 per person, in small glasses with a few spoonfuls of alcohol from the jar.

CRÈME FRAÎCHE

Crème fraîche is simply heavy cream in which the natural lactic acids contained in it are allowed to act until the cream has thickened considerably. It is then pasteurized. In most recipes, heavy cream may be used instead of *crème fraîche;* when there is a choice, this is indicated. If *crème fraîche* alone is given in the ingredient list, then it must be used, as its nutty taste and thick consistency are essential to the preparation involved. *Crème fraîche* can be found in some specialty stores, but it tends to be very expensive, so it is worth making it yourself.

When making *crème fraîche*, use pasteurized, *not* ultra-pasteurized, heavy cream if at all possible. The chemical substances in ultra-pasteurized cream tend to slow down the thickening process and give the *crème fraîche* a slightly unpleasant metallic taste.

INGREDIENTS FOR 1½ CUPS *CRÈME FRAÎCHE:*

1⅓ cups heavy cream
3 tablespoons buttermilk (active culture)

TO MAKE:

Place the cream and buttermilk in a saucepan, heat over low heat until lukewarm to the touch, then remove from the heat and allow to stand, covered, for 6 to 10 hours in a warm place. Gently stir the cream to see if it is ready—if a thick layer has formed on top, but the cream is still liquid underneath, it is done (do not let it thicken too much or it will sour). Place the cream in a jar, stir to mix well, cover, and place in the refrigerator overnight before using. The cream will finish thickening in the refrigerator and can be kept for up to a week before it starts to sour.

Recipe Index

333

Index

Fish *(cont'd.)*
    onnaise, 152–156
    Smoked
        Butter, on Toast, 19–20
        in Eggs Rosemonde, 54–56
        Terrine with Whipped Cream
            Sauce, 87–89
        Tarts with Fresh Herbs and Butter
            Sauce, 65–67
        Terrine, Hot, 84–86
        Terrine, Smoked, with Whipped
            Cream Sauce, 87–89
        See also specific types of fish
Floating Island, 293–295
Flounder
    Fillets with Carrots and Parsley,
        122–124
    Salad with Italian Parsley, 29–31
Foamy Butter Sauce
    for Hot Fish Terrine, 85, 86
    for Mussel Soufflé, 71, 72
    Puff Pastry with Asparagus and, 59–60
    for Salmon Tarts with Fresh Herbs
        and Butter Sauce, 65–67
Fraises caramélisés, crème anglaise au citron, 292–293
Fricassee
    of Asparagus, Scallops, and Oysters, 102–103
    Crayfish with Asparagus, 90–91
    Lobster
        with Cucumbers and Mint, 94–96
        with Fresh Peas, 141–143
    Rabbit with Tarragon and Garlic, 241–243
    Snails with Cream and Herbs, 83–84
    Spiny Lobster, with Morels and Asparagus, 143–146
    Spiny Lobster and Langoustine, with Baby Cabbage and Truffles, 147–149
Fricassée aux asperges, coquilles Saint-Jacques, et huîtres, 102–103
Fricassée d'écrevisses aux asperges, 90–91
Fricassée d'escargots à la crème, 83–84
Fricassée de homard au concombre et à la menthe fraîche, 94–96
Fricassée de homard aux petits pois frais, 141–143

Fricassée de langouste aux morilles et asperges, 143–146
Fricassée de langoustes, langoustines, truffles, et chou nouveau, 147–149
Fricassée de lapin à l'estragon et à l'ail, 241–243
Fritter(s)
    Anglerfish, 18–19
    Batter and Basic Deep-Frying Techniques, 266–267
    Chicken Dufour, 209–211
    Melon, with Strawberry Sauce, 290–291
Frogs' Leg(s)
    in Pastry with Chervil Butter Sauce, 79–81
    "Soup," 77–79
    Stew—Oyster, Langoustine, and, 82–83
    with Watercress, 75–77
Fruit(s)
    Fritters, 267
        with Strawberry Sauce, 290–291
    Salad, Tropical, 275–276
    Sauce, Snow Eggs with, 296–297
    Tartlets, Five Tropical, 314–315
    See also specific fruits

Galettes de pommes de terre rapées, 252–253
Garlic
    Chicken with 40 Cloves of, 207–208
    Cream Sauce, Sliced Lamb with, 172–175
    Mayonnaise, Mixed Fish Dinner with, 152–156
    Rabbit with Tarragon and, 241–243
Gâteau au café, 305–306
Gâteau au miel et aux noisettes, 320
Gâteau chocolaté aux noix et aux anandes fraîches, 321–322
Gâteau de foies de volaille à la crème de bacon, 107–109
Ginger
    Cream
        Pears with Chocolate Mousse and, 285–286
        Sauce, Lime and—Veal Cutlets with, 166–167
    in Squab Peking Style, 214–217

Index